History, Tourism, and Culture

Between Conservation and Commodification in Southern Africa

By

Joram Ndlovu and Henry Chiwaura

History, Tourism, and Culture: Between Conservation and Commodification in Southern Africa

Joram Ndlovu and Henry Chiwaura

The present binding first published in 2026.

Ethics International Press, UK

British Library Cataloguing in Publication Data
A catalogue record for this book is available from the British Library

ISBN (Paperback): 978-1-80441-461-3

ISBN (Ebook): 978-1-80441-231-2

Table of Contents

Preface

This book explores the relationship between local communities' heritage and tourism in Southern Africa. Local communities play an important role in shaping how natural and cultural resources are governed. Engaging local communities can help effectively align state development goals with local livelihoods and environmental sustainability. This book also examines the role of cultural heritage tourism in promoting community welfare. The themes explored in this book have broader application to the Southern African Development Community (SADC), as they address many of the challenges encountered in reconstructing cultural identities through heritage tourism and creating new heritage values aligned with development and the formation of national identity. Heritage tourism management in Southern Africa is conspicuously underrepresented in scholarly research. More importantly, the role of both personal and collective memory in tourism studies is neglected. This book contributes to the body of knowledge on heritage tourism in Southern Africa.

Situated at the nexus of the politics of culture, memory and identity, the book engages with heritage places as zones where tourism, culture, and memory intersect and construct notions of identity. The book navigates the contestations between conservation and commodification of heritage resources, which are often highly contentious. Conservation involves protecting heritage resources by safeguarding, maintaining, and sustaining historical, cultural, and natural assets in their original form, with particular attention to meaning, context, and community rights.

Commodification involves extracting economic value by turning history into marketable products or experiences (such as tourism, memorabilia, or branded experiences), often driven by profit, branding, or external demand. The book presents a structured approach which seeks to balance heritagization, livelihoods and economic development. The intriguing question is how to balance intrinsic cultural value (significance, memory, identity) with monetary value (tourism revenue, branding). The gap lies in who benefits from heritage commodification and how commodification can enhance or undermine conservation. Therefore, the analysis in this book is premised on the broader context of tourism-making, cultural appropriation, identity formation, nation-building, and governmentality.

The book explores the impact of social cohesion and identity by examining how commodified heritage activities can strengthen or fragment local identities and affect the transmission of intergenerational knowledge. The contention is on the fact that national identity is usually defined by dominant social groups and the political elite. While identity is constructed, it can also have primordial (traced from history), constructed (heritage factor) or imagined (heritage factor) premises. Cases from Southern Africa demonstrate how cultural heritage sites have frequently surfaced conflicting views among stakeholders, politicians, legislators, scholars, communities, heritage practitioners, and tourism officials, on the construction of personal and national identity, nationalism, ownership, development, and the political, economic, and other uses or misuses of heritage landscapes. At the heart of the conflict is the politicisation and commodification of memories as tourist attractions.

This book analyses and evaluates the relationships among heritage, memory, and identity in post-colonial Southern Africa. It examines how Southern Africa's historical sites are represented in local memorialization practices, heritage, and the (re)construction of local and national identities. Heritage tourism is a powerful force in the construction and maintenance of national identity because it relies on the nation's historical symbols to attract tourists. This book explores the production and consumption of tourism in Southern Africa, focusing on the influence of identity, memorialisation and the manifestation of nationhood. It examines the roles of tourists, communities, and state actors, such as the National Heritage Council and the National Department of Tourism in South Africa, that represent collective memories and leverage heritage tourism to forge national unity.

This book discusses the entanglement between tourism and heritage management in Southern Africa. This is reflected in inter and intra-community relations and contestations among stakeholders, including visitors, local communities, government authorities, tour operators, and institutions. The book also examines the historical, cultural, socio-economic and political processes through which communities or individuals construct identities and individual and collective memories about the commemorative representation of heritage sites.

In the post-colonial context, the state employs heritage as a tool for social cohesion, while local communities use it to demand rights and access to resources. This book demonstrates how heritage has become a platform for claiming resources and restitution for marginalised communities. It highlights debates over the representation and preservation of colonial and immigrant cultures in post-colonial contexts, as constructing a new, authentic national history and heritage is a key aim of the state. In this context, the practice of heritage becomes a form of cultural politics.

This book demonstrates how the state's use of heritage surfaces dissonant perspectives and privileges some memories while silencing others. In political contexts undergoing profound change, memories may be prioritised at both the state and local levels, leading to the formation of new identities and contestations. This book also explores how information about tourists' collective memory can reveal perceptions of quality that are not always defined by the supplier's objectives or generic criteria of excellence. Tourists become the audience for whom the past is represented in a specific way. They prefer certain destinations because of personal memories rather than marketing factors. The book also addresses the need for understanding the value of heritage from tourists' perspectives, which can be shaped and altered by present-day perspectives and identities.

Chapter 1
Introduction

This chapter introduces the topics of tourism, cultural heritage, and memorialisation, and explores the complex relationship among them. It provides an overview of the development of tourism from the ancient Empire era to the present. While mass tourism has dominated the industry in modern times, this chapter explores the special-interest sectors within the industry that focus on cultural, educational, heritage, and memorial tourism. It investigates how heritage and the memorialisation of history have been commercialised and commodified as tourism products, along with the accompanying benefits and risks. Focusing on Southern Africa, the chapter explores key features of the cultural heritage landscape and the packaging of cultural heritage, commemoration, and memorialisation for tourist experiences in this region.

The History of World Tourism

The travel, leisure, and tourism industry spans the globe and relies on significant infrastructure to ensure accessibility, safety, and the provision of utilities and services for tourists. Tourism impacts virtually every aspect of society, including politics, culture, and, most notably, the economy (Ndlovu, 2009; Gyr, 2010). According to the World Tourism Organisation, tourism generated approximately 1.4 billion international arrivals and total export revenue of US$1.9 trillion in 2024 (UNWTO, 2025). Tourism has the potential to generate jobs, enhance the local economy, contribute to the development of local infrastructure, and assist in the preservation of the natural environment, cultural assets, and traditions[1]. Tourism revenues can be used to fund roads, water, sanitation, health clinics, schools, and cultural preservation to enhance sustainable development.

Exploring the history of tourism across the centuries not only enables a deeper understanding of the past, but also the forecasting of the future that is needed to design viable tourism offerings[2]. The evolution of the tourism industry has been shaped significantly by Western culture (Towner, 1995). European elites pioneered early travel; as they encountered distant lands previously unknown to them, they formed stereotypes of other societies as exotic and primitive.

Scholars have classified the development of tourism into six periods: the Empire period (BC to the 5th century), the Middle Ages (5th to 14th centuries) the Renaissance (14th to 16th centuries), the Grand Tour period (1613 to 1785 A.D.), the Mobility period (1800 to 1944), and the Modern epoch, beginning in 1945 and continuing to the present (Gyre, 2010). The Empire era featured the Egyptian and Greek empires and ended with the collapse of the Roman Empire. During this era, people travelled for business, recreational, educational, and religious reasons (Gyr, 2010). A relatively wealthy population with the means to travel was attracted by the allure of safe, stress-free travel, strong

---

[1]Bakalo et al. Local tourism as a financial and economic development driver of the local economy: management aspects. 2025. World Development Perspectives. 38

[2] Christou, A. P., The History and Evolution of Tourism. 2022. CABI Publications.

and widely accepted currencies, a common language, and a legislative environment that protected individual rights[3].

Travel declined dramatically during the Middle Ages due to the greater risks involved. Without the broader frame of an empire, travellers faced greater barriers in transportation, currency, and language. Trade between regions was hampered by volatile exchange rates, hindering long-distance trade and budgeting. Cross-border trade became complex and costly as city-states and kingdoms minted their own currencies with varied standards[4]. Different weights and fineness required merchants to continuously weigh and assay coins or rely on expensive exchange rates. Rulers frequently devalued coinage by reducing their precious metal content to fund wars or deficits, resulting in more coins with lower intrinsic value[5]. Debasement inflated prices and eroded trust in money.

Marco Polo's extraordinary expedition to the Holy Land took place in the late 13th century. His voyages transformed distant, exotic places into tangible destinations in the European imagination, making the notion of travelling to far lands credible and desirable[6]. He travels in combined commerce and exploration. His ambitious travels of the Silk Road and maritime

---

[3] Christou, A. P., The History and Evolution of Tourism. 2022. CABI Publications.

[4] Flesher, Dale L, Trade and Commerce in the Ancient World. 2022. Economics. Research Starters. EBSCO.

[5] Flesher, Dale L, Trade and Commerce in the Ancient World. 2022. Economics. Research Starters. EBSCO.

[6] Mitchell, B.J., European Exploration. 2026. Britannica Editors.

routes were portrayed as journeys to gain knowledge, prestige, and opportunity.

In 1453, the Ottoman capture of Constantinople disrupted the overland trade of European merchants on the Silk Road[7]. The Portuguese established alternate maritime passages around Africa, providing direct access to Asia, with Bartolomeu Dias rounding the Cape in 1488 and Vasco da Gama reaching India in 1498. The Dutch, English, and later French and Spanish fleets expanded their networks across the Atlantic and Indian Oceans. Towards the end of the Renaissance era, trade routes were slowly revived as commercial ventures flourished and dealers expanded into new territories, generating interest in travel for both business and leisure.

The Grand Tour era, which began in the 16th century and continued into the 18th century, saw young European nobles and affluent visitors travel extensively across Europe to experience its art, culture, and history. This represented the start of tourism as an industry[8]. Educational journeys, called 'Bildungsreisen', became popular among the upper German-speaking middle-class professionals and played a significant role in the development of tourism from the Enlightenment to the 19th century (Gyr, 2010). People travelled by train and visited both rural and urban regions. They travelled to historical sites and landmarks to learn about art, culture, and the environment. Their travels also explored painting, sculpture, architecture, and manufacturing. Gyr (2010) explains: "The travels of the learned

[7] Barzun, J., History of Europe. 2026. Britannica Editors. History.

[8] Austin, G. From commodity to colonial currencies in the West Africa. 2025. African Economic History.

middle classes copied those of the prominent poets and philosophers of the time, such as Jean-Jacques Rousseau, Charles Baron de Montesquieu, Johann Wolfgang von Goethe, Gotthold Ephraim Lessing, Johann Gottfried Herder" (p. 1).

Tourists visited Italy and France in search of education, where they shared their knowledge and experiences through literary works and travel accounts. New segments of the population, such as younger clergy men, artists, and craftsmen, began to travel for educational purposes. A segment of the middle-class business sector travelled from various countries to Britain, France, and Germany to learn about technological advancements and industrial innovations. The affluent English pioneered the culture of visiting, which expanded throughout Europe as a symbol of status[9].

The Mobility Era began in the early 1800s and continued until 1944. It was characterised by rapid advancements in transportation technology, which made travel easier and more economical. Commercial aircraft transformed the way people travel. Thomas Cook, who has been called the 'father of tourism' pioneered the group travel package model[10]. In 1841, he organised the first tour for 570 members of a local temperance society from Campbell Street Station in Leicester to attend a temperance rally in Loughborough, England (Gyr, 2010).

---

[9] Flesher, Dale L, Trade and Commerce in the Ancient World. 2022. Economics. Research Starters.

[10] Norah, J. Thomas Cook History: The Tale of the Father of Morden Tourism. 2021. Travel History and Research. Independent Travel Cats.

The Modern Era began in 1945 and continues to the present. It has been characterised by mass travel to global destinations. The rise of package tours and affordable airlines has made foreign travel more accessible to the general public, and the Internet has simplified the process of booking and travelling[11]. As a result, tourism has emerged as a global economic leader, with intercontinental tourist arrivals estimated at 1.52 billion, nearly 60 billion more than in 2024, representing a 4% increase (UNWTO, 2025). While this has led to economic gains for many destinations, it has also raised concerns about overtourism—where the number of visitors to a destination surpasses its capacity to accommodate without compromising the environment, local quality of life, or visitor experience.

Special Interest Tourism

Since the end of World War II, special interest tourism has gained popularity, giving rise to new forms of tourism that meet the needs of tourists and hosts. Cultural tourism, educational tourism, heritage tourism, and memorial tourism are key special interest sectors within the tourism industry[12].

Cultural Tourism

The World Tourism Organisation (2012) states that cultural tourism is one of the most important and diversified sectors within modern tourism. It has shown innovation in response to

---

[11] Christou, A. P., The History and Evolution of Tourism. 2022. CABI Publications

[12] Brooks c. et al., Exploring the relationship between heritage tourism, sustainable community development and host communities' health and well-being: A systematic review. 2023. 18(3), e0282319.

tourists' demand for new experiences. While some claim that tourism degrades heritage sites (Kim, 2011; Zhuang et al., 2019), it can also be argued that cultural tourism results in tourists becoming more educated about the preservation and conservation of heritage sites and valuing the sites they visit. (Brooks, 2012; Ramli & Badarulzaman, 2023). As he appreciation of intangible heritage assets is typically part of the cultural tourism experience, some argue that the globalisation of heritage through tourism has resulted in a greater respect for both tangible and living culture than was previously achievable[13].

Tourism and globalization can also influence the aesthetics of places of a place by accelerating structural and visual changes, which often lead to a homogenization of urban landscapes while simultaneously creating new curated identities for visitors (Azcárate, 2025). Heritage and museum projects are affected by popular media, including earlier forms, to develop a lingua franca that spans national and international boundaries (Hlongwane & Ndlovu, 2019). Thus, globalisation has brought both opportunities and risks for historic and cultural heritage tourism destinations.

Educational Tourism

Educational tourism, or 'edu-tourism', refers to any program in which participants travel to a location, either individually or as a group, with the primary goal of engaging in a learning experience directly related to the site (Rodger, 1998). Educational tourism

[13] Brooks c. et al., Exploring the relationship between heritage tourism, sustainable community development and host communities' health and well-being: A systematic review. 2023. 18(3), e0282319

dates to the 18th century, when it became popular among the middle class to travel to Italy or France for education and leisure. Marunda (2014) identifies several types of educational tourism: countryside or ranch tourism, ecotourism, student exchange programs, and heritage tourism. Educational institutions and programs have used historical tourism sites, particularly those associated with famous individuals, for educational purposes[14]. In Zimbabwe, for example, schools organise field trips to National Heroes Acre and Chinhoyi Caves, among other places.

Heritage Tourism

'Heritage' has become a buzzword in South Africa, evoking a range of emotional associations and benefits for various stakeholders and local communities. Heritage is not a static concept, but rather a culturally and socially produced process (Smith, 2006). Heritage is open to different interpretations by different groups. Heritage is seen as a source of empowerment for the historically marginalised black majority (Marshall, 2010). It involves valuing and preserving cultural beliefs and values, honouring heroes and contributions, authenticating neglected stories and memories, and acknowledging suffering and sacrifice[15]. Heritage is also a loaded discursive marker of our time, one of the 'keywords' now commonly accepted to describe

---

[14] Abos, A.I. The importance of educational tourism in cultural heritage preservation and sustainable Tourism. Case study of the Mures Valley's cultural Heritage: Five Castles, Five Stories. 2023. Research and Education. 120-137.

[15] Bolarinnwa, O, F.O and Olaniyi, O.F. Participation in the preservation of cultural heritage and values: The Missing Link of Adult Education. 2021. 3(4), 2663-6743.

South African society, alongside race, culture, gender, tradition, and truth and reconciliation (Shepherd & Robins, 2008).

Cultural heritage encompasses both immovable and movable resources, including monuments and man-made things (Ndlovu, 2015). It also includes intangible customs passed down by tradition. UNESCO (2003) states that intangible cultural heritage takes the form of manners, activities, drama, visual arts, festive events, protocols and conventions regarding fauna and flora, and skills for producing traditional crafts, music, and dance. Cultural heritage and cultural landscapes are the most popular tourist destinations globally (Ivanovic & Saayman, 2013). A focus on cultural heritage in tourism can affirm the local and national identity of communities and indigenous groups (Zhang & Mohamad, 2025).

Heritage tourism has gradually become a feature of international tourism, particularly in countries looking to diversify their tourism industries[16]. Heritage tourism is closely tied to state formation, as it involves preserving and promoting monuments and symbols that are associated with a country's history and culture, legitimize authority, and foster collective memory (Ndlovu, 2015; Hlongwana & Ndlovu, 2019). Preserving buildings and symbols are ways that a state reinforces its identity and history while also encouraging its citizens to identify with the state and its principles.

---

[16] Zhang, Q., & Mohamad, D. B. Mapping identity dynamics in heritage tourism: a bibliometric and theoretical review. 2025. Cogent Social Sciences, 11(1). ttps://doi.org/10.1080/23311886.2025.2598726

Several writers have proposed definitions of heritage tourism. Zeppel and Hall (1992) describe it as a "special interest in travel, which ranges from the investigation of physical remains of the past and natural landscapes to the experiencing of local cultural traditions" (p. 49). Park (2014) defines heritage tourism as an interest in examining the material and non-material vestiges of a bygone era. Ndlovu (2015) and Palmer (1999) consider heritage tourism to involve visits to destinations deemed historically significant or heritage sites. McIntosh and Prentice (1999) describe heritage tourism as tourism based on a cultural legacy. Poria (2001:57) defines heritage tourism as "tourism to places categorised as heritage or historic places" and defines a heritage tourist site as "a place that attracts tourists by its heritage characteristics or by the heritage characteristics of the artefacts contained within it, which the tourists perceive as part of their heritage." This book uses Poria's definition of heritage tourism.

Memorial Tourism

States typically commemorate the histories and legacies of prominent individuals, thereby increasing their appeal as tourist attractions. Death and suffering sites have emerged as a niche in tourism, attracting an increasing number of visitors (Yuil, 2003; Lischer, 2019; Dresler & Fuch, 2021). Tourism that involves the sites of murders or other tragic deaths, natural disasters, death, and other tragedies has been called dark tourism (Lennon & Foley, 1996). Other terms for memorial tourism include thanatourism, black spot tourism, grief tourism, and atrocity heritage (Drvenkar et al., 2015).

Tourists are often motivated to visit memorials that connect with a part of their identity: for example, those whose families survived the Holocaust may be more likely to visit holocaust museums; battlefields are common destinations for those whose family or country fought in the battle[17]. Memorials can serve as 'sites of memory' for people affected by major disasters (Nora, 1989; Winter, 2009). Dark tourism acts as a mechanism for resuscitating mortality by providing recreated spaces for reflection and remembering tragedy and death (Stone, 2012). These curated spaces are often re-enacted and presented to symbolise suffering, war, confrontation, disasters or memorials to allow tourists to engage and remember the tragedy which is often ignored in traditional tourism[18].

In South Africa, some have advocated for the site of the 2012 Marikana massacre to be developed as a tourist destination (Henana, 2017). On August 16, 2012, the South African Police Service (SAPS) opened fire on a gathering of striking mineworkers in Marikana, North West Province. The police killed 34 mine workers, and 78 others were critically injured. The development of a Marikana Heritage Site is motivated by the need for a physical reminder of this tragedy as a warning to not allow it to happen again (South African History Online, 2013), August 16). Marikana is thus a potential dark tourism destination in South Africa's post-apartheid landscape that could be developed, commodified, and commercialised for both domestic and international tourism (Henana, 2017). In Zimbabwe, at the

[17] Ashworth, G.J., and Tunbridge, J.E. Dissonant heritage: The management of the past as a resource in conflict. (1996). Wiley.

[18] Henama, S.U. Marikana: Opportunities for Heritage Tourism. 2017. African Journal of Hospitality, Tourism and Leisure, Volume 6 (4) - (2017).

National Heroes Acre, tourists can view the tombs of War Heroes and read about the liberation struggle in the years leading up to independence.

Heritage and Memorial Tourism as Tourism Products

Heritage is an important tourist attraction and can thus drive tourism growth (Ching-Fu & Pei Chun, 2010). The expansion of historic tourism has affected the display and representation of tangible and intangible heritage within tourism. Heritage products provide potential for economic, social, and political progress in certain regions or countries (Boucher et al., 2018). In the context of tourism, the term 'heritage' refers to products (Santos et al, 2020), attraction (Liu et al, 2017), motivation (Changuk, 2001), resources (Chaudhary, 2000), industry (Light, 1995), business (Prentice, 1993b), and tourist segmentation (Getz, 19 91). Park (2014) and Ndlovu (2015) argue that the idea of heritage, which varies across political, economic, and socio-cultural contexts, must engage with globalised communities and societies. The same globalised cultures have been absorbed, yet they still strive to maintain their individual identities.

John Urry discusses the 'tourist gaze', which refers to how tourists visually consume, interpret, and shape locations through socially produced 'out-of-the-ordinary' experiences (Pomering, 2013). Gaze structure visitors' interactions with the other, bringing a sense of competence, pleasure, and structure to those experiences[19]. Similarly, the concept of authenticity in the construction of heritage assets for tourist consumption is neither

---

[19] Pomering, A. A review of: 'The Tourist Gaze 3.0'. 2013. Tourism Geographies, 15(4), 691–693. https://doi.org/10.1080/14616688.2012.699095.

static nor rigid. Amenities influence how tourists see and experience a site, often diverting their attention to well-serviced areas (Ndlovu, 2015). When planning heritage product routes, it is critical to create circuits that incorporate attractions with comparable characteristics to better please visitors. Tourism attractions include natural, man-made and intangible assets essential for tourism growth.

Chen and Chen (2010) suggest that the success of historical tourism depends not only on tourism policy, attractiveness, and distinctiveness, but also on local support for tourism development. Boucher et al. (2018) argue that stakeholder engagement is essential for the success of heritage tourism. Stories may be myths, folktales, simple narratives, songs, taboos, or proverbs and idioms. Myths describe the origins of specific qualities, beliefs, and traditions, as well as the interaction between the divine and human worlds. Myth and history are often considered antithetical modes of explanation (Heehs, 1994). The major myths are poetic representations of the profound perspectives of early people regarding the universe and life. Myths interpret creation, divinity, and religion; explain the meaning of life and death; explain natural events; and recount the exploits of ethnic heroes[20]. Myths are less historically based and contain more magical elements than legends. They are less concerned with moral teaching than with fables[21]. They explain the world's origins, natural phenomena, or cultural beliefs, featuring gods, goddesses, and supernatural heroes (Bascom,

---

[20] Heehs, P. Myth, History, and Theory. 1994. History and Theory, 33(1), 1–19. https://doi.org/10.2307/2505649

[21] South African History online. Oral tradition and indigenous knowledge. 2011. South African History online.

1954). Most myths are associated with social rituals, which are fixed forms and procedures in holy rites. Nevertheless, anthropologists dispute whether rituals originated from myths or whether myths have generated rituals.

Folktales are traditional stories with fundamental narratives of adventure, frequently centred on character and story components[22]. If a story involves magical beings who are not gods and is not part of formal mythology, it is generally regarded as a folktale. Folktales are mostly intended for entertainment, but they may also convey a life lesson. Folktales are transmitted orally as a means of passing culture down to current and future generations.

A legend is a fabricated story about a historical person or location. When the protagonist is human rather than a supernatural figure, the story is called a legend rather than a myth. Legends often exemplify the characteristics of highly esteemed individuals throughout a society's history[23]. Traditionally, a legend contains villains and protagonists that symbolise various roles and people and are intended to teach the listeners about acceptable and inappropriate behaviours. Legends can take the form of simple narratives, songs, taboos, or proverbs and idioms[24].

Poria (2001) considers heritage in terms of supply and demand, with the supplier wanting to supply something (legacy) and the

---

[22] South African History online. Oral tradition and indigenous knowledge. 2011. South African History online.

[23] Dahal, H. Folktales: A Moral Message from the Past to the Future generation. 2021. 4(10, 2705-4691.

[24] Dahal, H. Folktales: A Moral Message from the Past to the Future generation. 2021. 4(10, 2705-4691.

client potentially purchasing the supplied product (heritage). Four responses can occur between a provider and a consumer: the suppliers want to supply and the customers want to consume the suppliers' heritage; the suppliers want to supply but the customers have no demand for their heritage; the suppliers do not want to supply heritage but the customers want their heritage; and finally, the suppliers want to supply one type of heritage and the customers want a different type of heritage (Ndlovu, 2015).

History, Prominent People and Tourism in Southern Africa

In Southern Africa, case studies have shown that immovable cultural assets have long been contested by various stakeholders, such as politicians, lawmakers, scholars, communities, heritage practitioners, and tourism officials (Fontein, 2006; Ndoro, 2005). Typically, the debates revolve around topics such as the construction of personal and national identity, nationalism, ownership, development, and the political, economic, and other uses or misuses of cultural landscapes[25].

Hamilton (2011) advocates that the role of cultural heritage in the socio-economic development of people and their sense of identity and cohesion should be recognised. In South Africa, Marschall (2010) and Ndlovu (2015) observe that heritage has evolved into a resource with numerous advantages for all stakeholders, including local communities. Throughout the apartheid era,

---

[25] Yacoob, O.A. An examination of the relationship between identity and sovereignty: debates around the South Africa nation state from 1990 to 2010. 2017. PhD Thesis, University of Witwatersrand.

white South Africans easily associated with their own cultural symbols, while Black South Africans were forced to the margins as outsiders (Henana, 2017). In the democratic era, the state has used heritage to create social cohesion, while local organisations have exploited it to assert rights and access to resources (Collet, 1992; Eichler, 2020). Heritage serves as an avenue for marginalised communities to go beyond financial return to include symbolic, psychological and economic healing (Witz & Murray, 2015). Local communities have used it as a tool to redress historical inequalities, allowing them to reclaim stolen narratives, identities, sacred objects, and postcolonial contexts.

Across Southern Africa, European heroes have been immortalised, valorised, and canonised, then commercialised and packaged as tourist attractions. David Livingstone (1813-1973), a Scottish surgeon, missionary, and explorer who travelled across Southern Africa, is revered in Malawi, South Africa, Zambia, and Zimbabwe. He was the first European recorded to visit the Victoria Falls. Tourist sites in Malawi, Zambia, Zimbabwe, and the United Kingdom memorialise Livingstone. In Zambia, a town and museum have been named after him (Lewis, 2011). Cecil John Rhodes, the founder of the colonial Rhodesian state, is a notable figure in Southern African heritage tourism. Memorials to Rhodes are found in both South Africa and Zimbabwe. Monuments to Rhodes remained in public spaces in South Africa in the democratic era[26]. However, in 2015, students at the University of Cape Town debated the relevance of Rhodes in an independent South Africa. Today, Southern African

[26] Mushonga, M. From Barbarism to Civilisation: An Interpretation of Colonial Statues and Monuments in Southern Africa. Sabinet African Journals.

countries are expanding their tourism industries by focusing on heritage-based tourism as a speciality product, often capitalising on their struggle for liberation from colonial or white-majority rule.

One strategy for diversifying the heritage sector has been to use famous figures as tourism platforms. Examples across the region include heroes of the liberation struggles, such as Agostinho Neto in Angola, Seretse Khama in Botswana, Eduardo Mondlane and Samora Machel in Mozambique, Sam Mujoma in Namibia, Kenneth Kaunda in Zambia and Joshua Nkomo in Zimbabwe. In South Africa, struggle leaders such as Nelson Mandela, Robert Sobukwe, Steve Biko, Albert Luthuli, and Tiyo Soga have been memorialised. In Angola, the memorial to Antonio Neto is a modern, 120-meter Brutalist structure which often functions as a mausoleum and national monument[27]. Primarily, it is a tool of official doctrine and culture with a museum that reflects four aspects of Neto's work: poet, healer, liberator, and statesman. In some cases, heritage sites attract a substantial number of domestic and international tourists, making these tourism initiatives quite lucrative (Mgxekwa et al., 2019). In terms of gender, only a few women, such as Charlotte Maxeke in South Africa and Mbuya Nehanda in Zimbabwe, have been memorialised at sites that serve as tourist attractions. In some cases, the struggle history is complex, for example, Zimbabwe, where two competing

[27] Martins, V. and Cardina, M. A memory of concrete: Politics of representation and silence in the Agostinho Neto Memorial. Kronos, 45 (1), https://doi.org/10.17159/2309-9585/2019/v45a3.

liberation movements each promote their own narratives and identities[28].

Connecting cultural heritage monuments to tourism has led to increased employment and property values for local residents. Mgxekwa et al. (2019) conducted research to examine the qualities of the Nelson Mandela heritage sites and better understand why users are drawn to them. Nelson Mandela's home is one of the most iconic heritage sites in South African tourism. Visitors were classified as experience seekers, convenience experience seekers, and auxiliary experience seekers[29]. Experience seekers look for experiences that are deeply significant and immersive. They look for authentic interactions, novelty, and personal development. Convenience experience seekers seek experiential value characterised by exceptional ease, efficiency, and comfort[30]. For instance, they prefer guided tours or well-planned city tours that require less planning on their part[31]. Auxiliary experience seekers seek experiences that support, enhance, or complement the core experience by focusing on products that augment the primary activity. Comprehensive experience seekers were willing to pay higher rates for more memorable experiences.

---

[28] Ray, M.A. Zimbabwe's struggle for liberation. 1997. Global colonial studies.
[29] Kruger, M. et al., A Whale of time! An experience-based typology of visitors to a South African whale -watching festival. 2018. Journal of outdoor Recreation and Tourism. 24(2018) 35-44.
[30] Córdoba Azcárate, M. Tourism, space, and place: bridging past, present and future research. 2025. Tourism Geographies, 27(3–4), 735–755. https://doi.org/10.1080/14616688.2024.2404644
[31] Kruger, M. et al., A Whale of time! An experience-based typology of visitors to a South African whale -watching festival. 2018. Journal of outdoor Recreation and Tourism. 24(2018) 35-44.

Struggle heritage attractions have been reported to be the most distinctive and contentious cultural products in urban South Africa, forming an important part of the country's township or slum tourism sector (Khumalo et al., 2014; Marschall, 2006). Some communities believe that struggle sites honour important figures, such as Nelson Mandela and Oliver Tambo, while others remember state violence, displacement, and continued inequity. Robben Island and Liliesleaf have become major tourist attractions. Some scholars (Marschall, 2006; Mgxekwa et al., 2019; Henana, 2017) argue that this sanitises or commercialises trauma for profit by reducing attention to and diverting it away from ongoing injustices such as poverty, inequality, and land reform.

During the early post-apartheid period, the African National Congress (ANC) prioritised and displayed its own narratives. Communities historically excluded from decision-making have advocated for co-curation, community-led museums, and the reuse of sites to represent diverse experiences. The way representation and portrayal of identities is approached is central to post-apartheid South African heritage tourism (Marschall, 2006). The homes of Nelson and Winnie Mandela, Solomon Mahlangu and Steve Biko's parents have been converted into museums. Statues have also been erected in remembrance of struggle leaders such as Saul Mkhize (Hlongwane & Ndhlovu, 2019).

In Mozambique, liberation heritage has been memorialised by designating historical places associated with the country's struggle for freedom as national monuments. Jopela (2017) states that thirty years after independence, Mozambique began to memorialise liberation history through several initiatives. One, a series of publications titled 'Vida e obra' ('life and legacy'), was designed to raise the profile of national heroes and teach a philosophy of liberation by telling the stories of their lives and legacies, with the aim of strengthening national identity. Two founding fathers were memorialised: Eduardo Mondlane has a monument and statue in Maputo, and Samora Machel has monuments and sculptures in almost all the provincial capitals of Mozambique (Jopela, 2017).

Namibia has also developed its heritage tourism sector based on the memorialisation of struggle heroes such as Sam Nujoma, Hosea Kutako, Nehale Mpingana, Mandume ya Ndemufayo, and Limpumbu Ya Tshilongo. Some statues, such as the Sam Nujoma statue at the Independence Memorial Museum, have become important tourist attractions (Niezen, 2017; Becker, 2018), displacing the colonial memorial of the Windhoek Rider.

In Malawi, the tourism industry has also capitalised on the memorialisation of historical figures that embody the Malawian imagination and political change (Lipenga, 2009). Sculptures honour former presidents Dr Hastings Kamuzu Banda and Bingu wa Mutharika.

In Zambia, the legacies of Kenneth Kaunda and other iconic figures constitute part of the country's national heritage, conserved through museums and other forms of memorialization (Simakole, 2012; Mbewe et al., 2023).

It is important to understand the colonial history of Southern Africa because it brings people's experiences together and transcends geopolitical boundaries. However, despite the global expansion of heritage tourism, it remains underdeveloped in Southern Africa (Viljoen & Henama, 2017).

The Nexus between Memorialisation, Commemoration and Tourism

A complex relationship exists between memorialization, commemoration, and tourism. Commemoration and memorialisation are concerned with honouring the past. However, they differ significantly in their scope and duration. Commemoration involves specific events that are repeated frequently, such as ceremonies honouring certain people. Memorialisation is broader and refers to the continuous process of preserving memory by constructing physical or social structures (monuments, archives, and locations) related to war, trauma or tragedy. Nora (1996) argues that remembering, memory, and forgetting are all important aspects of memorialisation. Memorialisation involves preserving and honouring the memory of a person or event through physical monuments or symbolic gestures (Berliner, 2005), while commemoration refers to the public recognition and celebration of a significant person or event. In this book, the term 'memorialisation' refers to everything that contributes to the remembering of a person or event.

French historian Pierre Nora's seminal seven-volume work, *Les lieux de mémoire,* published in 1984, establishes memorialisation as the bedrock for the field of memory studies. The recognition of the relationship between memory and tourism resulted in the development of memorial tourism in France (Gonzales, 2018). Memorialisation has existed since time immemorial as one of humanity's first imaginative creations, honouring the lives of people or events via the preservation of their memory. Monuments, museums, public landscapes, and memorial museums have been built and dedicated to remembering the past (Ndlovu, 2015).

Some well-known examples of memorialization include the Great Zimbabwe Monuments, Stonehenge, and the Great Pyramids of Giza in Egypt. Common forms of memorialization include headstones and gravestones, remembrance trees, plaques, urns, remembrance ceremonies, war memorials, and charitable funds. New ways to memorialise include digital and virtual memorials, physical keepsakes and personalization, living and sustainable memorials, interactive and experiential tributes, and alternative ceremonies.

Memory and commemoration are inextricably interwoven with the heritage process, as they involve the selective use of the past (McDowell, 2008; Morgan, 2001). French philosopher Serge Thion (1993) posits that history is the reconstruction of the past using texts and physical evidence, while memory is the "story of the past based on personal remembrance and subjective feelings" (pp. 181–182). As the effects of economics, time, culture, and politics shape, direct and dictate the representation and interpretation of history, the message portrayed through memorial design is often better described as 'memory' than 'history', as multiple levels of remembrance and interpretation are represented. Philosopher and art critic Arthur Danto (1998) writes, "We erect monuments so that we shall always remember and build memorials so that we shall never forget" (p. 153). Paul Williams, in his 2007 book *Memorial Museums,* observes that while some scholars distinguish between 'memorial' and 'monument' based on their political function, "memorial often signifies loss and mourning, whereas monument signifies greatness or valour - we often see measures of both in any single structure, making this distinction fuzzy" (p. 8).

Memorialisation can thus take many forms, ranging from permanent expressions—such as graves, museums, and works of art, literature, or film—to temporary activities, including theatre, song, dance, or ceremonies (Steele, 2006). Place names represent another type of commemorative and instructive transcript in the practice of memorialization. Halbwachs (1950) views memorialization as an effort to revive public interest in national history at a time when such connections to the past are fading. Halbwachs (1947) describes this process as collective memory, which is "a reconstruction of the past [that] adapts the image of ancient facts to the beliefs and spiritual needs of the present" (p. 7).

A commemoration, which is a ritual or display intended to celebrate the memory of a person, a group, or an event, operates in the same way (Denis, 2015). It refers to the past in order to address the present. Commemorations, like individual memory, select, shape, and orient past experiences with a specific purpose. Commemorations can affect society, but they can also be influenced by the society in which they occur (Evaldsson & Wessels, 2003). Historical context can influence both commemoration and society at a particular point in their development.

Some commemorative purposes may be political, economic, or social (Ndlovu, 2015). In Southern Africa, independence celebrations and other national days are celebrated in many ways. National holidays contribute to the making of states and nations. Performances shape the state's role in national celebrations. The contested politics of memory shape the creation of any country's festival calendar[32]. Commemoration is sometimes marred by contestation over state control of national days and civic or popular participation.

Tourism is inextricably linked to national memorialisation or commemoration (West, 2010). Memorial tourism involves the combination of tourism, memorialisation, and commemoration through the transformation of historical trauma, war, or tragedy to a place of empathy, education and remembrance[33]. The intersection allows commodification of memory by engaging with the past for economic development[34]. Tourists may visit different locations that offer opportunities to reflect, learn, and engage with the past through memorials, museums, and historic sites.

---

[32] Mekonnen, H., Bires, Z. & Berhanu, K. Practices and challenges of cultural heritage conservation in historical and religious heritage sites: evidence from North Shoa Zone. 2022. Amhara Region, Ethiopia. Herit Sci 10, 172 (2022). https://doi.org/10.1186/s40494-022-00802-6

[33] Evaldsson, A and Wessels, A. To commemorate or not to commemorate: three important commemorative events in twentieth century South Africa. 2003. Journal for Contemporary History. 28, (1). https://hdl.handle.net/10520/EJC28270

[34] Madandola, M., & Boussaa, D. Cultural heritage tourism as a catalyst for sustainable development; the case of old Oyo town in Nigeria. 2023. International Journal of Heritage Studies, 29(1–2), 21–38. https://doi.org/10.1080/13527258.2023.2169332

West (2010) notes that memorialising often prompts memory, which manifests in the creation of museums and information centres. Paths, monuments, and memorial places may be reconstructed as tourist and hiking destinations (Repic, 2018). The construction of tourism facilities at memorial sites transforms these sites into tourism landscapes (Ndlovu, 2015). One example of building tourism facilities at memorial sites is in France, where, after World War I, the sites of many battles became places of pilgrimage (Gonzales, 2018). Landscapes in the Slovenian Alps, for example, have transformed from warscapes to landscapes of memory and history since World War I. Former military installations have been transformed into memorial sites and commemorative tourism through the construction of cemeteries and monuments (Repic, 2018). Memorials provide context for meaning-making and human involvement, both of which are essential components of tourism (Wagner-Pacifici & Schwartz, 1991). Researchers have investigated how memorial sites interpret violence or human rights violations (Isaac & Cakmak, 2016; Weaver et al., 2018).

Conclusion

The travel, leisure, and tourism sector has significant potential to contribute to global socio-economic and infrastructural development and social well-being. Tourism has had a profound impact on virtually every aspect of society, including politics, culture, and, most significantly, the economy. The rise of globalisation has had a far-reaching impact on nations worldwide. Hence, there are increasingly blurred boundaries between socio-cultural, religious, economic, and political life. Globalisation has created both opportunities and risks for historic and tourism areas. Tourism has become an important sector in many national economies. In the post-colonial era, the state has used heritage to promote social cohesion, whilst local groups have used it to seek rights and resources. Thus, heritage serves as a platform for marginalised populations to assert claims to resources and compensation.

Chapter 2
The Landscapes of History, Memory, and Culture in Southern Africa

This chapter discusses the importance of involving communities in the conservation of cultural landscapes. A disjuncture between national and local community interests often leads to epistemic violence. Cultural landscapes are multifaceted and provide linkages between people, place and their identities. The emphasis is placed on biocultural values and beliefs. Southern Africa has a rich history and culture, with deep-rooted memories that are associated with specific cultural identities. This chapter explores the diverse cultural landscapes that exist in Southern Africa. It examines the intersection of history, memory and culture to reveal the inextricable bond between culture and nature. The chapter describes how narratives create public memory by transforming chaotic historical events into structured, meaningful, and shared stories that define a group's identity. As a result, local ideas, values, and practices should be protected and reinforced as expressions of agency.

Theoretical Perspectives on the Relationship Between Heritage and Tourism

Using different theoretical lenses to explore history, heritage, memory, and culture in the context of tourism enables critical insights and relationships to emerge, resulting in a deeper understanding of phenomena. The use of theoretical frameworks allows researchers to interpret and model complex social, cultural, and historical phenomena. For this discussion of history, heritage, memory and culture in the context of tourism, structural-functional theory, conflict theory and symbolic interactionism provide a theoretical framework that facilitates an understanding of how a historical narrative is not just an assembly of facts but a selective, interpreted, and value-laden account.

Structural-Functional Theory and Heritage Tourism

Structural-functional theory focuses on how the different elements of a society function together to maintain stability. It provides a lens for seeing how heritage tourism can serve various roles in society, including cultural preservation, social integration, economic stimulation, and environmental conservation[1]. Communities can leverage heritage tourism to maintain and showcase their cultural identity. Cultural festivals and traditional performances can educate tourists while reinforcing cultural practices. Heritage tourism can foster economic stability by generating jobs and supporting local economies. Historical reenactments and preserved colonial architecture attract visitors, which, in turn, support local craftsmen, restaurants, and hotels. For example, in South Africa, Zulu communities employ cultural festivals and traditional performances to educate visitors while reinforcing their cultural practices. Cultural celebrations, such as the Diwali festival in South Africa, strengthen community ties while offering visitors opportunities to explore rich cultural legacies.

---

[1] Mason, M and Clarke. Poststructuralism and education. 2010. International Encyclopaedia of Human geography. 175-182.

Heritage tourism also has the potential to generate jobs and boost local economies. For example, Cape Town attracts visitors through historical reenactments and preserved colonial architecture, which benefits local craftspeople, restaurants, and hotels. In South Africa, a range of stakeholders, including local communities, government agencies, and civil society organisations, have developed memorial projects and established museums. Those initiating these projects have various perspectives on the importance of heritage and memorialisation (Hlongwane & Ndlovu, 2019). In the early years of social anthropology, structural functionalism viewed 'traditional' African civilisations as isolated, unchanging, and holistic systems. For instance, in South Africa, the apartheid ideology was premised on the institutionalisation of racial segregation and white supremacy. It reinforced the idea of separate development, creating artificial, rigid boundaries between racial and ethnic groups.

In Zimbabwe, the Rhodesia Front's ideology, founded on settler status concerns, supported a conspiratorial view of modern politics that highlighted virulent strains of Anglophobia, anticommunism, anti-internationalism, and anti-liberalism (Evans, 2007). However, modern critical studies in Southern Africa have rejected the notion that culture is fixed. Post-structuralists have argued that history, memory, and culture are actively formed, contested, and negotiated to meet present-day transformative demands[2]. Hence, counter-memories frequently compete for place alongside a dominant narrative that claims to

---

[2] Wood, k et al., Poststructuralism/Poststructuralist geographies. 2009. International Encyclopaedia of Human geography. 196-407.

promote nation-building and reconciliation. The official narrative claims that nation-building has led to a conceptualisation of a community that comprehends the truth about its traumatic past and has undertaken bold attempts at reconciliation (Hlongwane & Ndlovu, 2019). Memorialisation can create space for memories excluded from the official narrative to be held.

Heritage sites often serve an educational purpose. Museums and historical landmarks, for example, not only attract tourists and sustain societal ideals but also serve as educational institutions[3]. Communities may conserve their heritage while also supporting conservation efforts by fostering responsible tourism practices. At the Okavango Delta in Botswana, for example, tourism is used to support environmental conservation programs that benefit both the natural environment and the local economy.

Conflict Theory and Heritage Tourism

Conflict theory provides a useful lens for exploring which actors represent a culture in the context of tourism. At heritage sites, local communities may feel that their culture is being commodified for profit, leading to a conflict between the desire for economic benefits and the preservation of cultural integrity[4]. In some cases, traditional ceremonies have been altered to cater to tourists' expectations, sparking tension between local beliefs and commercial interests.

---

[3] Hein, G. 2005. The role of museums in society: Education and social action. Curator the museum Journal. 48(4). https://doi.10111/j.21516952.2005.tb00180.x

[4] Surata, K.I et al., The impact of cultural tourism on local traditions. 2024. JPPI (Journal Penellitian Pendidikan Indonesia) 10(4), 672-683.

Conflict theory illuminates the tensions arising from cultural appropriation, where dominant groups exploit the cultural symbols of marginalised communities without permission or understanding[5]. The use of Indigenous symbols in fashion often leads to protests from those communities, who assert their right to control their cultural narratives. There may be disputes over which narratives are presented and voices of local community members may be marginalised[6]. In some cases, the revenue generated by tourism is not shared equitably, leading to conflicts between local residents and external investors.

Conflicts also arise when tourism results in degradation of the natural environment, which affects the local communities that rely on natural resources. By analysing these conflicts, stakeholders can develop more equitable and sustainable tourism practices that respect and empower local communities while addressing economic needs.

Symbolic Interactionism and Heritage Tourism

Symbolic interactionism (SI) is a theory that can be used to examine how tourists and hosts co-create meaning through encounters with sites, objects, and the other. This perspective shifts the emphasis from objective historical facts to subjective experiences (Pansiri, 2023). It seeks to understand how tourists

---

[5] Dladla A et al., Incorporating cultural heritage into local tourism development strategy in KwaNdebele: A systematic review.2023. African Journal of Hospitality, Tourism, and Leisure.12(5SE), 1740-1753.

[6] Beach D and Vigo-Arrazola, M.B. Researching in solidarity with marginalised groups: A meta-ethnography about research for educational justice and social transformation. International Journal of qualitative studies in education. 37(10) 2981-2996.

perceive symbols (e.g., monuments, traditional ware) and negotiate and their identities during a visit. Pansiri (2023) writes:

> Objects are products of SI and are defined as anything that can be indicated, designated or referred to and could be classified for purposes of convenience into three categories namely: (a) Physical objects such as organizational policies, organizational tangible resources; (b) Social objects such as managers, subordinates, students organizational stakeholders, the human resource in general; (c) Abstract objects such as moral principles, social responsibility, organizational culture, vision and mission statements and philosophy. (p.353)

Pansiri (2023) notes that these categories are not inflexible, as all objects are created and shaped through the process of social interaction. As a result, all objects are social objects and are defined contextually. The function that people attached to a particular object or event makes it

meaningful and this meaning can change as the context changes (Oloidi, 2020). As a result, the meaning of an object to a community might change over time—not because its attributes vary, but because individuals modify their definitions based on their interaction with the object (Zhong et al., 2025).

Interaction with objects is the core activity of tourism. Pansiri (2023) observes that this "interaction can be with (i) social objects such as tourism company employees, host communities, tourists and/or guests; (ii) abstract objects such as ethics for tourism, tourism and culture, the responsible tourist, social responsibility in tourism etc.; and (iii) physical objects such as government laws/policies; the environment and an organizational or destination's tangible resources" (p. 354).

Cultures produce unique symbols that carried layered meanings. The symbolic interactionist perspective provides a lens for understanding how communities curate their cultural presentations[7]. During the face-to-face interactions that occur through tourism, communities build cultural presentations by co-creating meaning with tourists. Oloidi (2020) uses Clifford Geertz's argument about "local residents interpreting their culture for tourists through meaning (dress, rituals, symbols), language (words, expressions, verbal and non-verbal cues), symbolism (signs, gestures, behaviour norms), thought (social reality, methods, topics) and heritage sites" (p.47. These encounters enable hosts and tourists to shape and negotiate cultural identities in real time.

Tourists often seek authentic experiences. When they engage with local cultures through stories and traditions, they gain deeper insight into local beliefs, enriching their experience[8]. Tour guides serve as mediators of culture, guiding tourists through experiences that shape their understanding. The interaction between tourists and local communities can lead to the development of shared meanings. When tourists participate in traditional ceremonies, it may foster dialogue, mutual respect and deeper understanding[9]. Stakeholders in culture and heritage

---

[7] Carter, J.M and Fuller, C. Symbolic interactionism. 2015. Sociopedia. https://doi.10.1177/205684601561.

[8] Stevenson, N. Developing cultural understanding through story telling. 2018. Journal of Teaching in Travel and Tourism. 19(2), 1-14.

[9] Cathy, T. Tourism Culture and its implications: Intersection of Travel and Local Traditions. 2024. Journal of Tourism and Hospitality. 13(3), 10000551

tourism can find ways to make their culture 'better' from the visitors, to enable them to create engaging and respectful experiences that benefit both visitors and host communities.

Tangible and intangible heritage

An understanding of tangible and intangible heritage is important in tourism because it enables a deeper understanding of a destination's living culture. Engaging with both tangible and intangible heritage facilitates authentic experiences for visitors, which in turn can promote sustainable development and conservation, empower communities, and enhance cross-cultural understanding and education[10].

Tangible Heritage

Tangible heritage refers to the physical manifestation or symbol of the significant cultural expressions or traditions of an area[11]. It includes monuments, mosques, shrines, monasteries, and historic cities. Tangible heritage can further be classified as immovable or movable heritage. Moveable tangible heritage refers to objects such as pottery, furniture and musical instruments (Ruoss & Alfarè, 2013). Immovable tangible heritage includes buildings, monuments, memorials, archaeological sites, and cultural landscapes. Historical buildings are structures that have been the site of significant events and are referenced in historical

---

[10] Candeloro, G and Tartari, M. Heritage-led stainable development in rural areas: The case of Vivi Calascio community-based cooperative. 2025. Cities. 161. 105920. https://doi.10.1016/j.cities.2025.105920.

[11] Reshma, M.R. et al., Cultural heritage preservation through dance digitization: A review. 2023. Digital Applications in Archaeology and Cultural Heritage. 28. E00257. https://doi.org/10.1016/j.daach.23.e00257.

narratives[12]. Monuments and memorials are structures erected to commemorate historical events, figures, or cultures. Archaeological sites are locations that contain evidence of past human activity[13]. Cultural landscapes are areas where the interaction between human activity and the natural environment has resulted in a unique and meaningful landscape.

Intangible Heritage

Intangible heritage refers to the non-physical manifestations of the cultural expressions and traditions of a society that reflect the cultural values and practices of past generations. Intangible heritage includes oral traditions, social practices, traditional music, folklore, rituals and festivals, craftsmanship, language, foodways, and indigenous knowledge and practices concerning nature and the universe[14]. Oral traditions are stories, legends, and myths passed down through generations. Rituals and festivals are practices that connect people to their history and cultural heritage. Music, art, and crafts are expressive forms that reflect the cultural identity of a place[15]. Foodways refer to the culinary traditions and practices that are deeply rooted in a place's history. Intangible cultural heritage also encompasses living traditions or

---

[12] Rizzo, I and Prieto, H.C.L. Economics and Archaeological Heritage. 2024. Encyclopaedia of Archaeology (second Edition). 1, 617-625. https://doi.org/10.1016/B978-0-323-90799-6.00072-0

[13] Candeloro, G and Tartari, M. Heritage-led stainable development in rural areas: The case of Vivi Calascio community-based cooperative. 2025. Cities. 161. 105920. https://doi.10.1016/j.cities.2025.105920.

[14] UNESCO. What is intangible cultural heritage.

[15] Candeloro, G and Tartari, M. Heritage-led stainable development in rural areas: The case of Vivi Calascio community-based cooperative. 2025. Cities. 161. 105920. https://doi.10.1016/j.cities.2025.105920.

expressions that have been passed down from previous generations to the living members of a community.

The Nexus of Tourism, Heritage, Memory and Identity

Tourism, as an industry, exploits natural resources to attract visitors to destinations. The natural environment includes essential resources (rivers, lakes, oceans, wildlife, vegetation, mountains, and other characteristics) that can be freely used by all (Schlosberg, 2004). Natural heritage spaces, however, reflect a broader set of values for most people, including recreational, spiritual, and cultural identities. The belief that natural sites and features provide intangible, often undefinable, qualities is a fundamental motivation in the expansion of tourism—particularly, cultural tourism.

Cocksa et al. (2017) propose that a "biocultural diversity perspective of heritage not only recognises the inextricable relationship between nature and culture, but provide prominence to the beliefs, values and practices of local people, in strengthening their agency to safeguard their heritage in ways and forms that are relevant to them" (p. 3). Curated story-driven narratives and preserved landmarks are important for creating lasting interactive, emotional and educational experiences. The use of history, heritage, and memorialization are strategies that can be used for exploring the past in the present. They link current issues and with past experiences and highlight patterns in society. The understanding of historical perspectives can help society to trace the evolution of problems and foster and predict future trends.

Heritage tourism can facilitate intercultural exchange between people, countries, and regions. Park (2014) asserts that historical tourism fosters social connections among people. It enables a conversation between the present and the past, with multiple voices debating the reality of the past.

Memory is regarded as the primary conduit for intangible cultural assets, while identity serves as the channel for knowledge and action, and tourism acts as an intermediary for articulating identity (Ndlovu, 2015). As a result, memory serves as both a source and a repository of identity. Sturken (20080 notes that "memory is the product of continual activity by individuals and groups through memorialisation, ritual acts, shrine and construction" (p. 74). However, in nonliterate groups, memory as practice or lived experience becomes an important source of heritage knowledge (Keitumetse et al., 2011).

Memorialization can either reinforce or challenge current historical and mythical meanings. These processes frequently occur between contenders of unequal strength, with differing levels of significance given to history and memory (Hlongwane & Ndlovu, 2019). Keitumetse et al. (2011) state that memory-based heritage identity construction differs from traditional heritage management practices. Traditionally, people consider themselves to be part of their landscape. They do not just live on the land, but they also live through it by materially and symbolically shaping it while it also shapes their identities and relationships. The existing connection results in place attachment, with the surrounding environment becoming part of an inseparable personal and collective identity. Therefore, their worldviews and spirituality are deeply intertwined with their natural environment.

The relationship between heritage and tourism is both conflicted and cooperative (McKercher et al., 2003) with the prospect of financial sometimes in tension with heritage values (Urry, 1990). The balancing of cultural conservation and historical or cultural assets with financial gains may result in negative equity. Very often, the pressure to increase the number of tourists in a destination can result in physical degradation of the environment and displacement of communities. Wanjohi (2002) writes about the influence of cultural tourism on Kenya's Maasai community. He claims that, due to the economic benefits of tourism, traditional performances are being stage-managed and removed from the surroundings that give them meaning. Tourism thus reinterprets culture and integrates it into the economic production process (Ndlovu, 2015).

It is, however, possible for tourism to strengthen heritage (McKercher et al., 2003). The experience at heritage sites encourages visitors to connect with multiple identities and their sense of identity. It is this aspect of the phenomena that distinguishes these locations or attractions, particularly because they challenge both tourists and destination operators to broaden their sense of space and time based on their worldview (James, 1996).

Sacred natural sites are part of a broader collection of cultural values that different social groups, traditions, beliefs, or value systems attach to places and which, as Putney (2005) states, "fulfil humankind's yearning to comprehend and relate in meaningful ways" (p. 132). Mountains, hills, woods, groves, rivers, lakes, lagoons, caves, islands, and springs are some of the natural features found at sacred natural locations. These features might be modest, such as a single tree, a little spring, or a single rock formation, or large, such as landscapes and mountain ranges. Sacred historical places have a significant impact on the preservation and protection of national culture and tradition. The cultural and traditional qualities of sacred sites have an impact on the tourism industry, which necessitates a careful balance between commercial use and preservation of tradition.

A diverse range of actors, including politicians, travel agents, regional governments, policy makers, and hotels, make up the extensive network of intermediaries that supports the socio-cultural aspects of heritage tourism. Furthermore, heritage tourism offers a platform for comprehending discourses, images, and representations of the 'other'.

Benefits and Negative Effects of Cultural and Heritage Tourism

Cultural and heritage tourism offers numerous benefits to destination areas. It is a fast-growing and high-yielding sector that tends to attract tourists interested in cultural activities who often stay longer and spend more money that other types of tourists.

Many developing countries have placed a major focus on cultural and heritage tourism as a channel for stimulating economic growth and enhancing the socio-economic well-being of their people. Economically, cultural and heritage tourism contributes to a nation's Gross Domestic Product (GDP), as spending by tourists directly and indirectly injects new money into the economy through the multiplier effect. Taxes generated by tourist spending can be used to develop communities and raise their standard of living. The tourism industry is a labour-intensive sector that generates employment opportunities, through indirect gains like improved infrastructure, education, health, and environmental preservation. Tourism can stimulate entrepreneurship and small businesses and promote the diversification of the local economy. The growing tourism sector may contribute to pro-poor growth compared to other sectors. Tourism can thus play a significant role in alleviating poverty (Saayman et al., 2012).

The use of tourism as an important route to poverty reduction has been reported frequently in the literature. However, there is no agreement among scholars on the most effective way to use tourism to address poverty (Woyo & Musavengane, 2023). Researchers argue that pro-poor tourism contributes to poverty alleviation while others are of the opinion that tourism growth and development is exploitative. Their argument is based on the premise that tourism revenues do not benefit the poor due to leakages (Woyo & Woyo, 2018). Some have argued that countries can develop appropriate policy instruments to reduce external leakages.

Socially, cultural and heritage tourism provides opportunities for greater understanding and communication between people of diverse backgrounds, as residents of local communities interact with tourists, reducing stereotyping and prejudice[16]. It facilitates cultural exchange between host populations and tourists, thereby promoting the preservation of local traditions, customs, and culture[17]. Cultural and heritage tourism provides opportunities for work placements, research, and education for students interested in expanding their knowledge base. It also reinforces local and national identity (Estonian, 2001).

Environmentally, cultural and heritage tourism encourages a culture of preservation among local communities, as the livelihood derived from tourism depends on the attractions being kept in a pristine state[18]. It further raises awareness of the significance of tourist sites and attractions, teaching residents and visitors to be mindful of their impact on both the natural and built environments.

Despite the many benefits of cultural and heritage tourism, it can also have significant negative impacts on tourism destinations. For example, social pressure and environmental issues appear to be significant challenges at many cultural heritage sites (Huibin & Marzuki, 2012). Residents who resent tourist interference or profit-sharing gaps may oppose conservation efforts or advocate for commodification that undermines heritage integrity. Activists may oppose tourism initiatives they perceive as damaging or demand better stewardship, clashing with other stakeholders.

---

[16] Salama, E.M. Exploring the sociocultural influence of cultural heritage Tourism. 2024. International Journal for Holistic Research. 2(1), 20-39.
[17] Candeloro, G and Tartari, M. Heritage-led stainable development in rural areas: The case of Vivi Calascio community-based cooperative. 2025. Cities. 161. 105920. https://doi.10.1016/j.cities.2025.105920.
[18] Wijayanti, A. et al., Community Based Heritage Tourism Management Model: Perception Driven participation. 12(4), 1630-1645.

Given these factors, stakeholders in the cultural and heritage tourism industry need to develop policies that optimise the benefits offered by tourism and implement long-term measures to mitigate negative effects[19].

Blurring the Boundary between Materiality and Intangible Heritage

The relationship between heritage, memory, and identity is multifaceted, deep, and mutually beneficial (Ndlovu, 2015; Park, 2014). In 2003, the UNESCO Convention for the Safeguarding of the Intangible Cultural Heritage was adopted to ensure that indigenous and minority rights are recognised and protected. Despite being important for identity, cultural heritage has been exposed to public discourse and homogenising language that continues to hinder its integration. Although debates have revolved around material heritage and respective legal regimes, intangible cultural heritage has continued to face challenges in being fully integrated into both academic curricula and professional practitioners. Cultural heritage has been criticised for its neocolonial approach, which prioritises the written forms of heritage and neglects the cultural human dimension of practice[20]. Consequently, the Global South has demanded reforms to international law, arguing that cultural preservation is currently rooted in a Western-centric framework of individualistic and liberal traditions, insufficient to address

---

[19] Brooks, C. et al., Exploring the relationships between heritage tourism, sustainable community development and host communities' health and well-being: A systematic review. 2023. 18930, e0282319.

[20] Wijayanti, A. et al., Community Based Heritage Tourism Management Model: Perception Driven participation. 12(4), 1630-1645.

systemic inequalities, structural domination, and collective harm (Eslava & Pahuja, 2020).

In Southern Africa, the boundary between materiality and intangible heritage has become increasingly blurred due to objects, practices, and spaces that disrupt simple classifications. The meanings of the region's material culture are carried through different artefacts as vessels[21]. These include sacred sites, landscapes, pottery, beadwork, and rock art that carry meaning through time. Living traditions, songs, dance, storytelling and crafts are displayed in different material forms. The blurring is demonstrated across people, places and the media, which shows the need to offer a more holistic understanding of heritage that is visible, portable and negotiated within contemporary contexts[22].

The Blurring of Symbolic Boundaries

Different communities in Southern Africa demonstrate the integration of discrete objects through a combination of rich, longstanding traditions and manufactured, imported, or recycled materials[23]. For instance, in Mpumalanga, the Ndebele people have used their colourful beadwork to encode social status. Beads are used to signify marital eligibility and tell communal history. Granddaughters have been taught by grandmothers how to design bead patterns for certain ceremonial dresses. The dresses

---

[21] Sanchez-Climent, A. Materiality and Immateriality: Exploring material culture in the Construction of Cultural Meanings. 2024. Global Journal of Cultural Studies. 3, 116-125.

[22] Wang, Z. Tourism Imaginaryband Landscape at Heritage Sites: A case in Honghe Hani Rice Terraces, China. Land. 10(4)439.

[23] Dladla A et al., Incorporating cultural heritage into local tourism development strategy in KwaNdebele: A systematic review.2023. African Journal of Hospitality, Tourism, and Leisure.12(5SE), 1740-1753.

are won, photographed, and exhibited through various media platforms, thereby transforming private knowledge into public narrative. Materiality is symbolised not only through tradition; it is transmitted, adapted and communicated across generations and borders[24]. The rock art and landscapes in Namibia, South Africa, Zimbabwe and Botswana blur boundaries, transforming physical spaces into intangible narratives. The Drakensberg Mountains in South Africa and Lesotho, the Cederberg Wilderness Area of South Africa, the Matobo Hills of Zimbabwe, the Tsodilo Hills of Botswana, and Twyfelfontein in Namibia are perceived as pedagogical canvases with rich cosmological stories of origin and survival performed on site. At the sites, engravings and pigments are complemented by rituals that immerse visitors in meaning and interpretation carried through oral history. These arts are not confined to museums; they are alive as oral historical accounts shared with visitors. Researchers and visitors participate in memory work, which extends the sites' significance in contemporary economic growth.

The Blurring of Social Boundaries

Wel et al. (2022) argue that heritage tourism "plays a central role in developing, promoting, and strengthening national identities among domestic and even international tourism" (p. 8798). Performances are part of intangible heritage, materialised through music. In Zimbabwe, mbira music is a form of social ritual in Shona communities. The mbira is an ancient instrument with metal keys, often placed in a large gourd (*deze*) to intensify

---

[24] Sanchez-Climent, A. Materiality and Immateriality: Exploring material culture in the Construction of Cultural Meanings. 2024. Global Journal of Cultural Studies. 3, 116-125

its resonance and reverberation. The music is bound to social rituals and healing practices, and it is played particularly during communal gatherings. The act of playing, singing, and dancing brings the community together. The mbira is believed to be a spiritual instrument, and its timbre is said to convey the voices of the ancestors (*mbira dzavadzimu*).

In South Africa, a cappella groups that blend close-harmony singing with synchronized, tiptoe choreography, called isicathamiya choirs, use wind-and-drum ensembles to transform urban and rural spaces[25]. These groups have commodified performances by transforming performances into memory through migration histories and social aspiration. The performances have transformed the intangible heritage through dress, music, and instruments into a material and economic phenomenon. This blurring is underscored by the ethical dimensions of repatriation and conservation.

Museums provide temporary exhibitions, while monuments serve as backdrops for activities such as music and theatre performances (Hlongwane & Ndlovu, 2029). For instance, Laurajane Smith acknowledges that museums and heritage objects are not merely rooted in the past, but are active agents in shaping contemporary identities and economies (Menozzi, 2024).

There are talks between Germany and Namibia, and Zimbabwe and Britain, about the repatriation of sacred objects, human remains and significant cultural items[26]. The current debates

---

[25] Mihalka, M. Isicathamiya. Music in World Cultures.

[26] Batt, F. The repatriation of African Heritage: Shutting the door on the imperialist narrative. 2021. African Human rights yearbook. 328-350.

reignite discussions on how material claims can either support or undermine intangible rights and communal governance. This has been complicated by digital technologies, which have turned living practices into tourism products without engaging local communities. Therefore, the blurring requires policy interventions to build a strong relationship between living practices and material heritage[27]. This calls for integration and representation of diverse voices in decision-making to support customary memory.

Merriman (2000) believes that heritage tourism can be used to construct new national and ethnic mythologies and inform new identities to mould together historically distinct groups. The intricate interdependence between objects, sites, and stories should be preserved through ethical data sharing, co-curation and community beneficiation. To nurture a more inclusive and creative heritage sector, Southern Africa should start to understand the mutually constitutive nature of materiality and intangibility.

Tourist Attractions and Interests in History and Heritage

The unique stories and memories associated with a place can draw visitors from across the world. The issue of authenticity is crucial to scholarly discussions of historic tourism (Wang, 1999). The concept of authenticity is often used to explain visitors' motivations and experiences in a general sense. Thus, genuine

---

[27] Banda, L.O.L. et al., Preserving landscape changes in the built environment at World Heritage Sites: Lessons from Bukovina, Romania. 2021. Journal of Destination Marketing. 20, 100583.

and believable cultural constructions and representations are important in various heritage contexts[28]. Tourism service providers may construct authentic experiences to appeal to authenticity seekers (Salazar & Graburn, 2014). Tourists who visit heritage sites often focus more on an authentic experience than on the underlying local reality (Marshall, 2013). Tourists are typically unaware of the broader political, economic, and sociological contexts within which heritage tourism operates (Salazar, 2005). In South Africa, for example, tourists may not be aware that the Zulu cultural villages that serve as tourist destinations may have been established solely for that purpose.

The globalization of the tourism industry has spurred alternative visitor experiences, which include the international movement of sites of conscience[29]. Sites of conscience are historical sites of oppression or mass atrocity that are utilised to foster remembering, discourse, and action in order to defend and promote human rights. Sites of Conscience are most commonly linked to the International Coalition of Sites of Conscience (ICSC), which is a network that assists in the conversion of former prisons, ghettos, battlefields, slave-trade ports, and other violent sites into educational and centres of community activism[30]. This movement aims to remember and trace the legacies of contestations for justice through civic engagement programs (Hlongwane & Ndlovu, 2019). The International Coalition of

---

[28] Labadi, S. Representations of the nation and cultural diversity in discourses on World Heritage. Journal of social archaeology. 7(2), 147-170.

[29] Heath, E. Globalisation of tourism industry: Future trends and challenges for South Africa. 2001. South African Journal of Economic and Management Sciences, 4(3), 542-569.

[30] Un, Report on the Special Rapporteur in the field of cultural rights, Farida Shaheed. UN General Assembly.

Historic Sites of Conscience includes individuals and remembrance institutions from all across the world. In South Africa, these include Robben Island Museum, Constitution Hill, and the District Six Museum in Cape Town. Kolmanskop, in Namibia, and the National Heroes' Acre, in Zimbabwe, are also sites of conscience.

In Search of Meaningful Experiences

Heritage tourism allows visitors to connect with the past, fostering understanding and appreciation of a location's cultural heritage (Salazar & Graburn, 2014). Many tourists seek authentic heritage, which can include undisturbed landscapes, traditional indigenous performances, private community spaces, and ethnic festivals. Heritage of liberation struggles can promote civic engagement in post-conflict cultures. Heritage places offer opportunities for oppressed individuals to confront their past and address social justice issues (Hlongwane & Ndlovu, 2019).

What counts as authentic varies from one tourist to another, as authenticity is not static but is negotiated between the guest and the destination before, during, and after the journey[31]. Authenticity also has different meanings in different societies. Nicolaides states that "the modern tourist does not simply travel to feel satisfied, but it is important to have a true reflection of the destination that they are visiting. Pseudo-events are by their nature inauthentic, and when tourists partake in them, they are essentially replicating the false patterns that comprise their daily

---

[31] Yeh, S. et al., Destination authenticity influence on tourists' behavioural intentions, involvement, and nostalgic sentiments. Tourism review. 80(2) 456-471.

existence" (p.3). Authenticity implies that tourists seek a connection to something genuine, unspoilt, and unique to a specific place. Authenticity must be tied to the place and situated within the local community. This shows that authenticity creates significant development prospects for local communities, increasing the number of sustainable tourism initiatives (Gundlach & Neville, 2012). Tourist destinations should thus contribute to the benefit of local communities and to the authenticity of their offerings. Visitors may experience disorientation when they travel outside their usual environment, which increases their emotional and cognitive engagement with the destination, making their tourism experience more authentic (Tiberghien et al., 2020).

Community Development and Local Identity

In Southern Africa, historical, cultural, and memory landscapes are inextricably linked with community development (Cocks et al., 2017), as well as social cohesion and economic growth. Cultural landscapes are shaped by human interaction with geographical areas. These interactions include natural and spiritual places that are used for creating local identity, developing tourism, and community empowerment in post-conflict settings[32]. Heritage tourism can empower local communities by preserving their cultural heritage and creating economic opportunities. Heritage sites have been monetised and made into consumable products to improve the visitor experience, which has been criticised for resulting in a loss of

---

[32] Kasmin, K. Sustainable tourism Development Based on Community Empowerment through local culture. 2025. SHS Web of Conferences. https://doi.10.1051/shsconf/202522601007.

meaning and authenticity[33]. Tourists utilise their purchasing power to shape their imagination and consumption preferences, thereby shaping how places are depicted and represented.

Implications of Landscapes of Memory in Southern Africa

In Southern Africa, landscapes of memory relate to how sites—such as museums, monuments, ruins, graves, streets, and even agricultural fields—encode and mobilise communal memory about colonialism, apartheid, liberation, and postcolonial struggles. They have far-reaching consequences for politics, society, culture, and policy.

Monuments and memorials contain a narrative about national identity. South Africa has worked actively since the end of apartheid to reshape its commemorative landscape through the creation of new memorials and monuments that symbolise the liberation struggle and promote reconciliation (Salazar, 2005). Tributes commemorating the anti-apartheid movement—such as Robben Island, District Six, and Freedom Park—influence who is regarded as a legitimate national hero. Landscapes of memory are interlinked to land rights. Sites of forced removals, such as District Six in Cape Town, and restitution programs show the relationship between memory and land restitution, and this can be integrated into rebuilding communities and preserving these sites as a testimony.

---

[33] Yeh, S. et al., Destination authenticity influence on tourists' behavioural intentions, involvement, and nostalgic sentiments. Tourism review. 80(2) 456-471.

Memory landscapes can be used as tourist attractions to stimulate economic activities and preserve local cultural norms[34]. Schools and museums employ memory landscapes to teach history and shape young people's sense of responsibility, identification, and pride. The preservation or erasure of memory in urban and rural areas can impact people's daily livelihoods[35]. Although the establishment of preservation rules can safeguard gravesites and cemeteries, these rules can also impede growth or property rights, particularly if they are not balanced with the needs of the community. Although emphasis is placed on the importance of recognising and protecting local cultural landscapes as reflections of and for local people's cultural heritage, this should not preclude efforts to generate outside interest in, and a better understanding and appreciation of, cultural landscapes (Cocks et al., 2017). Ecotourism can generate wealth and economic growth by attracting visitors to a place to enjoy local landscapes and culture, and to foster community pride.

Conclusion

In conclusion, landscapes are active, contested, and intensely personal centres of memory, power and identity. They play a central role in both the marginalisation of the past and the empowerment of communities, as well as connecting cultural identity to socioeconomic progress. Traditionally, they have been used to express power, wealth, and colonial histories. Despite

[34] Heath, E. Globalisation of tourism industry: Future trends and challenges for South Africa. 2001. South African Journal of Economic and Management Sciences, 4(3), 542-569.

[35] Dai, Y et al., From memory to really: Preservation and Transmitting Collective Memory in urban Historic Neighbourhoods. 2026. Sage Journals. 16 (1), https://doi.org/10.1177/21582440261424596.

being marginalised, sacred places are frequently employed to oppose coloniality and preserve indigenous memory. When properly managed, cultural heritage can drive economic growth and stimulate long-term development. The use of eco-tourism has a potential inspire pride while also providing economic returns for local communities. However, the success of heritage management depends on an inclusive approach. Heritage preservation should move beyond Eurocentric approaches and focus more on living heritage. The new approach should focus on transforming heritage by empowering local communities to steward their natural and cultural landscapes.

Chapter 3
The Development of Cultural Heritage in Southern Africa

The theoretical concepts of rationality and preference can serve as valuable lenses to understand the evolution of heritage tourism in Southern Africa. Through heritage tourism, tourists, local communities, and policymakers interact through a complex tapestry of sites and memories. Considering demand, rational actors consider the costs and benefits of visiting places. Tourists' preferences for authenticity, education, and unique cultural experiences can influence their choice of tourism destinations. Considering supply, destinations respond to choices by investing in information centres, conservation, and accessible infrastructure. Rational choices drive realistic projections of tourism flows, revenue generation, and employment creation. In Southern Africa, the institutional landscape is distinct in terms of public funding, community-based management and international tourism networks. The combination of rationality and preferences can shed light on the emergence of specific flagship routes in southern Africa. Policy design and economic incentives shape long-term conservation and equitable community benefits. This chapter critically discusses the development of cultural heritage in Southern Africa and individual tourist choices and preferences. This chapter will critically examine the roles of tourism and development in Southern Africa, focusing on key aspects, including economic development, cultural and heritage tourism, and community-based tourism (CBT). It will also examine how tourism marketing and promotion impact regional competitiveness, while maintaining political stability and safety remains crucial for attracting tourists.

Rational Choice Theory, Preferences and Heritage Tourism

Orthodox economists have used preferences as if they have an equal right to be fulfilled in mainstream economic theory (Jackson, 2013). Individual preferences have played a central role in economics, explaining and predicting the behaviour of groups and individuals. As such, they have been used to evaluate and aggregate behavioural outcomes[1]. The basic concept underlying microeconomic theory is the rationality postulate, which posits that consumers always choose the alternative they prefer from a set of available options (Cherchi, 2009). Individual choices regarding environmental goods and services are reflected in individual preferences, which economists use to infer individuals' economic values[2]. Orthodox economics places greater emphasis on individual preferences and conceptualizes them as relatively autonomous and atomistic (Loewenstein & Prelec, 1993; Davis, 2003). Thus, they assess whether any change that occurs is beneficial or detrimental and evaluate the extent to which an outcome is positive or negative.

In traditional economics, individuals are viewed as rational agents who seek to maximise their preferences. The assumption is that if an agent is uncertain about the outcomes of their choices,

---

[1] Blackburn, W.D and Ukhov, A. Individual vs Aggregate preferences: The case of a small fish in a big pond. 2013. Management Sciences. 59(2), 470-484.
[2] Dutt, A.K. et al., Individual preferences, efficiency, and Coost Benefit Analysis. In: Economics and Ethics. Palgrave Macmillan, London.

they will evaluate other available options, provided they know what the end chances look like. The model assumes that the agent's preferences can be measured numerically in terms of utility (Adler et al., 2003). The individual's awareness is disconnected from reality. Janssen-Lauret (2018) explains that the individual is separated from the world in a dualistic manner, which signifies a separation between the internal mind and the external real world[3].

Individual preferences are assumed to be modelled by utility functions (which order their preferences) relating their consumption of goods or, more generally, the state of the world (which could include how much leisure time they have, or how clean the environment is), to their level of satisfaction or utility[4]. The assumption is that an individual's utility level increases with the amount of goods and services consumed but decreases with the time spent working. In this case, Individual preferences are used to evaluate overall global social states.

For orthodox economists, individual preferences are important insofar as they allow people to make choices over goods or, more generally, 'over states of the world' (Kontoleon et al., 2002). In contrast, heterodox economists view individuals as embedded in socio-economic relationships. They view the economic tradition of preferences as being primitive, consistent, and immutable (preference rationality); consumers are seen as behaving as if they

---

[3] Janseen-Lauret, F. Elisabeth of Bohemia as a Naturalistic Dualist. In E. Thomas (Ed.) Early Modern Women on Metaphysics. Pp.171-187. Cambridge University Press.

[4] Broome, J. Economics and Ethics. International Encyclopedia of the Social Behavioural Sciences. 4146-4152. https://doi.org/10.1016/B0-08-043076-7/01025-1.

possess the formal tools with which to calculate the optimum adequately (perception-rationality), and the cognitive process is simply about preference maximization, given the market constraints (process-rationality) (Cherchi, 2009).

The economic model understands preference as an agent's ranking of their choices and the various possible outcomes of those choices (Kornhauser, 2003). When faced with a situation that requires action, people tend to choose courses of action that are likely to yield the best overall outcome. Rational choice theory posits that individuals are likely to act in a way that balances costs and benefits to maximise their benefits[5]. The concept of rationality is used to define homo economics, which assumes that individuals possess a mental ordering of preferences that enables them to have perfect information about all available options and the possible consequences of their actions (Cherchi, 2009).

In contrast to orthodox economists, neoclassical economists classify and understand an individual's behaviour as a choice behaviour, with beliefs, tastes, and preferences originating from within the person and introduced endogenous preferences[6]. The major difference between the two perspectives is their understanding of society (or the policy maker or the courts) on whose preferences matter when making decisions (Kontoleon et al., 2002; Semov, 2009). For instance, in his preference model, Veblen posits that preferences are socially determined,

---

[5] Paternoster, R. et al., Rational Choice Theory and Interest in the Fortune of Others. 2017. Journal of Research in Crime and delinquency. 54(6). https://doi.101177/0022427817707240.

[6] Lorek, S et al. Consumption and Savings. Encyclopaedia of Social movement. 471-480.

depending on the social hierarchy an individual occupies in society[7]. The lack of consensus among economists on a universal model of preferences creates significant challenges for individuals in making decisions, as there is no single framework for correctly valuing choices (Specian, 2015).

Psychologists view decision-making as dynamic and individual behaviour as local, adaptive, learned, context-dependent, mutable, and influenced by complex interactions of perceptions, motives, and attitudes (Cherchi, 2009). The best choice for a rational agent, then, is the choice that maximizes their preferences or utility, adjusting for the probabilities of which she is aware of obtaining specific outcomes (Adler et al., 2003).

Economists' approach to preferences is inherently instrumentalist and anthropocentric. Rational choice theory offers an operational framework that illuminates mixed-motive settings where incentives for cooperation and conflict coexist (Ainsworth, 2020; Ogu, 2013). The argument that people make choices under constraints, such as time, information, and income, is not only narrow but also contradictory. Numerous variables influence an individual's choices and preferences. This contradiction is justified by the notions of trade-offs and economic value. Economic value is the amount individuals give up in exchange for something (Arrow, 1951). However, this assumes that the choices people make over bundles of things are merely choice realisation. When an agent's actions fail to maximise their preferences or utility, the agent is perceived to be rational as long as the actions were selected based on the prior intention or

[7] Karaarslan, N.O. An Illustration of Social Type: The Idle in Veblen Sociology. Ictimaiyat. 9(1) 538-555.

context. For instance, economists argue that rational agents may adopt plans that involve suboptimal actions when comparing the cost of complying with the plan to the net benefit it provides (Adler et al., 2003). The rationality of an agent may be based on the benefits of use and non-use. Yet, there is no evidence that suggests that values are, in fact, non-specific to goods and do not vary with the nature or size of the good (Kontoleon et al., 2002).

Orthodox economists assume that individuals are actors in society and everywhere and will act rationally in a self-calculating, self-maximising and self-interested manner for the ultimate good of the larger society[8]. There is a need to consider the range of economic habits that drive economic motives that are not always self-regarding. The assumption that an agent can be risk-averse or risk-loving, considering the components of outcomes, does not differentiate the behavioural traits of individuals, such as economic situation, personality, lifestyle, occupation, self-concept, and age[9].

Individuals choose their actions optimally, given their preferences and the opportunities or constraints they face (Ogu, 2013). Optimality occurs when an individual has no preferred course of action other than the one chosen. Economic models allow agents to have greedy preferences that are wholly focused on the agent's consumption and ignore other preferred features of outcomes (Schelling, 1978; Bikhchandani et al., 1998). Thus,

---

[8] Lorek, S et al. Consumption and Savings. Encyclopaedia of Social movement. 471-480.

[9] Karaarslan, N.O. An Illustration of Social Type: The Idle in Veblen Sociology. Ictimaiyat. 9(1) 538-555.

intuitively preferred outcomes—such as accomplishment, relationships, fair dealing, and emotions—are often overlooked.

While rationality is the predominant assumption of rational choice, models of rational choice vary in sophistication, with a foundation in individual, goal-oriented behaviour (Morrow, 1994). Choice is sometimes constrained by the environment to the point that it becomes unrepresentative of the individual's decision or preferences, rendering it unpredictable or impossible to evaluate[10]. Others have employed the 'complexity of the good' argument, which acknowledges that economic value is a valid concept but not applicable to heritage products, as they are too complex to be commodified (Kontoleon et al., 2002). Within a complex society, individuals are defined by and choose groups or ideologies based on their affiliations with socio-economic and cultural groups. Therefore, if individuals shift their binary positions to another during the period of analysis, the completeness condition of rational preferences can be violated. Individuals often lack complete control over their own preferences due to external factors.

To be clear, the at least as good as' relation can order complex, multidimensional issues, but complex, multidimensional issues allow strategic actors to debate the relevance of one dimension over another (Ogu, 2013). Transitivity can be challenging to maintain under certain conditions, casting doubt on the existence of rational preferences. There is agreement that aggregating transitive group preference orders is more challenging than

---

[10] Paternoster, R. et al., Rational Choice Theory and Interest in the Fortune of Others. 2017. Journal of Research in Crime and delinquency. 54(6). https://doi.101177/0022427817707240.

homogeneous preferences. To derive favourable results, ordinal preferences are needed to order the market basket from most preferred to least preferred; however, this information may not always be available (Rabin, 1998). The information can only be derived from cardinal preferences, which describe how the market basket is preferred to other baskets. The utility of a product should reflect underlying preferences. As additional money is secured, utility increases at a diminishing rate, thereby reflecting the individual's attitude towards risk[11]. This is problematic, considering that the agent demand function generates mentalist utility variables, such as subjective tastes, which determine the consumer's choice and are potential substitutes at the same price.

Individual choice may sometimes have social implications resulting from externalities associated with the choice (Dutt & Wilber, 2010). When humans make choices or reveal their preferences, they must appeal to considerations of motive, reasons and utility, if their choices are to be explained or understood by themselves and others. The problem is that decision-making is organised around preferences that implicitly conform to postulated rationality. Balancing potential trade-offs between inclusionary and redundancy is the main challenge (Ishida, 2021). Hence, experimental economists reject the notion that people make clear decisions and possess a complete set of preferences when faced with problems (Keita, 2012; EPA, 2010). In most cases, decisions are not made randomly; individuals calculate and consider options before making a choice. The point

[11] Russo, S. et al., Understanding Patients' preferences: A systematic Review of psychological Instruments used in Patients' Preference and decision studies. Value in Health, 22 (4) 491-501.

is that consumer behaviour cannot be explained solely by preferences, given an individual's budgetary constraints for purchasing certain goods and services.

The application of rational choice theory and consumer preferences to heritage tourism enables a deeper understanding of how tourists act as decision makers, performing a cost-benefit analysis in order to maximise their utility and minimise costs[12]. Heritage sites are perceived as collections of attributes that tourists evaluate to select the option that provides the highest value. Before tourists travel, they look at the benefits of visiting the site (educational value, image, photos) against the costs involved in getting to the destination (mode of travel, distance, time taken to travel, popularity)[13]. Tourists make informed decisions based on information from various sources (e.g., travel guidebooks, websites, travel magazines, and social media). Tourists calculate the risks involved and measure them against the rewards associated with the experience of visiting a particular site[14]. Preferences differ from one individual to another; for instance, some people may be interested in colonial history while others may value artefacts, which implies that heritage site managers should develop experiences that are tailored for different tourist profiles.

---

[12] Paternoster, R. et al., Rational Choice Theory and Interest in the Fortune of Others. 2017. Journal of Research in Crime and delinquency. 54(6). https://doi.101177/0022427817707240.

[13] Paternoster, R. et al., Rational Choice Theory and Interest in the Fortune of Others. 2017. Journal of Research in Crime and delinquency. 54(6). https://doi.101177/0022427817707240.

[14] Ruan, W. Measuring destination image. Sustainability. 2017. Sustainability. 9(9)1501.

Tourism and Economic Development

Tourism plays a significant role in the economic development of Southern Africa, contributing substantially to the GDP of several countries in the region[15]. In nations like South Africa, Botswana, and Namibia, tourism is a key driver of economic growth, providing both direct and indirect employment opportunities[16,17]. For example, South Africa's tourism sector contributed approximately 8.8% to the GDP in 2024 and supported over 1.68 million jobs (RSA, 2026). The sector also stimulates other industries, such as agriculture, construction, and retail, creating a ripple effect that benefits local economies, especially in rural and underserved areas.

Despite its economic potential, the development of tourism in Southern Africa faces several challenges[18]. Rural communities often remain underdeveloped and have limited access to the benefits of tourism, while urban areas and well-known tourist destinations flourish. Development plans should thus aim to ensure equitable and sustainable growth for all countries in Southern Africa to optimise the benefits of tourism (Snyman, 2017). The tourism sector is also vulnerable to global factors such as political unrest, economic downturns, and international health

---

[15] Muchapondwa, E. and Stage, J. The economic impacts of tourism in Botswana, Namibia and South Africa: Is Poverty subsidising? Natural Resources Forum. 37(2), 80-89.

[16] Rivi, J.D and Momoh, Z. Effects of Tourism on Economic Growth in Africa. Quaestus Multidisciplinary Research Journal. 53-63.

[17] SA, Economic Impact of the Tourism Sector: Tourism is a key economic driver and it is on the rise. Southafrica.net.

[18] Muchapondwa, E. and Stage, J. The economic impacts of tourism in Botswana, Namibia and South Africa: Is Poverty subsidising? Natural Resources Forum. 37(2), 80-89.

emergencies, such as the COVID-19 pandemic, that influence global travel trends.

Culture and heritage are widely recognized as crucial to sustainable development efforts. This sector advocates for the development of local markets for cultural goods and services, the safeguarding of Indigenous traditional knowledge and community environmental management approaches and capacity building to foster a dynamic cultural and creative landscape. Tourism has significant potential for poverty alleviation, protection of natural and cultural assets, and sustainable development. The sector can convert local, historical, and cultural landscapes into revenue-generating opportunities for rural communities. Tourism is regarded as a more sustainable development option than intensive agriculture, forestry, and mining in many countries (Garidzirai & Pasara, 2020). This is especially true in Southern Africa, where the region holds vast potential for economic and environmental development that is currently constrained by structural, infrastructural, and governance challenges.

Adequate infrastructure, such as airports, roads, and accommodation, as well as effective services, is needed to enable access to tourism destinations. Tourism-related infrastructure development can create jobs and other economic benefits across industries such as construction, hospitality, and transportation[19]. By encouraging prudent resource management and environ-

[19] Chiwawa, N. and Wissink, H. Sustainable Tourism for Local and Regional Development in Southern Africa: Unlocking Economic Potential Through Responsible Tourism Strategies 2023. African Journal of Hospitality, Tourism and Leisure. 12(3), 1163-1175.

mental preservation, tourism infrastructure development may also help sustainability (Gonda, 2024). Tourism initiatives may provide special accessibility for the elderly, families with young children, and those with disabilities, making destinations more inclusive. The local economy benefits from accessible tourism, which attracts a wider range of visitors and boosts spending at nearby businesses. Improvements in lodging, transportation, and other services may increase demand for complementary services, such as dining options and tourist attractions[20]. Accessible tourism promotes sustainable practices by aligning social inclusion with environmental and economic resilience, ensuring that everyone, regardless of ability, may benefit from travel (Khadaroo & Seetanah, 2008). Therefore, tourism infrastructure and visitor facilities at heritage sites should be carefully planned, sited, designed, and periodically upgraded to maximize visitor appreciation and experiences without negatively impacting heritage values.

Consumers may see cultural commodities, such as art or music, as investments. Individuals may weigh the advantages of participating in a culture, such as social status or financial gain, against the potential backlash from appropriation[21]. For example, a company may logically decide to include elements of indigenous art into a product line if the financial benefits outweigh the risks of alienating specific populations. In the digital age, creators frequently use social media platforms like

---

[20] Dutta, I. Adapting to change: Exploring contemporary issues in Tourism and Hospitality. 2024. International Journal of Advanced Academic Studies. https://doi.10.33545/27068919.2024v6.19a.1262

[21] Sampaio, C. et al., Hospitality and Tourism Demand: Exploring Industry Shifts, Themes, and Trends. Societies. 14(10)207.

TikTok to determine which cultural content connects with people[22]. A sensible choice could be to create content that aligns with popular themes, such as when artists produce songs that incorporate viral challenges, thereby increasing their reach and impact. These examples demonstrate how rational choice theory can shed light on the decision-making processes that drive cultural commodification, emphasising the importance of balancing personal worth, market dynamics, and social implications[23].

The Development of Cultural and Heritage Tourism

In many countries, tourism has been a strategy of choice to revive local economies (Acha-Anyi, 2014; Lepp, 2007). In most instances, this has been successful, as tourism-led development has created jobs, increased family incomes, and boosted the country's GDP, among many other benefits (Acha-Anyi, 2014). However, the consistent development of cultural and heritage tourism simultaneously contributes to economic growth. Similarly, cultural and heritage tourism development contributes to job creation and income generation and offers other benefits. It also motivates the protection and preservation of both natural and man-made heritage (Acha-Anyi, 2014; Connell et al., 2009).

---

[22] Alam, M.M. et al., The power of social media in the digital era in keeping cultural Traditions alive. International Journal of Social Science Research and Review. 8(10), 68-88.

[23] Bleier, A. et al., On the role of social media platforms in the creator economy. 2024. International Journal of Research in Marketing. 41(30, 411-426.

Culture and Heritage Tourism in Southern Africa

In South Africa, cultural heritage has grown tremendously as a niche tourism area. There is evidence of an increase in the number of people visiting cultural heritage sites and attractions, particularly KwaNdebele in Mpumalanga, which is renowned for its vibrant culture, unique artwork, colourfully decorated huts, and traditional attire (Dladla et al., 2023).

Tourism development is sometimes hindered by conflicts among stakeholders' interests. Communities are sometimes concerned about the influence of outside cultures, which may undermine the authenticity of their cultural and natural landscapes (Mutanga et al., 2025). Tourism development has also lagged due to conflicts of interest among different stakeholders. Poor infrastructure and lack of community involvement have strained relationships among different tourism stakeholders, restricting the overall development and growth of the sector[24].

Locations such as Mapungubwe and the Great Zimbabwe Ruins offer prospects for sustainable development. At the Chinhoyi Caves, the main attraction at the location is the limestone, dolomite caves and the sinkhole[25]. The Wonder Hole—a ‘swallow hole’ or vast cavern with a collapsed roof—is the cave's primary attraction. The biggest sinkhole leads to a pool about 20 meters below ground level. This is the 'Sleeping Pool' of Chinhoyi. The pool is known as 'Chirorodziva' in Shona, which

---

[24] Fong, S and Lo, M. Community involvement and sustainable rural tourism development: Perspectives from the local communities. 2015. European Journal of Tourism Research. 11, 125-146.

[25] Kabote, F. and et al., Tourists activities and their impacts on Chinhoyi Caves Heritage Site, Zimbabwe. 2023. Chinhoyi University of Technology.

translates to 'pool of the fallen'. The name was given after an invading Nguni tribe attacked the local Shona people living near the caves and tossed them into the pool, where they were never found. A common myth about the Chinhoyi Caves is that if you toss a stone across the Sleeping Pool, it will never strike the wall, and if you keep trying, the stone will return and hit you. This is believed to be due to a curse from the ancestors.

There is a fine line between preserving authenticity and advancing culture. If customs are modified to accommodate tourism, they may lose their original significance. Western influence and tourism have altered traditional heritage, in some cases transforming lived practices into commodified hybrid assets[26]. For example, while Eswatini has preserved its royal ceremonies, such as the Umhlanga reed dance and the Incwala ceremony, Lesotho is facing the degradation of sites due to changing lifestyles and development. Often, local communities reap no direct benefits from tourism and are not included in decisions. The San people in Botswana, for example, have complained about being excluded from projects that highlight their cultural heritage (Timothy, 2009).

The development of the heritage industry is further hampered by political and economic uncertainties in countries like Zimbabwe, which can deter both investors and tourists. However, it should be noted that inclusive development in Southern Africa could be fuelled by cultural and heritage tourism. Hence, governments

---

[26] Marbun, S. The commodification of Culture in Global Tourism: Balancing authenticity, sustainability, and ethical practices amidst disruption.2025. Proceeding of International Seminar of Culture and Tourism. 1(1). https://ojs-akbi.org/inex.php/proceedings/index.

and stakeholders need to address infrastructure, funding, skills training, authenticity, and community involvement to effectively utilise them to their advantage.

In South Africa, the KwaZulu-Natal coastline attracts visitors to its beaches, diverse marine life, and vibrant culture. The establishment of attractions along the Durban coast generates significant economic benefits but also causes environmental strain, including coastal erosion, pollution, and habitat loss due to the removal of vegetation to create space for building projects (Wong, 1993). It is crucial to find a balance between tourism growth and the well-being of the environment and local communities for lasting success. Therefore, beach tourist sites should consider avoiding new construction development projects to preserve the integrity of the physical landscape[27]. To mitigate the impact of tourism development on natural environments, local governments should adopt laws that promote the reuse and rehabilitation of existing buildings rather than the construction of new ones (UNWTO and UNEP, 2005). Another strategy is to use fresh, imaginative architectural designs that enhance rather than change the natural surroundings. Recreational activities like hiking should be actively regulated to prevent environmental degradation, and coastal activities should be monitored where necessary to preserve coral reefs (UNWTO and UEP, 2005). Tourism businesses should conduct environmental impact assessments and develop strategies to minimise environmental

---

[27] Pawestri, P. et al., The restrictions on Beach Tourism Destination Development as an effort for environmental preservation. 2023. IOP Conference Earth Environmental Science. 1181012014.

damage, such as reducing the use of hazardous chemicals and utilising fewer polluting modes of transportation (Tapper, 2010).

By eliminating middleman fees, local communities gain more money from direct tourist spending, enabling them to receive payments from tourists. Purchasing local mementoes enhances visitors' genuine experiences by fostering memories of the place they visited[28]. This is due to the hosts' dual role as intermediaries between guests and the local environment, and as co-creators of genuine experiences based on direct contact with local community members who bring knowledge and added value to the visit (González-Reverté et al., 2025) promoting cultural tolerance, cultivating an appreciation and respect for local customs, and increasing cultural knowledge (Swanson, 2014). If people recognise the benefits of tourism, local communities can embrace its growth (Muganda et al., 2013).

In Southern Africa, demand has shifted from large-scale, uniform accommodation to small-scale, unique lodgings that offer high experiential value, personal hospitality, and regional cuisines. The expansion of the tourism sector also encourages job creation, increased investment, and the use of tourism-derived income to finance the construction of essential infrastructure, such as roads, energy, water, transportation services, hospitals, and retail establishments (Hassan, 2000). Furthermore, since tourists frequently strain these resources, the expansion of the tourism sector should not impede local communities' access to resources, services, and supplies (UWTO and UNEP, 2005).

---

[28] Sthapit, E. et al., The memorable souvenir-shopping Experience: Antecedents and outcomes. 2018. Leisure studies. 37(5), 628-643.

According to UNWTO and UNEP (2005), sustainable tourism requires the travel and tourism sector to create local jobs accessible to all individuals, regardless of gender, race, religion, or disability, to pay a fair wage, and to provide decent working conditions. Improved working conditions can lead to better performance; therefore, policies should address labour relations (Dabphet, 2012). To better prepare local populations for the skills required in the tourism and hospitality industries, tourism companies should offer career advancement opportunities (UNWTO and UNEP, 2005).

Nature and Wildlife Tourism

Countries such as South Africa, Botswana, and Namibia have leveraged their abundant natural resources to promote environmental and wildlife tourism. For example, South Africa's Kruger National Park and Botswana's Okavango Delta are internationally renowned for their biodiversity (Rogerson, 2017). Nature-based tourism promotes conservation by offering economic incentives to protect species. It also promotes rural development by creating work opportunities in regions where there might otherwise be few (Rogerson, 2017). However, there are significant hurdles to developing such businesses sustainably. Political instability in some southern African countries discourages investment and tourism. Zimbabwe, for example, has experienced fluctuations in visitor numbers due to political uncertainty (Rogerson, 2017). Poor infrastructure in rural locations also hinders access to natural reserves. There is also the possibility of excluding local communities from the benefits of tourism. Large businesses can sometimes dominate the industry, leaving indigenous communities with limited financial resources (Ovelli, 2016).

Furthermore, climate change poses a long-term threat, with shifting weather patterns harming ecosystems vital to wildlife tourism. One significant challenge is environmental degradation. High tourist numbers can lead to habitat degradation, pollution, and increased pressure on water resources. Concerns about water use in Botswana's Okavango Delta have increased due to tourism developments (Novelli, 2016). Another issue is poaching, which endangers wildlife populations, despite the fact that the fees charged to tourists contribute to conservation efforts. Travel and tourism are significant export sectors in developing countries, contributing substantially to foreign exchange earnings and job creation. It has the potential to generate significant global revenue for environmental conservation and to provide economic value to cultural assets.

Community-Based Tourism (CBT)

Community-based tourism (CBT) plays a significant economic role by providing direct and indirect jobs in guiding, hospitality and craftwork to local people. CBT stimulates local business growth as tourists purchase goods from local shops and use local services. Furthermore, it reduces leakages by ensuring that tourist spending benefits the local community rather than large external corporations. CBT also empowers communities, giving local people more control over local affairs and decision-making. It can also encourage the preservation of local culture and traditions, such as dance, music, and crafts, which are often of interest to tourists. Additionally, CBT encourages community well-being by generating funds and development that can be invested in local infrastructure, such as schools, hospitals, and roads (Blackstock, 2005). CBT also promote conservation by making it financially beneficial for local people to protect their natural environment. It encourages sustainable practices, such as conserving water and energy, to protect the environment. In simple terms, CBT helps local people earn money, preserve their culture, and protect their environment. CBT initiatives often involve training local community members in a range of skills, including hospitality, guiding, management, and marketing. This enhances their capacity to participate in and benefit from tourism activities, leading to long-term economic benefits. CBT fosters interaction between tourists and local communities (Goodwin, 2005).

The Role of Culture and Sacred Sites

A cultural holiday is a cultural tourism product that involves an organised tour aimed at fostering knowledge of the culture (in both narrow and broad senses) of the countries being visited. Countries like South Africa, Namibia, and Zambia have worked diligently to harness their natural resources (including national parks, wildlife reserves, and coastal areas) to bolster their tourism industries. South Africa's tourism sector, for example, has become a major contributor to its economy, with areas like Kruger National Park and Cape Town's coastal tourism attracting significant numbers of visitors (Republic of South Africa, 2021). Namibia also attracts international tourists with its stunning deserts and diverse wildlife by promoting sustainable, conservation-supportive tourism (Meyer, 2019).

Despite these achievements, Southern Africa's tourism industry faces challenges, particularly in terms of marketing and promotion. Limited marketing budgets, poor infrastructure, and a lack of a cohesive branding strategy often hinder the region's ability to compete effectively with other global tourist destinations (Gordhan, 2018). Additionally, tourism in Southern Africa is influenced by social issues and broader economic trends. Political unrest, as observed in Zimbabwe and parts of South Africa, can deter potential visitors due to safety concerns. Furthermore, global economic downturns and crises, such as the COVID-19 pandemic, have underscored the tourism industry's vulnerability (Harrison, 2020). The heavy reliance on international tourists, who are often influenced by global trends and events, leaves the sector exposed to instability. To overcome these obstacles, tourism marketing strategies must adapt by showcasing the region's unique offerings while emphasising safety, sustainability, and accessibility (Republic of South Africa, 2021). Despite these challenges, the potential for tourism to drive economic development in Southern Africa remains strong, provided efforts are made to overcome the barriers and promote a positive, attractive image of the region.

Sacred Sites and Tourism

Tourism and the natural physical environment are inextricably linked, as most tourist destinations centre on natural features. Environmental management is one of the most pressing concerns facing the world today, given the challenges posed by global warming, which has led to significant climatic shifts. Butler (2000) asserts that there is little doubt that tourism and the environment are inextricably linked, though some scholars have challenged this link. Mihalic (2000) contends that a well-managed destination can effectively advertise itself. Monteiro and Dayanand (2016) report that the rites and rituals performed at holy sites attract tourists, and the number of annual visitors, the size of the sacred location, and the method of site administration indicate different stages of tourist development. Sacred and natural places can be effective tools for protecting biodiversity through community participation and tourism marketing. Tourist amenities, which include a variety of basic traveller services and interpretive facilities, can help visitors make the sacred site experience more meaningful while also boosting the local economy.

Politics, Safety and Stability

Tourism and development in Southern Africa have a significant impact on the region's economy and political stability. On the one hand, tourism generates funds, provides jobs, and fosters cultural interchange, all of which contribute to economic growth and development[29]. However, safety concerns may deter guests. In South Africa, for example, high-profile crimes and safety issues have impacted tourism (Zama & Linda, 2020). In Zimbabwe, political instability and economic decline have negatively affected the industry (Siambombe & Hupile, 2024). Heritage promotes a sense of collective belonging to a nation, fostering what Anderson (1983) calls an "imagined political community". This affects how heritage is handled, displayed, and interpreted.

---

[29] Marbun, S. The commodification of Culture in Global Tourism: Balancing authenticity, sustainability, and ethical practices amidst disruption.2025. Proceeding of International Seminar of Culture and Tourism. 1(1). https://ojs-akbi.org/inex.php/proceedings/index.

Heritage can become a source of conflict between different interest groups when it is shaped by political or economic goals. Critical heritage studies have recently challenged this way of thinking about and doing heritage.

Heritage tourism encourages tourists to become more interested in distant cultures and societies and their preservation. Furthermore, heritage tourism is often encouraged to foster national pride and patriotism, as well as to disseminate propaganda to international visitors (Timothy & Boyd, 2006). Heritage tourism may boost local pride by highlighting local values and cultural memories, while also connecting communities with the world (Edson, 2004). Effective collaboration between governments, local communities, and tourism operators is crucial in addressing these challenges and promoting responsible tourism practices (Chiwawa & Wissink, 2023).

Environmental Sustainability

While tourism plays a vital role in the economic development of Southern Africa, it also poses significant challenges to environmental sustainability. Although ecotourism projects, such as those in Botswana's Okavango Delta, may encourage conservation, tourism can also lead to pollution, habitat degradation, and stress on water supplies (Ovelli, 2006). Striking a balance between growth and environmental preservation remains challenging due to a lack of infrastructure, inadequate policy implementation, and pressure for immediate financial gain. Long-term ecological monitoring, environmental evaluations, and integrated planning, including local populations, are all necessary for sustainable tourism development[30]. Heritage offers numerous opportunities to experience and appreciate the past in alternative ways (Boniface & Fowler, 1993). Both cultural and natural heritage can drive tourism expansion, but tourism can also generate funding for preservation efforts (NWHO, 1999).

Additionally, the sustainability of tourism in Southern Africa is increasingly threatened by climate change. Many tourist destinations, including Victoria Falls, rely heavily on natural water cycles that are being affected by severe droughts and shifting rainfall patterns (Becken & Job, 2014). In addition to making places less appealing, this environmental instability significantly impacts local economies that rely heavily on tourism. Deforestation and biodiversity loss result from an ongoing disregard for ecological sensitivity in the construction of infrastructure such as highways and hotels. Another cause for the lack of adequate measures to conserve the values of heritage properties is an underdeveloped awareness, and thus a lack of appreciation, of the heritage value of precious cultural or natural resources by both local populations and tourists[31]. To overcome these obstacles and guarantee that tourism makes a constructive contribution to sustainable development in the area, regional collaboration and the implementation of green tourism strategies, such as community-based tourism and low-impact lodging, are crucial.

---

[30] Marbun, S. The commodification of Culture in Global Tourism: Balancing authenticity, sustainability, and ethical practices amidst disruption.2025. Proceeding of International Seminar of Culture and Tourism. 1(1). https://ojs-akbi.org/inex.php/proceedings/index.

[31] Fong, S and Lo, M. Community involvement and sustainable rural tourism development: Perspectives from the local communities. 2015. European Journal of Tourism Research. 11, 125-146.

The future of sustainable tourism development is heavily influenced by sustainability, particularly in economically and environmentally significant locations such as KwaZulu-Natal's coastal districts. Sustainability ensures that tourism not only prospers now but also endures for generations to come by combining economic viability, community empowerment, and environmental protection[32]. Prioritising sustainability in tourism initiatives is not only advantageous but also necessary to promote long-term prosperity and ecological balance in coastal areas.

Tourism in southern Africa plays a pivotal role in driving economic growth, creating employment, and promoting cultural and environmental conservation. However, the region faces significant challenges, including inadequate infrastructure, uneven distribution of benefits, political instability, and environmental degradation. Addressing these issues requires inclusive policies, sustainable practices, and robust infrastructure development to ensure equitable growth. Community-based tourism and cultural heritage preservation must be prioritised to empower local populations. Effective marketing strategies and regional collaboration are crucial for enhancing competitiveness and attracting tourists. Political stability and safety measures are critical to rebuilding traveller confidence. By striking a balance between development and sustainability, Southern Africa can unlock the full potential of tourism to foster long-term prosperity while preserving its natural and cultural treasures for future generations.

---

[32] Huseynli, E. Sustainable tourism and its environmental, economic and social benefits to host destinations. 2022. https://doi.10.13140/RG.2.2.2.31912.03845

Conclusion

The growth of cultural heritage tourism in Southern Africa is driven by tourists' choices and preferences when visiting a destination. The application of rational choice theory can help balance the costs and benefits associated with a site. Preferences are driven by identity, memory, and authenticity of experiences. When choosing a destination, tourists consider safety and access, which can boost demand for heritage products. On the supply side, destinations respond to these choices by investing in information centres, conservation, and accessible infrastructure. Proper management of cultural heritage sites can drive economic growth and stimulate long-term development. Eco-tourism can generate economic returns for local communities and encourage them to participate in tourism when they are involved in decision-making. Therefore, the use of heritage as a conservation strategy should go beyond Eurocentric approaches by focusing on living heritage. The transformation of heritage management should seek to empower local communities to become stewards of their own natural and cultural assets. To deliver economic development outcomes, infrastructure and accessibility are critical to ensuring that the region has reliable transport, well-maintained facilities, multilingual information centres, and greater local participation and reduced leakage. Public-private partnerships should be pursued to ensure community ownership is prioritised in heritage preservation planning. The integration of visitor choices, preferences, and experiences is essential to achieving sustainable community livelihoods. Linking heritage to sustainable practices provides a blueprint for ecological, resilient tourism in Southern Africa.

Chapter 4
Critical Heritage Studies and the Future of Southern Africa

Critical Heritage Studies (CHS) examines monuments, museums, historical sites, archives, and memory to understand how memory is created and challenged. It investigates the use of power, memorial legislation and the financing of museums to legitimize power and national narratives for economic purposes. It moves beyond just celebration by defining the past, determining inclusion and exclusion, who gets support for infrastructure, and challenging socio-economic injustices. While heritage emphasises resistance, censorship, and performance, tourism is more concerned with the negotiation of legitimacy, development, and identity. The future of heritage in Southern Africa is closely linked to postcolonial stories, land reforms, and regional identity. Therefore, heritage should be used as a resource to achieve sustainable development, education, and social justice. The success of heritage management lies in collaborative stewardship of resources. Neoliberal heritage conservation views heritage as cultural capital that promotes tourism at the expense of local needs. The sustainability of contemporary heritage requires adopting new approaches that reconcile memory by including contested representations and marginalised postcolonial and Indigenous voices.

Critical Heritage Studies

Within the field of heritage studies, critical heritage studies (CHS) is an emerging approach that seeks to problematize the effects of the production, use, and consumption of heritage to address contemporary world challenges. The approach aims to address complex heritage issues through a critical analytical perspective (Winter, 2013). The CHS approach recognises contestations, memory, and identities. It is used to analyse complex, multi-vector challenges that require an interdisciplinary approach to solve problems (Winter, 2013).

Critical heritage studies highlight that pivotal heritage changes arose within colonial environments and consider how post-colonial systems respond to and recalibrate these legacies[1]. Critical heritage studies highlight how the most significant changes in heritage have occurred in colonial environments and how post-colonial systems re-interpret these legacies. CHS crucially highlights how the most significant advances in heritage have occurred due to the specific degree of heritage development in colonial settings and how the independent systems responded (Harrison & Hughes, 2010). Silverman (2014) points out that the re-theorisation of heritage discourse as critical heritage studies centres several topics of concern in the humanities and social sciences: bodies of knowledge, class, colonialism and post-colonialism, dominant rhetoric and authoritative discourse, gender, globalisation, identity, ideology, institutions, memory work, nationalism, and tourism, among others. Winter (2013) argues:

> At its most significant level, it means better understanding the various ways in which heritage now has a stake in, and can act as a positive enabler for, the complex, multi-vector challenges

---

[1] Giblin, D.J. Critical Heritage approaches to Post Colonial Heritage. In: The Palgrave Handbook of Contemporary Heritage Research. pp.313-328.

> that face us today, such as cultural and environmental sustainability, economic inequalities, conflict resolution, social cohesion and the future of cities (p. 533).

In this chapter, the critical heritage studies perspective is used to analyse the complex relationships between tourism and heritage. Winter (2013) states that, "heritage is both enmeshed in, and constituted by, complex, entangled and contradictory processes. The question thus arises, then, is the professional heritage conservation sector adequately equipped to address and respond to these challenges?" (p. 536). In recent decades, the concept of a single national culture has been eroded by the presence of multiple cultures representing diverse identities. Modernisation, the lure of modernity, and rapidly growing economies are liquifying existing social structures and detaching people from place, whether through their own mobility or the radical transformation of their physical environment, in ways that destabilise and redefine relationships between past and present (Winter, 2013).

Tourism, in some cases, has been linked to the rehabilitation of personal and collective memories through the revival of traditional cultures. It can expand memory to include marginalised groups, while dominant groups may continue to influence the official narrative. Certain rituals, crafts, or storytelling can be emphasised over others[2]. The creation and consumption of memories can be shaped by how culture is revived, packaged and branded as a tourism product. The revival

---

[2] Datta, R. Traditional Storytelling: An effective Indigenous research methodology and its implications for environmental research. 2018. Alternative, An international Journal of Indigenous Peoples. 14(2).

can spark conflicts about who is prioritised in postcolonial or post-conflict contexts[3]. States may finance the revival of traditional cultures to establish national identity and empower communities while suppressing dissenting histories.

The widespread trend towards incorporating cultural quarters or hubs into planning processes means that museums, historic waterfronts, historic properties, and urban parks, which together constitute urban heritage, help position cities in these regions on the global stage. In Southern Africa, colonial heritage policies sought to separate Indigenous people from their language, lifestyle, and territories[4]. Heritage research has shown that there is a complex and nuanced relationship between the settler and Indigenous populations in colonial settings. Despite attempts by colonial administration to distance indigenous people from their way of living, they remained connected with their indigenous languages and environment. When teaching and administration were conducted in European languages, ecological knowledge (plants, animals, seasonal cycles) was passed from one generation to the next through oral history, clan stories, proverbs, and songs[5]. For certain languages, missionaries and researchers created dictionaries and scripts, while traditional leaders kept oral archives (genealogies, praise poetry, oral histories) that encoded environmental information in a permanent form. The San (Bushmen) and Khoikhoi kept comprehensive ecological

---

[3] Banda, L.O.L. et al., Preserving Cultural heritage: A community-centric approach to safeguarding the Khulubvi Traditional Temple in Malawi. Heliyon. 10(18), e37610.

[4] Hitchcock, K.R and Vinding, D. Indigenous people's rights in Southern Africa: An introduction. International Workgroup for Indigenous Affairs.

[5] Layden, J.T. et al., Confronting colonial history: towards healing, just and equitable indigenous conservation futures. 2025. Ecology and Society. 30(1), 33.

knowledge of tracking animals, understanding their behaviour, water supplies, and edible plants. Once colonized countries gained their independence, it was assumed that government would establish more inclusive forms of heritage that reflect the complex ethnic and cultural mix of the postcolonial states (Harrison, 2008). The indigenous challenge to colonialism and the methods of cultural heritage management in postcolonial countries have been influential in shaping policies regarding ownership and control of the past. The activism of Indigenous communities and the global-scale migrations of people, ideas, and technologies call into question the established systems and discourses of power that underpin group, community, or national identities, as well as the meaning of heritage[6].

Heritage emerges as a factor in many policies and debates on sustainable development, climate change, conflict resolution, multiculturalism, and innovation. Heritagization is a selective, dynamic, and sociopolitical process of identifying, classifying, and relocating items, locations, or cultural practices into heritage. While it recognises items or activities from the past as significant, the process is shaped by whoever performs the valuation, their motives, and how it is viewed and consumed. Heritagization is a performative act that involves the active, affective, or artistic expression of individual and community notions of self. It can be regarded as a process of cultural creation in which people make sense of their world and place by strategically establishing their voices in the public sphere (Ashley & Terry, 2018). It promotes careful site management to prevent damage due to increased

---

[6] Gomez-Mera, L. Indigenous people and the new generation of climate activism. 2024. Conference: Youth in international Relations. Brussels, Belgium.

visitor activity. Heritagization can result in over-commercialization and distortion of heritage narratives. If tourism becomes the main economic activity, there is a risk of gentrification or displacement of locals. As a result, tensions arise between preserving a place's authenticity and meeting tourist expectations.

Critical Heritage Theory and Modernism

Modernism frequently emphasises the search for objective truth and universal narratives, especially in the context of development and civilisation. Critical heritage theory, on the other hand, advocates subjective historical readings, arguing that heritage varies across cultural contexts. Modernism typically employs a top-down approach to historical management, with specialists determining what is considered valuable[7]. Critical heritage theory challenges this authority by highlighting the value of community engagement and grassroots perspectives. Modernism frequently idealises a shared cultural vision. In contrast, critical heritage values diversity and pluralism, recognising that heritage can reflect a wide range of histories and identities. Critical heritage serves as a counterbalance to modernist ideals, advocating for a more inclusive and diverse perspective on the past. Critical heritage studies use modernism to analyse dominant narratives about heritage, revealing how they reflect specific power dynamics. Heritage sites can be reinterpreted to promote marginalised voices, such as Indigenous viewpoints on colonial monuments.

---

[7] Nwachuku, A. Models and approaches to change management in Morden organisations. 2023. Journal of Management Indonesia. 8(2), 109.

Tools for Critical Heritage Studies

Critical heritage theorists argue that scholars, practitioners, and policymakers must critically engage with their proposition that heritage studies need to be rebuilt from the ground up by questioning power relations and inviting the active participation of people and communities who have previously been marginalized in the creation and management of heritage (Ashley & Terry, 2018). Critical heritage studies challenge the power structures underlying heritage practices and highlight the potential of utilising tangible and intangible heritage to address historical and structural inequities as a social-activist strategy.

Critical heritage studies employ various theoretical and analytical frameworks to examine who preserves memories and controls narratives. For instance, postcolonial and decolonial frameworks are used to critically analyse, criticise, and reconstruct how cultural, historical, and natural legacies are understood, managed, and presented. Other frameworks for critical heritage studies include UNESCO's Memory of the World (MoW), Laurier's heritage as social process and Tim Ingold's materiality. In challenging gendered and normative histories, critical heritage studies use feminist, intersectional, and queer perspectives. Critical scholars argue that "the historical notion of heritage heavily draws on privileged masculine positions, practices, and perceptions that have dominated definitions, interpretations, preservation, and values of heritage" (Lähdesmäki & Vlase, 2023, p. 746). Other concepts include memory studies and collective memory.

Critical scholars use community-centred and participatory methods, such as participatory action research (PAR) and community-based heritage production. Scholars and practitioners are questioning established notions of heritage by revealing power dynamics and including the needs, interests, and values of historically marginalised communities (Kryder-Reid, 2018). To achieve a more democratic, inclusive, and activist approach, it is necessary to shift away from top-down, officially sanctioned concepts of heritage and adopt techniques that promote such practices. The studies also illustrate a gradual but positive transition of participatory heritage from the periphery of activist academics to the mainstream discourse on heritage, where the basic principle of inclusion is prioritised[8]. Scholars use curatorship and participatory methods in collaboration with community stewards. To fully realise the promise of this paradigm shift, the discipline must establish effective techniques to include diverse populations in discussions about heritage and give them decision-making power.

Ethnographic and qualitative research tools follow participant observation to understand the contextual meanings of heritage sites. This includes the use of critical discourse analysis to understand the meanings of signs, policy rhetoric and the media[9]. Critical heritage studies challenge traditional notions of heritage by highlighting dichotomies between nature and culture, the tangible and the intangible, the formal and the informal, and the

---

[8] Chirikure, S and Pwiti, G. Community Involvement in Archaeology and Cultural heritage Management. An Assessment from case studies in southern Africa. Current Anthropology. 49(3).

[9] Tenorio, H.E. Critical discourse analysis: An overview. Nordic Journal of English Studies. 10(1)183-210.

global and the local aspects of cultural heritage. Archival ethnography traces how archives shape memory and what gets preserved. Critical heritage studies view heritage as a dynamic process of interpretation, contestation, and representation (Borges et al., 2020). In this process, the past is contested, negotiated, and recreated in the present. Spatial realities are re-valued and produced, rather than remaining static and locked in the past.

Harrison (2015) explains that heritage is not the inscription of meaning onto blank objects, places, and practices created by this process, but rather the material and social possibilities, or 'affordances', of collectives of human and non-human agents, material and non-material entities in the world. Critical heritage uses digital humanities and data analytics tools such as text analysis and visualization, network analysis with Gephi or Cytoscape and other qualitative data management tools. These emphasise the relationships between people, nature, and artefacts. Any connection with heritage from this perspective implies dealing with heritage across multiple disciplines. This approach enables the sensitive exploration of the past and the management of cultural and natural resources.

Other tools include digital, multimodal, and public-facing tools for digital storytelling, oral history platforms, and community media. CHS addresses the complex socio-political aspects surrounding heritage, which are often overlooked by conservation professionals[10]. Challenging the divide, several CHS scholars have explored new methodological approaches to

---

[10] Winter, T. Clarifying the critical in critical heritage studies. 2013. 19(6)532-545.

heritage, enabling them to unpack the socio-political complexities that intersect with heritage and reveal its critical relationship to global challenges such as climate change, pollution, over-population, and species extinction (Borges et al., 2020). Critical heritage uses open-access archives and platforms that support participatory curation. Others include GIS/space analysis to map displacement, site significance, and access. In this regard, emphasis should be placed not only on the characteristics of the pre-existing urban environment but also on the processes and performances that contribute to its creation[11]. While critiques of policy approaches and ideologies will always be essential, critical heritage studies should focus on addressing the key concerns that face the globe today, as well as the broader issues that are influenced by and extend beyond heritage (Winter, 2013).

Museology, curatorial practice, and policy tools are decolonial curation approaches used to exhibit designs that foreground contested histories. Heritage plays a crucial role in addressing complex challenges, including cultural and environmental sustainability, economic inequalities, conflict resolution, social cohesion, and the future of cities[12]. Policy analysis and heritage impact assessments interrogate governance, funding, and stakeholder power. They should also acknowledge the essential obstacles and rewards of safeguarding heritage, which are sometimes ignored or dismissed in critical heritage theory.

---

[11] Chana, K. et al., Aesthetic components of urban environments and their relation to well-being: a scoping review. Cities and Health. 1-23.

[12] Banda, L.O.L. et al., Preserving Cultural heritage: A community-centric approach to safeguarding the Khulubvi Traditional Temple in Malawi. Heliyon. 10(18), e37610

Ethical guidelines are important when conducting oral history studies, managing data governance, and ensuring benefit-sharing with communities. In academia, it is easy to overlook that most institutions and resources dedicated to natural and cultural assets are focused on their conservation and preservation. Conservation is a billion-dollar sector that is rapidly developing[13]. Therefore, the use of ethical and governance instruments is essential in getting informed consent in data-sharing agreements and community benefit agreements. For instance, the use of rights-based approaches to repatriation and negotiations for cultural materials. To make an impact, critical heritage studies must develop a language that transcends academic and industry boundaries[14]. Many countries now incorporate heritage into discussions and policies related to climate change, sustainable development, human security, multiculturalism, and conflict resolution (Winter, 2013).

Scientific Materialism and Conservation

Scientific materialism emphasises the value of real, physical facts and empirical data in interpreting the world, frequently favouring scientific and technological approaches. This perspective, which focuses on the physical features of heritage sites and artefacts, can significantly shape how we evaluate and manage cultural heritage. It focuses on physical and evidence-based preservation, basing conservation decisions on observable features such as the material record's stability, reversibility, and authenticity. Scientific materialism offers a rigorous, evidence-

---

[13] Ashworth, J.G. Heritage and economic development: Selling the unsellable. Heritage and Society. 7(1), 3-17.

[14] Winter, T. Clarifying the critical in critical heritage studies. 2013. 19(6)532-545.

based framework for comprehending and caring for tangible remnants of culture[15]. It allows for accurate diagnosis, testing, and action in conservation. Conservation approaches grounded in scientific materialism may prioritise material significance over intangible cultural qualities, such as community narratives or spiritual significance. To engage with heritage fully, it should be combined with other approaches that consider the intangible meanings associated with living communities. This should result in holistic stewardship of both the material aspects and the cultural meaning assigned to it by the community.

The relationship between scientific materialism and conservation in critical heritage studies is complex. While scientific materialism may offer valuable methods for preservation, critical heritage studies stress incorporating cultural contexts and meanings into conservation. Informed by scientific materialism, conservation of a heritage site may approach the rehabilitation of a site by using modern materials and procedures to maintain structural stability, potentially overlooking previous construction methods that have cultural significance[16]. Critical heritage studies, in contrast, advocate for a more comprehensive approach, recognising that history encompasses not only physical things but also the meanings and values that communities attach to them. Critical heritage studies thus support conservation approaches that strike a balance between

---

[15] Torrissen, W. and Lovoll S.H. Exploring creative wellbeing frameworks in context: Nature, culture, and sustainable futures. 2024. https://doi.10.4324/9781003294498.

[16] Torrissen, W. and Lovoll S.H. Exploring creative wellbeing frameworks in context: Nature, culture, and sustainable futures. 2024. https://doi.10.4324/9781003294498.

scientific rigour and cultural sensitivity, such as involving local communities to ensure their perspectives and values are heard.

Heritage as a Tourist Resource

Tourism research demonstrates how heritage sites, narratives, and artefacts attract visitors, drive local economies, and alter local identities. CHS examines how attractions are chosen, packaged, and sold, often privileging histories while marginalising others. CHS emphasises who has a say in heritage decisions (indigenous populations, local communities, and minorities) and who benefits from tourism development[17]. Tourism studies assist in analysing stakeholder roles, tourist expectations, and governance frameworks that influence site interpretation and management. Tourists frequently seek crafted experiences that align with their expectations, shaped by the lens through which they view the world.

CHS questions authenticity, provenance, and cultural commodefication, while tourism studies focus on tourist experiences, satisfaction, and behaviour regarding perceived authenticity at heritage sites[18]. Resorts now offer wellness packages marketed through glossy brochures and social media, compelling consumers to purchase not just a vacation, but an idealised lifestyle. Tourism planning is used to exploit heritage to attract visitors. The rise of 'Sites on Instagram' encourages destinations to sell visually appealing spots that boost a tourist's social media

---

[17] Park, H. Critical approaches to tourism heritage and culture. Tourism planning and Development. 19 (1) 37-49.

[18] Sampaio, C. et al., Hospitality and Tourism Demand: Exploring Industry Shifts, Themes, and Trends. Societies. 14(10)207.

presence, changing the experience into a consumable commodity. CHS is more concerned about democratic, equitable planning that involves local people and non-dominant narratives.

Digital Cultural Heritage, Narratives and Interpretation

Digital cultural heritage aims to complement and broaden conventional cultural heritage. The shared goals include preserving history, promoting awareness, and establishing lasting and accessible documentation of cultural artefacts, locations, and traditions for future generations (Yükseka & Sökmenb, 2018). Digital cultural heritage refers to the use of digital technologies to enhance, supplement, or preserve the experience of historical or cultural sites or objects. It seeks to increase access and inclusivity, support research and education, and enable discovery and engagement. Record provenance can help verify legitimacy and prevent forgery by ensuring the authenticity and integrity of the archival context. Digital assets include texts, still and motion photos, music, graphics, software, and web pages (Cameron & Kenderdine, 2017). There are two approaches to studying encounters and interactions (Staiff, 2013). The contingent approach suggests that representative narratives shape both heritage and tourism. The contingent approach claims that heritage is neither static nor unchanging.

The importance of heritage and meanings are shaped by individuals, events, circumstances, and power relationships at a particular time. Therefore, contingencies determine whether a site retains or loses its heritage designation. These factors include political changes, economic pressures, social movements, memory politics, and material circumstances. The negotiated approach asserts that heritage and tourism are dynamic and are not constrained by representative narratives. Meanings are co-constructed rather than merely discovered or imposed. Heritage is produced through continuous negotiation between stakeholders with multiple interests, values, and power[19]. Digitising cultural heritage aligns with the negotiated approach to understanding tourists' encounters and interactions. The historical development and social context of visits can provide insight into the interaction between heritage and tourism. Heritage tourism focuses on interactions between tourists and heritage sites.

Digitisation not only preserves cultural heritage but also enhances the tourist experience by making it more interactive and informative (Aurindo & Machado, 2016). Some argue that digitisation enhances the tourist experience, while others argue that audiences should experience the originality, development, and context of heritage sites in person (Kidd, 2019). There is also an argument that digitisation should not overshadow the heritage it represents, and advocates that the emphasis should be on the mediating role of digitisation in the transfer of cultural heritage. Digitisation offers significant benefits to both cultural heritage suppliers and buyers. Digitisation enables museums to preserve cultural assets and artefacts that have been destroyed or lost due to disasters such as wars. Projects such as Google Arts & Culture enable users to visually navigate places by utilising 3D scanning to create lifelike representations of historical sites

[19] Park, H. Critical approaches to tourism heritage and culture. Tourism planning and Development. 19 (1) 37-49.

(Bianchi, 2006). Digital presentations can help museums overcome the time constraints that visitors face. Museums and historical sites can offer virtual tours that enable worldwide audiences to explore exhibits from the comfort of their own homes, thereby breaking down geographical barriers (Aurindo & Machado, 2016).

Institutions are utilising platforms like Instagram and TikTok to engage with younger audiences and foster connections to their cultural heritage. The Smartify app enhances visitors' experiences and knowledge of cultural items by enabling them to scan artworks for detailed information and associated content. Libraries and archives digitise rare manuscripts and historical documents to ensure their preservation and accessibility for research and education. Digitisation has the potential to provide an alternative solution for disadvantaged populations, such as the disabled and the elderly (Caffo, 2014). Critics of digital cultural heritage highlight the dichotomy between the transient nature of digitisation and the long-lasting value of heritage.

Heritage Reproduction and Representation

The UNESCO World Heritage Centre and UN Tourism (formerly UNWTO) have led efforts globally to strike a balance between preservation and visitation, encompassing visitor management, heritage destination planning, and heritage interpretation. Stojcic et al. (2026) have developed a model to strike a balance between tourism development and the preservation of cultural heritage, taking into account overcrowding, infrastructure congestion, and stakeholder tolerance. Stakeholder groups may have competing goals and priorities, making it challenging to reach consensus on heritage management, interpretation, and appropriation (Salazar & Zhang, 2013). Uncontrolled tourism can have negative impacts, including environmental damage, social disruption, and the commercialisation of cultural heritage. Site managers and authorities may be unwilling to restrict access or implement preservation measures due to tourism-related infrastructure improvements (Salazar, 2005).

The use of landscape can impact the stories told in film, literature, and the arts. For example, memory is often depicted using ancient towns or mines in post-colonial literature novels, theatres, and cinemas to capture wars, conflict, heroes, loss and complicity[20]. However, heritage tourism often presents planning challenges, including demolition of buildings, congestion, traffic management, and parking issues. Developing countries often suffer from limited financial resources and inadequate institutional capacity. Balancing tourism development and preservation can be a challenging task, often leading to tensions and conflicts among stakeholders[21].

In the broadest sense, the interaction between heritage sites and people can be called a dialogic communicative act. However, this 'conversation' between visitors and heritage sites is complex[22].

---

[20] Masri, A.A.A. et al., The role of memory and trauma in Post colonial literature: a critic examination of Chinua Achebe and J.M. Coetzee. Evolutionary studies in Imaginative Culture. 8(3), 724-734.

[21] Fong, S and Lo, M. Community involvement and sustainable rural tourism development: Perspectives from the local communities. 2015. European Journal of Tourism Research. 11, 125-146.

[22] Torrissen, W. and Lovoll S.H. Exploring creative wellbeing frameworks in context: Nature, culture, and sustainable futures. 2024. https://doi.10.4324/9781003294498.

For many decades, the distinction between visitors and tourists has been blurred within the heritage sector, but this contested dynamic has produced a strong critique of the ongoing exchange between heritage sites and visitors (Waterton, 2013). Furthermore, the individual experience of heritage is fundamental to the dialogic link between heritage locations and people, where generalities give way to the particularities of geography, place, and culture.

A collection of brochures and other materials can be utilised to create an official image of a heritage tourism site. Although they are intended to reflect the physical reality of a location, they can also convey hidden meanings and tensions (Reading, 2015). Tourist attractions are infused with heritage discourse, while also providing tourists with a limited range of potential tourist acts and roles. On a more personal level, it is crucial to understand the implications of this representation, particularly the interconnected notions of belonging and identity (Watson and González-Rodríguez, 2015). The heritage/tourism relationship is reinterpreted under the banner of dialogue, thereby stimulating contemplation of the numerous communication acts between heritage sites and their visitors. Tourism and heritage sectors are increasingly linked to inclusiveness and harmony in political discourse.

Reflecting on the Future of Heritage Tourism

A new paradigm is emerging in the tourism sector, prompting a critical examination of how heritage may shape the future[23].

---

[23] Park, H. Critical approaches to tourism heritage and culture. Tourism planning and Development. 19 (1) 37-49.

Rather than having only an economic or cultural impact, heritage tourism can be seen as a social movement that strengthens local communities. Heritage tourism can be viewed as a worldwide political and ethical enterprise linked to the power of dominant actors and the hopes of marginalised people (Xu, 2021). Heritage tourism raises several significant political issues, including imperialism, capitalism, multiple definitions of authenticity, exploitation and displacement, nationalism, and cultural elitism[24]. Heritage tourism has become a tool for cultural and economic imperialism, promoting aristocratic ideologies and value systems (Zhu, 2021). Cultural narratives are created for heritage tourism to advance national political objectives.

Heritage tourism should prioritise the respect of community perspectives and rights during the recognition, interpretation, and management processes (Zhu, 2021). International organisations can use heritage tourism to promote cultural acknowledgement and resource redistribution, empowering local populations to influence social, economic, and political aspects that affect their lives. Co-production should be employed to promote community-centred collaboration that incorporates planning, design, and management to advance and foster social trust, equity, empathy, and community resilience (McConnell, 2022). This strategy reframes heritage tourism by prioritizing the rights and social well-being of local communities while offering platforms for visitors to respect and appreciate others' pasts.

---

[24] Zhu, Y. Heritage tourism: from problems to possibilities. 2021. Elements in Critical Heritage Studies. Cambridge University Press.

Conclusion

Critical heritage studies have been reframed by a dynamic conversation between communities, scholars and stewards. The emphasis on power dynamics, representation and benefit sharing has challenged notions of authenticity and uncontrolled economic growth in the heritage tourism industry. Southern Africa has acknowledged the contested nature of memory and heritage. By moving beyond nostalgia towards inclusive narratives, agency, and sustainable livelihoods, the region can achieve social cohesion and development. History and museums should be co-managed, and community-owned museums and Indigenous knowledge centres should be controlled by indigenous communities to drive development. In the future, the region should balance innovation with preservation to increase accessibility and inclusivity. Critical heritage should help preserve sensitive sites, provide support, conduct research, and facilitate engagement. Governments need to develop legislative frameworks that return revenue to local communities. Academics and practitioners should foster collaborations by adopting critical views that contribute to a sustainable future for locals and tourists.

Chapter 5
Cultural and Heritage Tourism at Memorial Sites

Cultural and heritage tourism that involves memorial sites combines place, meaning, and memory to create an engaging travel experience. These include museums, mausoleums, battlefields, or memorial parks. They offer more than historical education; they encourage visitors to consider issues of shared identity, values, and the human consequences of migration, violence, and resiliency. When visiting memorial sites, audiences connect personal memories with broader cultural meanings through reinterpretations, living archives, and guided storytelling. To ensure respectful conduct, inclusive interpretation, and physical access for a diverse range of people, effective memorial tourism strikes a balance between solemnity and accessibility. To support economic viability, local communities often use memorials to uphold cultural customs, handicrafts, and culinary traditions, thereby promoting preservation. Ethical guidelines prioritise continuous engagement with the descendant population to ensure factual accuracy and transparency of sources. Memorial sites serve as centres of education, remembrance, and intercultural understanding when they are linked to discussions of peace, justice, and heritage.

The Construction of Identity

Identity theory explores the dynamics of identity construction. Social identity theory postulates that identities are social constructs that influence behaviour and group interaction. A person has multiple layers of identity, including the attributes of age, sex, gender, religious and political affiliations, and many other aspects. A person may express different aspects of their identity more strongly in different situations. Identities are expressed through symbolic objects and behaviour, including dress, decorations and food[1]. Identities form naturally when a group is isolated or when constructed in response to an external threat or competition.

Mamdani (2013) argues that colonial administrations did not merely conform to existing African social structures. Instead, they created, formalised, and frequently rigidified 'customs' and 'tribes' to align with their administrative model of indirect rule. The colonial political economy demanded the commodification of labour and land. To enable this, colonial states constructed market-oriented identities. Mamdani (2013) argues that colonial identities were not revived by colonialism but rather constructed by the state to rule. This chapter explores the form and nature of identities constructed through heritage and heritage tourism around memorial sites. Many historians have described how colonialism disrupted and bound the fluid, multicultural and multi-linguistic networks of interaction and identity that existed in the places that were colonised.

The conversion of historical legacies into heritage elements necessitates a careful consideration of past errors. The concept of 'negative heritage' refers to challenging heritage sites that preserve historical records while examining their evolving meanings and associated values over time (ICOMOS, 1999). It

---

[1] Brodsky, E. A. and Marx, M.C. Layers of Identity: Multiple psychological senses of community within a community setting. Journal of Community psychology. 29(2), 161-178.

departs from the traditional definition of legacy as a curated collection of celebratory, beautiful, or nationalistic monuments. Instead, it sees locations of trauma, conflict, and humiliation as important archives that require serious consideration. Places of cultural heritage function as protectors of elements which people have transmitted over time. Active cultural site visits combined with traditional oral practices and heritage rituals allow people to express their native ties. This could be done by offering workshops where tourists can learn traditional skills, such as pottery or weaving. For example, in Vambo Village, Namibia, a workshop was created that allows tourists to make their own mats while learning about the cultural significance of these crafts. Communities facilitate storytelling sessions in which local elders discuss stories and legends. For example, in San Village, a museum in Namibia, tourists can gather around a fire to hear traditional stories, gaining a deeper understanding of the culture. Cultural immersion programs connect travellers with local families for homestays. Visitors to rural Zimbabwe can stay with a family that observes traditional ceremonies, offering a personal experience of Zimbabwean culture. Guided walks with local experts are led by local historians or cultural practitioners. In cities such as Harare, guided walks are arranged with archaeologists that shed light on the historical value of lesser-known locations.

Several southern African cities, particularly in South Africa, host collaborative art projects that involve tourists and locals. Cape Town, with its vibrant street art scene, is a prime example, offering opportunities for both residents and visitors to participate in artistic expression. Other cities, such as Durban, Johannesburg, and Port Elizabeth, also embrace creative initiatives that foster collaboration and artistic engagement, resulting in a shared cultural expression. These initiatives utilise constructivist ideas to foster active engagement and personal connections to cultural assets, thereby making tourists' experiences more meaningful.

Memorial Sites as Cultural Tourist Gateway

Memory plays a crucial role in preserving historical records, alongside customs and experiences, as it establishes continuity between the past and present, thereby shaping cultural preservation and shared identity[2]. The memorialisation of figures from the South African liberation struggle through sculptures and museums keeps the significance of their sacrifices in the public eye (Barsalou & Baxter, 2018). Memorial activities serve two purposes: they allow people to experience relief from trauma and help communities reconnect. According to Du Plessis (2023), early San rock art in the Cederberg area chronicles life and religion through artworks, establishing connections between contemporary cultures and their ancient origins. Historical cultural heritage elements enable present-day communities to connect with their ancestral roots.

Southern Africa uses literature as a powerful instrument for documenting shared memories throughout the region. Keletso Mopai and Angela Makholwa utilise their literary works to present detailed stories that challenge traditional historical records while exploring diverse perspectives on social groups and racial relations (Winstanley, 2022). In South Africa, the strong

[2] Sthapit, E. et al., The memorable souvenir-shopping Experience: Antecedents and outcomes. 2018. Leisure studies. 37(5), 628-643.

ideological ties between European fascism and Afrikaner nationalism materialised during the apartheid era in the Voortrekker Monument in Pretoria, which is a religious monument commemorating the Great Trek (Coombes, 2003). After all other colonial governments in Africa had been replaced by majority rule, South Africa further entrenched colonial power through the structures of apartheid, which claimed religious morality as a basis for structuring society along the lines of race and privilege.

In the contemporary formation of nationhood, African heritage assumes a crucial new significance, as evidenced by the national motto and coat of arms. African heritage plays a multifaceted role in shaping modern national identity, particularly in post-apartheid South Africa[3]. It emphasises that heritage is no longer just about the past, but is also an active tool for social, political, and economic development. This is exhibited in state medals and awards, in governmental discourse, the burgeoning of museums and heritage sites, exhibitions and archaeological endeavours, innovative curricula in education, arts and crafts initiatives, and a multitude of developmental projects. National mottos, coats of arms, and state prizes are being revamped to incorporate indigenous values and African heritage. The expansion of museums and heritage sites seeks to reclaim history while also creating economic prospects for local communities through

---

[3] Reid, R. World Heritage Sites in South Africa and why to visit them. 2024. Available online from: https://www.roxannereid.co.za/blog/world-heritage-sites-in-south-africa-and-why-to-visit-them. Accessed on: 16/02/2026.

tourism[4]. The emphasis on indigenous knowledge and history, innovative curricula, and archaeological projects contributes to correcting colonial imbalances. Arts, crafts, and other developmental programs use cultural heritage to provide jobs and promote community self-reliance. These activities are intended to bridge historical divisions and encourage national reconciliation and social cohesion.

The United Nations Educational, Scientific and Cultural Organisation (UNESCO) recently declared Mapungubwe National Park a World Heritage Site. The park features Mapungubwe Hill, the site of a powerful pre-colonial kingdom (1200–1290 AD) known for trade with Egypt, India, and China. Mapungubwe was home to a powerful tribe that thrived on trading with nations such as China and India, and it witnessed the growth and fall of this great civilisation about 700 years ago. This is where archaeologists discovered the famed golden rhino and other remnants of a prosperous African kingdom (Reid, 2024). The park is hailed as a model that blends heritage conservation with social transformation and black economic empowerment in South Africa.

The Value of Promoting Memorial Tourism

Southern Africa's cultural and linguistic diversity spans countries like South Africa, Botswana, Namibia, Zimbabwe, Mozambique, Lesotho, and Eswatini, reflecting a rich mosaic of peoples, languages, and traditions. Southern Africa has numerous

---

[4] Hugentobler, L. Memories Set in Stone—How Visitors Make Sense of Memorials On-Site and Online Experiences of Public Memory at Two Dr. King Memorials in DC. 2025. Universität Zü rich, Zü rich, Switzerland: Springer.

beautiful cultural heritage sites that showcase evidence of long human occupation. However, the trust region has relied on and promoted natural heritage more than cultural heritage (Manwa, 2007).

Twelve official languages have been recognised in South Africa to promote inclusiveness and diversity (South African Government, 2023). The Constitution requires that all official languages be valued and treated equally and fairly. Similarly, Zimbabwe's Constitution, adopted in 2013, recognises 16 national languages. Shona, Ndebele, and English are considered more important for practical, widespread use, education, and government administration (Chimhundu, 2016). Language is a means of communication but also a key vessel for the transference of cultural values, oral tradition, healing, spiritual healing, and identity (Maseko & Vale, 2016). In South Africa, the Pan African Language Board (PanSALB) was established primarily to promote the development and use of all official languages, including the Khoisan languages, which have been historically neglected. The Pan South African Language Board (PanSALB) was established in 1995 as a statutory body to promote multilingualism and protect language rights in South Africa (PanSALB, 2020).

The multilingualism of African societies, particularly in South Africa, complicates the development and implementation of indigenous language programs. Using indigenous languages in education appears to pose several obstacles for both teachers and students (Sibanda & Tshehla, 2025). The debate over the use of the mother tongue in education has raged for years. The dispute stems from several factors. The contention is based on the complexities of improving and integrating indigenous languages into education. Children who receive instruction in their mother tongue display greater success in complex cognitive activities and literacy than those taught just in a second language (Hilgart, 2024). Mother-tongue education has been widely accepted as a means of promoting cognitive development and cultural identity (UNESCO, 2016). However, this remains a challenge in much of Southern Africa. For instance, Botswana's education system emphasises Setswana and English, often at the expense of languages such as Kalanga and !Xóõ, which are spoken by minorities (Mautte, 2004). In South Africa, to address the language problem in schools, researchers and educators have advocated for mother tongue education, a crucial component of quality education, especially when adopted early in schooling (Sibanda & Tshehla, 2025). Zimbabwe has implemented policies that encourage mother-tongue instruction in the early years of schooling (Nyika, 2009), but implementation is uneven.

The use of local languages in the media contributes significantly to the ongoing maintenance of cultural identity. Community radio stations in rural areas of South Africa and Zimbabwe present programs in indigenous languages, honouring local storytelling, music, and oral traditions (Finlay, 2015). Digital innovations, such as mobile apps and online language-learning platforms, are helping to transfer indigenous languages like Setswana, isiNdebele, and Shona to the next generation. Cultural festivals provide a space for communities to showcase their heritage. Masilela and Hoogendoorn (2023) observe that cultural tourism can be seen as a means of developing rural communities, as it creates employment opportunities without requiring extensive development of infrastructure construction.

The Harare International Festival of the Arts (HIFA) in Zimbabwe and the National Arts Festival in South Africa celebrate local music, dance, and crafts, building awareness and pride in cultural traditions (Maseko & Vale, 2016). Regional organisations, such as the Southern African Development Community (SADC), and international bodies, such as UNESCO, have promoted measures to protect indigenous cultures and languages. UNESCO's International Decade of Indigenous Languages, which runs from 2022 to 2032, calls on Southern African countries to increase funding for programs aimed at revitalising languages (UNESCO, 2021). The cultural and linguistic endowments of Southern Africa are a significant asset for national development and the global heritage. The protection of this diversity through inclusive education, facilitative policies, community media, and the promotion of cultures is imperative for realising human rights and building cohesive, resilient societies. While constitutional recognition is a step of progress, the realisation and committed investment from the community should ensure that culture and linguistic heritage survive for generations to come.

Experience of Visitors at Memorial Sites

Through physical monuments, historical relationships become accessible to communities that wish to learn about past events, influential personalities, and cultural traditions. The nation achieves unity through shared history and values because monuments reflect its collective past. The protection of landmarks drives economic growth through tourism, thereby sustaining the generation of conservation funds. Through conservation activities, people from local communities gain employment opportunities in eco-tourism roles and take on responsibilities for eradicating invasive species and participating in environmental education programs. Support for protecting natural heritage is received through sustainable tourism operations. Hugentobler (2025) notes that understanding individuals' experiences at memorials is a practice that is part of a larger (active or passive) engagement with the narrative and the site, situated within a context of experiences. Purely studying the means of communication (the memorial), the text (the narrative of public memory), or the reception process (the moment of viewing the memorial) falls short of the complexity of experience. Hugo (2023) identifies five types of heritage tourist: "1) the purposeful heritage tourist who seeks a deep, meaningful learning experience, 2) the sightseeing heritage tourist who seeks a shallower, entertainment-orientated learning experience, 3) the casual heritage tourist who happened to visit the site but has little engagement, 4) the incidental heritage tourist where cultural tourism plays a small or no meaningful role in the destination decision-making process, and 5) the serendipitous heritage tourist who also experiences cultural tourism as playing little or no meaningful role in the destination decision-making process, but ends up having a deep, meaningful experience" (p. 2). Guided tours, human testimony, and multimedia presentations depicting struggles and resilience shape visitors' narratives and educational experiences. The physical landscape at Isandlwana, or the chilly wind on battlefields, creates an authentic and memorable atmosphere.

Memorial Landscapes and Everyday Practice

Everyday heritage is frequently associated with unofficial heritage: commonplace, vernacular, and living heritage. Everyday life, including our routine interactions with heritage, as well as conceptions of everyday heritage, suggests that the everyday is gaining greater currency across various academic domains, artistic activities, and policy contexts (Ireland et al., 2025). The concept of everyday heritage is a people-led approach to urban heritage and placemaking, which can positively impact urban design. Hugentobler (2025) explains that "...the commemorated individuals are not so much remembered for the entirety of their personhood or achievements, but rather for specific qualities that the dominant, contemporary culture deems useful for creating and reinforcing national identity" (p. 62).

While they may focus on inclusivity and diversity, methods such as significance assessment, heritage lists, and inventories often overlook everyday life domains, which include family histories, domestic-scale gardening, culinary, craft, and work activities. These activities can highlight overlooked narratives of low-income communities and historically marginalised groups. Critical heritage studies view history as a way for people and civilisations to determine their present and future by selecting what is remembered and what is forgotten (Meskell, 2018). Official heritage management and assessment methods still rely on positivism and universalism, which have been replaced by more nuanced heritage practices that consider local communities lived realities (Ireland et al., 2020). To create more inclusive and holistic place-making, consideration should be given to the relationships among street fabric, activities, and users, as well as other special and temporal factors (Skoura, 2023). Everyday heritage is more authentic than authorised heritage because it is unconsciously created by ordinary people in their daily lives; whereas official, designated heritage is instrumental and ideological, like public and private heritage (Ireland et al., 2025). Everyday heritage, unlike public heritage, is rooted in everyday life and supported by individual sensibility rather than by visiting authorised heritage sites.

Reframing Memorials for the Future

Poor planning, corruption, and incompetent administration all contribute to the infrastructure of ever-expanding metropolitan regions that are unable to meet the demands imposed upon them. Cities of all sizes will face challenges related to energy, water, waste, population, health, housing, and transportation infrastructure. While the quality of life for many people will surely improve, hundreds of millions will continue to live in substandard homes without access to basic amenities. The discourse of sustainable development has brought conservation closer to capitalism and wealth creation in countries such as those in South America, Africa, and Asia, which prioritise rapid economic growth (Winter, 2013). A critical approach to heritage should therefore not be limited to being aware of contestation, competing values, economics, or the growth of critical theory in areas such as memory, consumption, and identity.

As critical heritage studies expand their reach, they should address current challenges. Even though monuments, memorials, and memories are currently receiving considerable attention, many serious challenges are often overlooked in the industry[5]. To make the most of scarce academic resources, it is important to prioritise knowledge generation for heritage that addresses current problem domains and their diverse ramifications. Critical heritage studies must account for their relationship to today's regional and global transformations in ways that legitimise their conceptual development while also responding to emerging globalisation ideologies (Winter, 2013). This domain of knowledge production addresses critical concerns by expanding beyond traditional epistemologies.

Connecting Heritage, Environmentalism and Well-being

A sense of connection to one's heritage can benefit both personal and planetary well-being. Connection is a key factor in human health and well-being. Humans, as social animals, are typically focused on social connections. A sense of place can be linked to both well-being and environmental stewardship[6]. Hence, connecting with the natural environment enhances well-being and reduces the effects of social isolation. Engagement with the natural environment increases prosocial behaviour, which is an important aspect of hedonic and eudaimonic wellbeing (Meskell, 2018). Hedonic well-being aims to maximise pleasure, happiness, and life satisfaction while minimising pain. Eudaimonic well-

---

[5] Masilela, N., Hoogendoorn, G. & Visser, G. Cultural Tourism in South Africa: A Case Study of the Experiences of Employees. 2023. African Journal of Hospitality, Tourism and Leisure, 12(1):326338. DOI: https://doi.org/10.46222/ajhtl.19770720.370

[6] Sen, A., & Nagendra, H. The role of environmental placemaking in shaping contemporary environmentalism and understanding land change. 2019. Journal of Land Use Science, 14(4–6), 410–424. DOI: https://doi.org/10.1080/1747423X.2020.1720841

being, on the other hand, focuses on complete function, personal progress, purpose, and self-realisation. Hedonic signifies feeling good (short-term gratification), whereas eudaimonic indicates living well (long-term success).

While the historical characteristics of a place are thought to play an important role in developing place attachment, particularly in shaping a sense of place identity, there has been limited research on the broader concept of heritage in forming ties to a place (Ireland et al., 2020). Heritage combines and expands the concept of place to include relationships with the past that can help people locate themselves in the present. While the relationships between different thresholds of valuing heritage are important for understanding everyday heritage, formal heritage listings and registrations frequently fail to engage with the everyday (Richardson et al., 2025).

Balancing Diverse Cultural Heritage in Southern Africa

Given its diverse indigenous populations, colonial past, and multicultural influences, Southern Africa has a rich and varied cultural heritage. This legacy encompasses customs, languages, music, dance, art, and historical sites that capture the region's dynamic present and complex past. In Southern Africa, the preservation of indigenous practices such as the San (Bushmen) rock art or storytelling traditions not only connects modern communities with ancient civilisations but also reinforces pride in local heritage. These practices are not simply relics of the past but are robust elements integrated into living social structures.

Museums, historical monuments, and heritage places are physical reminders of our shared past[7]. They provide an account of our identity, history, and future vision. They play a crucial role in shaping how people perceive the past, particularly in relation to the struggle for democracy. These locations offer foreign tourists a glimpse into a nation's resilience and complexity. Cultural sites, such as museums, historic waterfronts, properties, and parks, play a crucial role in positioning cities on the global stage. Heritage economies emphasise unique elements of the past to attract visitors, business travellers, and tourists.

Heritage sites are living institutions that shape our national identity, inspire our youth, and foster a sense of community pride. They have also become popular tourist destinations, attracting visitors from around the world who want to experience Southern Africa's rich history and diverse cultural tapestry[8]. In this sense, heritage sites have a twofold benefit: they educate and inspire while also contributing to the local tourism economy. Cultural heritage is important for teaching both tourists and local communities about the region's social, political and historical development. The history of Southern Africa teaches deep lessons of struggle, resilience, and liberation. Historical sites such as the Johannesburg Apartheid Museum or the Robben Island Museum offer places where people can witness the injustices endured and learn about the necessity of reconciliation and freedom. For local

---

[7] O'Connor, D. The role of Cultural Heritage in shaping Morden identity: A comparative study of Easten and Western perspectives. 2024. Journal of education, Humanities, and Social Research. 1(1). 37-45.

[8] McGregor, J. and Schumaker, L. Heritage in southern Africa: Imagining and Marketing Public Culture and History. Journal of Southern African Studies, 32(4)649-665.

communities, preserving these sites fosters a sense of history, enabling all people, especially children, to learn about their cultural narratives.

The educational dimension of culture and heritage attracts tourists and to deepen their understanding of the complexities of the Global South. UNESCO World Heritage Sites, such as the Great Zimbabwe Ruins, the Island of Mozambique, and the Richtersveld Cultural and Botanical Landscape in the north-western part of South Africa, are good examples of how heritage preservation can generate tourism revenue. These landmarks draw international tourists as well as local residents looking to reconnect with their history.

Heritage tourism creates job opportunities in rural communities, ranging from guiding to selling traditional arts and crafts. Preserving cultural heritage ensures that local economies benefit from long-term tourism growth, while also providing a platform for communities to showcase their unique customs and lifestyles. Cultural heritage conservation in Southern Africa is tied to sustainable development[9,10]. As the tourism industry expands, there is an increased emphasis on responsible tourism that respects local cultures and habitats.

The anti-apartheid movement, led by figures such as Nelson Mandela, adds a powerful historical and political dimension to South Africa's heritage. Tourists and visitors are drawn to

---

[9] Ashworth, J.G. Heritage and economic development: Selling the unsellable. Heritage and Society. 7(1), 3-17.

[10] McGregor, J. and Schumaker, L. Heritage in southern Africa: Imagining and Marketing Public Culture and History. Journal of Southern African Studies, 32(4)649-665.

heritage sites such as the Cradle of Humankind, the Cape Town Jazz Festival, and the Zulu Reed Dance. Heritage preservation gives marginalised groups a sense of pride and identity. For instance, projects like the !Khwa ttu San Heritage Centre presents the San origin stories and art, alongside archaeological and genetic findings about their origins. The National Heritage Council (NHC) recognised the centre as a finalist in the Golden Shield Heritage Awards. The NHC fosters employment creation and skills development by supporting community-based cultural activities. Local communities make money through traditional art, handicrafts, and cultural events. South Africa's economy benefits from these creative industries.

Evaluating the Impact of Memorial Tourism in Southern Africa

Rapid urbanisation, climate change, economic hardships, and political unrest are among the factors that have raised concerns about threats to Southern Africa's cultural heritage and preservation. Numerous historical sites, artefacts, and indigenous knowledge systems are in danger of being destroyed because of deliberate actions like land development and the illegal trafficking of cultural goods, as well as neglect. Modernity and globalisation have led to a decline in traditional languages and customs, making it more difficult to transmit cultural heritage to future generations. At the same time, balancing conservation with modern development is a complex issue, as infrastructure improvements and tourism expansion must be managed sustainably to prevent long-term damage[11]. Climate change-induced natural disasters, such as droughts and floods, exacerbate the problem by destroying historical sites and artefacts. Poor policy implementation and inadequate funding have further stalled effective conservation efforts[12]. To overcome these dangers, officials on the ground must come together with other non-state actors and international organizations to bolster legal frameworks, enforce sustainable conservation practices, and educate the public on the need to preserve Southern Africa's rich cultural heritage for future generations. World Heritage sites face many challenges, including climate change (rising sea levels, floods, and droughts), underfunding, mismanagement, and inadequate maintenance[13]. Due to a lack of funding, historic buildings are subject to extreme weather events, which increase humidity and threaten rock art with biodeterioration, erosion, and irregular maintenance.

Conclusion

The use of heritage to commemorate and connect the past and present through inclusive narratives blends well with telling authentic stories that lead to effective stewardship and interpretation. Cultural and heritage tourism at memorial sites

---

[11] Marbun, S. The commodification of Culture in Global Tourism: Balancing authenticity, sustainability, and ethical practices amidst disruption.2025. Proceeding of International Seminar of Culture and Tourism. 1(1). https://ojs-akbi.org/inex.php/proceedings/index.

[12] Chirikure, S. Heritage conservation in Africa: The good, the bad and the challenges. South African Journal of Science. 109(1/201-3.

[13] Reid, R. World Heritage Sites in South Africa and why to visit them. 2024. Available online from: https://www.roxannereid.co.za/blog/world-heritage-sites-in-south-africa-and-why-to-visit-them. Accessed on: 16/02/2026

provides opportunities for tourists to learn about history, human values, and to critically reflect on the shared responsibility for the future. The conservation of African heritage encompasses both positive and negative aspects that pose significant challenges. Moving forward, African universities must incorporate heritage conservation into their curricula, drawing on their local experiences. Such teaching should draw from other disciplines, such as planning, environmental studies and conservation, to best prepare graduates to conserve heritage. As a result, conservation efforts must be intensified for the benefit of future generations. Memory should be celebrated through memorial tourism, without sensitisation, to achieve collective commitment that fosters dialogue and reconciliation, informing civic safeguard action for generations to come.

Chapter 6
Toponymic Politics and Symbolic Landscapes in Southern Africa

Toponymy is not a neutral administrative act, but a powerful expression of memory, identity and authority embedded within symbolic landscapes. This chapter examines how place naming influences tourism development in shaping both visitor perceptions and host community experiences. Drawing on social constructionism, it explores how meanings attached to the places are socially produced and continually negotiated positioning tourism as an active agent in construction identity and memorialisation. While the theory provides a useful lens for understanding symbolic meaning, the chapter also critiques its limitations in addressing material and structural dynamics. In Southern Africa, toponymic practices are often tied to colonial legacies, post-independence nation-building and contemporary political agendas, frequently generating contested, traumatic and controversial memories. These dynamics are particularly evident in heritage site which function as contact zones where tourism, culture and memory intersect to shape notions of identity. The chapter contributes to the broader body of knowledge on heritage tourism, which is underrepresented in the literature. By situating the discussion within the broader frameworks of tourism, governmentality and nation-building, the chapter highlights the role of toponyms in constructing cultural heritage aligned with development and national identity goals.

Social Constructionism

Social constructionism posits that knowledge and meaning are socially constructed. Our understanding of our environment is shaped by our social and cultural ways of life. Reality is neither fixed nor objective; rather, it is created through social interaction and the construction of shared meanings[1]. The development of social constructionism as a theory has been influenced by the work of philosophers such as Karl Marx, Émile Durkheim, and George Herbert Mead and was shaped by several trends in the discourse in the early 1860s[2]. Marx, Durkheim, and Weber, the founders of sociology, studied how social structures are produced, maintained, and experienced in modern capitalist society, focusing on conflict, solidarity, and rationalisation, respectively[3]. Marx viewed society as built through economic competition, Durkheim through common moral standards and social truths, and Weber through rationalisation and bureaucracy. A key influence was Thomas Kuhn's proposal that scientific outcomes are not objective but rather partial, reflecting the particular communities that produce them (Vinney, 2021). Social constructionism was put forward as a theory by Peter Berger and Thomas Luckmann in 1966.

Butowsk et al. (2021) comment that social constructionists take "the ontological viewpoint that the meaning of the social world

---

[1] Damaschin, G.A. 2014. An introduction to social constructionism. Social Research Reports.

[2] Korumaz, K.E. The crisis of the individual in the Morden society: An analysis of the works of Marx, Durkheim and Weber. 2019. Sosyoloji Dergisi Sayi:40 Yil:2019.

[3] Little, W. Theoretical perspectives on the formation of modern society. 2023. 3rd Canadian Edition.

cannot be discovered but is rather constructed by humans along with their histories, societies, ideas and languages" (53). Social constructs that gain prominence in specific historical periods are often shaped by institutions and cultures. The dependence of social constructs on economic, historical, and political situations can lead to their transformation.

Social constructionists typically agree on three key ideas. A community's understanding of truth, reality, and value is sustained by its members. This knowledge is transmitted to new members of the community and informs the development of ideas, policies, and perspectives on power and honour, which are then codified. These socially constructed concepts then generate a sense of social representativeness and, if they are not observed, they begin to appear permanent and unalterable (Vinney, 2021).

Social Construction in Tourism

Social constructionism has been applied in tourism research to understand how tourists' experiences and perceptions of travel and leisure are shaped by social and cultural factors. Bukowski et al. (2021) explain that constructionism enables a "conceptualisation of tourisms that encompass multiple worldviews and cultural differences as well as research praxis that recognises and reflects the plurality of multiple positions, practices and insights" (p. 62). This theory suggests that the meaning is not fixed but arises and develops through the relationships between tourists and the people and places they encounter. For example, a tourist's perceptions of a destination may be influenced by how it is portrayed in the media or by their own expectations based on cultural stereotypes. Pernecky (2012, cited in Butowsky et al.,

2021), argues that tourism illustrates how meaning is socially constructed for objects—such as tickets and souvenirs, places, or social roles—such as host, guide, or guest. This understanding of tourism has implications for how destinations are marketed and for the experiences of both tourists and locals.

Social Construction of Identity

Social constructionism posits that identities are not fixed or innate but are shaped by social and cultural influences, including power and privilege. Thus, identity is not something that exists independently of the social world; instead, it is a product of the interactions and relationships that individuals have with others. Rather than identity being derived from a 'true' or 'essential' self, it is fluid and dynamic. Constructionism aims to 'denaturalise' the social world, providing an understanding of how identities, institutions, and practices are created, and to observe social phenomena within the social context in which they are embedded (Hopf, 1998). In construction theory (social constructionism and critical theory), to denaturalise is the process of critically investigating, criticising, and revealing the social, historical, and political origins of phenomena that are often viewed as 'natural', 'normal', or 'fixed'.

It seeks to challenge the notion that contemporary social arrangements are unavoidable or inevitable outcomes of human nature. Denaturalisation promotes a shift from accepting reality to acknowledging that it is created and can be changed through political action[4]. By unmasking power relations, it examines how certain groups maintain power by defining their own goals as either 'natural' or 'universal'. Constructionists postulate that social organisations not only have administrative but also constitutive effects on people, leading them to reinvent their identities and interests through interaction[5]. Historical contextualisation of social reality is not a fixed or natural fact but a product of history. Constructionist theory posits that the identities and interests of nations are not fixed or predetermined by nature but are socially constructed through ongoing interaction, communication, and shared understandings with other players.

This proposition that identities are not static but can be influenced by social factors has significant implications for the study of identity. Constructionism can serve as a useful analytical tool (Hopf, 1998). Constructionist approaches help to explain how individuals, communities, and nations contribute to shaping and remaking identities. Heritage tourism enables people to perceive, envision, and affirm their connection to a country (Palmer, 2005). Heritage tourism sites thus play an important role in building national identity (Pretes, 2003). Visits to heritage sites strengthen people's sense of connection, ethnicity, nationality, and identity, as well as diverse meanings, multiple interpretations, and a sense of belonging to their country's past.

---

[4] Ongaro, E. et al., Integrating philosophical perspectives into the study of public administration: The contribution of critical realism to understanding public value. Public policy and administration. 40(3)477-496.

[5] Hosking, M.D. and Morley, E.I. Social constructionism in community and applied social psychology. Journal of community and applied social psychology. 14(5), https://doi.10.1002/casp.801

It is important to examine the unofficial and informal mechanisms of identity formation in heritage tourism. Park (2010) posits that "the socio-psychological dimensions of heritage are of paramount importance in understanding how personal perceptions, individualised meanings and subjective sentiments concerning collective social memories contribute to the long-standing tourism appeal of heritage institutions" (p. 120).

Thomas (1996) defines national identity as "a shared structure of feeling, a largely imagined consciousness that is reinforced both through life's daily routines as well as through ritualised, symbol-laden, celebrations of nationhood" (p. 1). In Zimbabwe, the ruling elite, particularly ZANU-PF, derives political legitimacy from ancient myths, historical events, and prominent figures from the past by constructing a narrative that positions them as the rightful heirs to ancestral legacies. They use ancestral and spiritual narratives to link their authority to ancient figures, implying that their rule is guided by the country's forefathers, a claim disrupted in the late nineteenth century. The immortalisation and elevation of Mbuya Nehanda, a Shona tribal symbol and the 'national spirit-medium' credited with galvanising the struggle against colonialism, are informed by social constructivism (Mhlanga, 20213, p. 52). The elite have led efforts to rewrite history and toponymy by changing place names to reflect pre-colonial identities, resulting in a 'commemorative landscape' that proclaims a particular, ethnocentric interpretation of national history. Most narratives about who should be considered a national hero and which historical events inform the nation's identity are controlled by the powerful political elite[6].

Soon after independence, the Zimbabwe ruling elite embarked on a nation-building exercise which involved the use of symbols. Symbols are sometimes fabricated to claim connection between the modern state and an affluent and autonomous pre-colonial past. In Zimbabwe, revered figures such as Joshua Nkomo were accorded national hero status and buried at the National Heroes Acre. The Hero's Acre was constructed as a symbol of anti-colonialism and national identity. Mpofu (2016) states that "attached to the Heroes' Acre is a permanent physical symbol of nationhood, which is attached to war Heroes and Heroines who died during and after the war and the living who participated in the war" (p. 63). The site is designated as a national monument under the NMMZ Act. According to Mpofu (2017), "the National Shrine has historically served as a space where nationalist teachings encourage selective memory, allowing for politically expedient forms of remembering and forgetting" (p. 66). Some individuals who otherwise would have been buried at Heroes Acre have been denied burial on racial, political, sexual orientation, or ethnic grounds (Mpofu, 2014). The structure partly conveys selected memories, which are designed to communicate selective historical narratives and memories (Mpofu, 2017).

In the first decade of Zimbabwe's independence, the Heroes Acre played a pivotal role in shaping the nation's identity, alongside Great Zimbabwe. Onslow (2011) suggests that heroes are not just

[6] O'Connor, D. The role of Cultural Heritage in shaping Morden identity: A comparative study of Easten and Western perspectives. 2024. Journal of education, Humanities, and Social Research. 1(1). 37-45.

historical figures but spiritual forebearers who passed down values, ideals, and a moral compass. They represent the "soul" of the nation by defining and consolidating the imagined nation through narratives that make people feel part of the "imagined community" (Mpofu (2017, p. 63). In times of political strife, economic turmoil, and social unrest, people look to these heroes for endurance and guidance to inspire, unify, and reassure the nation (Anderson, 1991). Nkomo and Heroes Acre have been used by the ruling ZANU (PF) party to construct national identity narratives.

Constructionism is also used to analyse ethnic identities. A person's ethnic identity may be influenced by their family's history, the community they live in, and the broader political and historical context[7]. Citizens in any nation are viewed as being loyal because of the progressive society and the formation of its vision, instead of the primordial case in which the community's vision is anchored in the myths of the past (Brown, 1999). Conversi (2006) argues that "this perspective suggests ethnicity is externally controlled and manipulated by elites for strategic, secular goals like political power or economic resources, rather than being a primordial identity" (p. 16). Constructionists believe that ethnic identities evolve in both content and boundaries within a changing nation, adapting to circumstances rather than being fixed, and are socially constructed and negotiated through interactions with others.

---

[7] O'Connor, D. The role of Cultural Heritage in shaping Morden identity: A comparative study of Easten and Western perspectives. 2024. Journal of education, Humanities, and Social Research. 1(1). 37-45

Constructionists argue that ethnic and nationalistic aspirations are at the mercy of political elites who continuously redefine and reconstruct them (Özkırımlı, 2010). Brass (cited in Özkırımlı, 2010) posits that the study of ethnicity and nationality is, in large part, the study of politically induced cultural change. More precisely, it is the study of the process by which elites and counter-elites within ethnic groups select aspects of the group's culture, attach new value and meaning to them, and use them as symbols to mobilise the group, defend its interests, and compete with other groups. Özkırımlı (2010) observes that "ethnic and national identities become convenient tools at the hands of competing elites for generating mass support in the universal struggle for wealth, power and prestige" (p. 88). This perspective has been influential in the study of multiculturalism, as it suggests that ethnic identities are not necessarily fixed or bounded and can be shaped by a variety of factors, including culture, language and religion.

Ethnic minority groups often have a strong sense of their identity. This identity, however, does not necessarily correspond to that ascribed to them by the majority. Wagley and Harris (1958) identify five characteristics that distinguish a minority group, including unequal treatment, limited power over their lives, awareness of subordination, involuntary membership in a group, and distinguishing physical or cultural traits. Issues such as institutional mechanisms that control or attempt to control relations between governments and minority groups affect minorities within complex, stratified societies (Mpofu, 2017). Ethnic politics involves promoting or defending the central values of an ethnic group or advocating for its material interests, without necessarily bringing it into direct contact with others.

The politicisation of identities occurs at both social and national levels, and these politics essentialise and create conflict. In Zimbabwe, tensions have always existed between Shonas and Ndebeles regarding their ethnic identities. Competition for political or public offices has tended to assume an ethnic dimension and has spilt into memorialisation practice. Depending on the context of the issues being articulated, explanations take a constructionist approach to Nkomo's identity and heritage. The social constructionist approach used in this chapter also helps explore the implications of transforming Nkomo's legacy into a tourism space through the lens of ethnic identity. Joshua Nkomo rose from the Ndebele people to become a national icon. Even within the Ndebele ethnic group, it is widely accepted that Nkomo originated from the Sotho but adopted a Ndebele identity by construction (Nkomo, 1984). Nkomo's ethnic identity has been the subject of debate, with some claiming that he is a Kalanga (The Herald, 2015).

Memorialisation practices in Zimbabwe have been marked by contestations rooted in ethnic identities. During Robert Mugabe's rule, there were arguments that he favoured the Zezuru clan at the expense of other ethnicities. Some high-ranking members of the Zimbabwe African People's Union (ZAPU) were not accorded national hero status and were buried at the Lady Stanley Cemetery in Bulawayo (Magadzike, 2011). The same questions have been raised about the implications for democracy and constitutionalism, particularly regarding the protection and promotion of human rights and the rule of law, in relation to the 2017 coup in Zimbabwe (Nyathi & Ncube, 2020). Through memorialisation practices, the so-called 'New Dispensation' have recognised individuals who were not recognised by the Mugabe regime, seeking to establish political legitimacy. The "New Dispensation" refers to the political era in Zimbabwe that ousted Robert Mugabe with military backing in November 2017, leading to the establishment of the 2nd Republic led by President Emmerson Mnangagwa. The new government introduced a mantra aimed at repositioning Zimbabwe as open for business, promising economic transformation, international re-engagement, and democratic openness (Masunda, 2023).

Nationalist discourse and social construction are inextricably linked in Zimbabwe. The ruling party (ZANU-PF) has historically shaped the country's social reality, identity, and political consciousness through curated narratives, particularly by emphasising the liberation struggle (*in Shona it is referred to as Chimurenga*). For instance, Mhlanga (2013) states that "Zimbabwe's Shona-dominated nationalist discourses tend to follow the social constructivist path, which publicly dismisses the existence of ethnicity while clandestinely embracing it for dubious political purposes" (p. 47). Nationalist discourse uses emotion or nationalist historiography to call on citizens to participate in the national project to "reinforce a sense of common destiny, and therefore a common future" (Harris, 2009, p. 59). Ndlovu-Gatsheni and Willems (2009) and Ranger (2004) argue that for nationalist discourse to be effective, it must invoke strong images, traditional stories, memories or feelings to prepare the nation to face new challenges. Harris (2009) concurs, stating that "the core function of nationalist discourse is to actively create and leverage collective memory and shared narratives to forge a unified national identity" (p. 59). In Zimbabwe, this is achieved through national commemorations, narrative construction, the conferment of hero status, public media, and institutional mediation, among other means.

Hutchinson et al. (1983) contend that "nations are not ancient, primordial entities, but rather modern constructions (imagined communities) created to integrate disparate populations through state education, industrialisation, and bureaucratic centralism" (p. 124). The constructionist ideal frequently seeks to transcend ethno-cultural barriers (primordialism) to establish a 'cosmopolitan' or civic nation, a state in which membership is determined by adherence to common, often rationalised, political institutions rather than shared bloodlines (Mpofu, 2014). Monuments may strengthen ethnic, national, or place identity through official narratives or rhetoric, inspiring extreme sentiments among their visitors.

Özkırımlı (2010,) suggests that "competition also influences the definition of the relevant ethnic groups and their persistence . . . because the cultural forms, values and practices of ethnic groups become political resources for elites in their struggle for power and prestige" (p. 89). Ethnic identities can be transformed into nationalism to gain political power. These symbols can easily be used to facilitate the construction of political identity and generate political support (Mpofu, 2014).

A key aspect of creating and preserving national identity is using domestic tourism to shape and sustain it, transforming the imagined concept into a tangible, felt experience (Pretes, 2003). Heritage tourism sites may function in a manner similar to museums, in line with Benedict Anderson's (1983) study of nationalism, offering the defining traits of nationhood and providing historical evidence of its existence. The government's plan to establish culture houses in every province in Zimbabwe soon after independence was intended to neutralise ethnic divisions and promote political unity.

Social Constructionism and Memorialisation

The social constructionist perspective has important implications for the study of memorialisation. The theory proposes that memorials and commemorations are not neutral or objective. Memorials are not just about the past; rather, they are tools that shape and influence how the past is remembered and understood[8]. Social constructionism theory has been widely used in qualitative research. This approach provides an inclusive framework for understanding tourism, identity, and memorialization practices. Therefore, it facilitates the understanding and analysis of representations in tourism and their impact on memorialization. Guzzini (2000) states that social constructionism is underpinned by the view that socially meaningful objects and events are embedded in interpretations about the world.

According to Oztig (2021), representations act as the pivot for the memorialisation of distant events, including violence, through museum exhibitions, tour guides, images, statues, and graves. Ozitig (2021) argues that constructionism offers an innovative perspective on the literature by providing an account of how heritage tourism sites, particularly memorial museums, function

---

[8] Denis, P. Memory and commemoration as a subject of enquiry for African Christianity scholars. 2015. Studia Historiae Ecclesiasticae, 41 (3), https://doi.org/10.17159/2412-4265/2015/450

as intermediaries between people, tourism, and memorialization practices and processes. Verztberger (2005) asserts that both sovereign states and opposition groups use and abuse the commemoration of traumatic events to challenge political systems that produce ethnic cleansing, violence and war.

Criticism and Relevance of Social Constructionism Theory

Social constructionist theory provides a useful lens for understanding tourism, identity, and memorialisation. Butowski et al. (2021) note that "some scholars believe that by asserting that knowledge is socially constructed and not the result of observations of reality, social constructionism is anti-realist" (p. 57). It can be difficult to determine whether something is truly socially constructed or whether it represents an objective reality. Social constructionism has also been critiqued for its relativism, which holds that all opinions are equally valid[9]. By asserting that no objective truth subsists and that all social constructions of the same process are equally authentic, no construct can be more legitimate than another. This can be challenging in the context of research, as there are no clear grounds for establishing meaning or value, and thus no clear pathway for research to make a meaningful impact on society. An unscientific explanation about a practice may be as valid as empirical research about that phenomenon.

Social constructionist theory has also been criticised for simplifying complex processes and important elements in its modelling of national identity construction. Brown (1999) argues

[9] Damaschin, G.A. 2014. An introduction to social constructionism. Social Research Reports.

that constructionist nationalists employ the language of ancestry and nature in referring to the past, thereby linking civic nationalism and cultural nationalism. Myths and historical continuity significantly influence memorialization practices. Despite these critiques, social constructionism offers a valuable perspective for understanding the world. For instance, after 1994, South Africa's ruling ANC government sought to create a new state that transcended racial, ethnic, and linguistic differences[10]. The new government actively established a non-racial, non-sexist, democratic vision for the country, conceptualised as a 'rainbow nation' that celebrates diversity and a shared sense of history, suffering, and destiny, without encroaching on individual rights.

Understanding Trauma and Historical Grief

The scholarship on traumatic events is extensive and diverse. Feakinsa et al. (2024) note that "as 'trauma and truth telling' discourse is embraced globally, there is a marked increase in the recognition of heritage connected to trauma, suffering and tragedy. Yet, despite the breadth and depth of research in this space, psychological trauma has been largely unexamined in the field of heritage studies" (p. 857). When the term 'trauma' is used, it usually refers to a general feeling of pain, suffering, and brutality, but it has increasingly been used to apply to a broader range of victims and has gained popularity. In fact, trauma is widely applied to cultural complexes, and in Southern Africa, the term is used metaphorically to refer to widespread experiences of

---

[10] Sokani, A. Making South Africa's government of National Unity a Sustainable approach towards Building a Capable, Ethical, and Developmental Sate: Public perspectives and Pathways to success. Journal of Public Administration. 60(3).

suffering, including war, genocide, and other forms of violent conflict. In the broader trauma studies landscape, debates continue around the representation of trauma and whether focus should be placed on lived experiences of pain and suffering or survival, resilience, and recovery (Feakinsa et al. 2024,)

Post-traumatic stress disorder (PTSD) is a mental health condition that occurs after experiencing or witnessing a traumatic event, such as war. It is distinguished by chronic symptoms that interfere with daily life, such as intrusive thoughts, avoidance behaviours, unfavourable changes in thinking and mood, and heightened alertness and reactivity. These symptoms can persist for more than a month, causing substantial distress and impairing a person's ability to function. Conscious remembrance and articulation of traumatic experiences, aided by public memory sites, may result in the formation of a group organisation or the construction of a coherent group identity[11]. Incorporating trauma tales can be a powerful technique for identity politics and recognition. However, minority groups may challenge dominant narratives, while institutionalised remembering of traumatic events and historical grief can also shape national identity.

Traumatic, Contested and Controversial Memories

Collective memory refers to narratives of previous experiences created by and for specific groups, providing a sense of identity and empowerment. Collective memory, together with supporting

---

[11] Evaldsson, A and Wessels, A. To commemorate or not to commemorate: three important commemorative events in twentieth century South Africa. 2003. Journal for Contemporary History. 28, (1). https://hdl.handle.net/10520/EJC28270

institutions and practices, shapes individuals' sense of identity, history, place, and belonging (Weedon & Jordan, 2012). Nation-states and their social and cultural institutions face challenges controlling collective memory due to ethnic diversity, anti-colonial struggles, religious transformations, and globalisation. Groups develop collective memory using historical narratives that are told through books, libraries, museums, monuments, archives, cinema, and television. The emergence of new media has significantly increased the potential for articulating new and marginalised forms of collective memory. The development of digital technologies such as the Internet have contributed to the democratisation of cultural production, making it easier to articulate marginalised forms of collective memory[12]. The focus on collective memory has been fuelled in part by a desire to recall the painful events of the past—particularly, wars. These interests also influence how we articulate collective memory. Within traumatic memory, history acts not as a passive record of the past, but as an active, disruptive force that shapes present identity, behaviour, and social structure.

Contestations of memory arise around historical issues such as human rights violations committed by liberation movements against their own members, killing of suspected spies, torture in liberation movement camps, civilian victims of comrades' bomb attacks, or sexual abuse of women within the movement. Political memory refers to how a society collectively remembers and interprets the past, and how these interpretations shape current political narratives and actions. It includes what is remembered

[12] Alsaleh, A. The impact of technological advancement on culture and society. 2024. Sci Rep. 14(1)32140. https://doi.10.1038/s41598-024-83995-z.

and what is forgotten, as well as the political power relations that shape these narratives. Political memory can be defined too broadly or too narrowly, excluding crucial components of public life. Political leaders, their supporters, and their opponents may attempt to derive meaning from the past and transmit or impose it on other parts of society (Verovšek, 2016). The primary challenge of political memory studies is mediating between institutional understandings of the politics of memory that are too narrow, ignoring the important role that broader debates in civil society and the cultural sphere play in influencing political expressions of collective remembrance, or that are too broad, lacking analytical rigour and making comparison across studies impossible (Verovšek, 2016). Because trauma is often defined by its invisibility, failing to acknowledge it in heritage-making is deeply problematic. Overlooking these experiences risks traumatizing or re-traumatizing individuals and communities through words and actions.

Commodification of Monuments and Memorial Sites

Private firms and commercial zones are increasingly aligning with well-known icons of the struggle through naming, statue placement, and the sale of branded products aimed at tourists. Well-known icons of the struggle include anti-apartheid leaders in South Africa and broader liberation movements who sacrificed their freedom, lives, and careers to fight oppression[13]. At heritage sites across South Africa, the presence of tourists, particularly

[13] Evaldsson, A and Wessels, A. To commemorate or not to commemorate: three important commemorative events in twentieth century South Africa. 2003. Journal for Contemporary History. 28, (1). https://hdl.handle.net/10520/EJC28270

foreigners, appears to substantially foster the commercial exploitation of the celebrated event through the creation and sale of postcards, books, souvenirs, and struggle chic (Marshall, 2010). Although some tourists object to such commercialisation, others choose to buy souvenirs that symbolically embody, prolong, and preserve their visitor experience while also contributing to the local community's socioeconomic well-being.

Monuments built in the past might stagnate over time, but they can be rejuvenated when used as part of a spectacle, memorial event, or ceremony. The public can experience mythological history through planned commemorations and carefully orchestrated spectacles. The way a mythological history unfolds reflects the power dynamics in society at the time (Mitchell, 2003). The term 'monument' has been associated with elitist, Eurocentric notions of memorialization, while 'heritage' is more inclusive and acknowledges and celebrates previously overlooked aspects of the past as valid and valuable, and fosters the interest and identification of local communities with the conservation of their cultural heritage (Marshall, 2010). While some (Winberry, 1983; Denis, 2015) view monuments as deeply meaningful, others (Jokilehto, 2017; Cudny & Appelblad, 2019) see them as reminders of societal divisions. They often fail to foster a shared understanding of history or a living sense of citizenship.

Monuments and Public Space

Monuments represent a community's growth and serve as a tangible part of its cultural environment. Monuments and their surroundings create a symbolic environment in urban areas, which is reflected in urban morphology. Their relevance stems from the variety of purposes they serve in modern cities (Cudny & Appelblad, 2019). The effects of public art are heavily influenced by the relationships between monuments and urban public space. They have an aesthetic influence on both the tangible and intangible components of urban space, including the cultural, symbolic, social, and economic domains of cities (Cudny & Appelblad, 2019). Winberry (1983) states that a monument is a structure, usually made of durable material, that serves as a symbol or commemoration. Progressive generations may perceive a monument differently.

Public art can enhance urban regeneration by fostering a sense of community, place, and civic identity, addressing community needs and social exclusion and providing educational benefits (Hall & Robertson, 2001). When architecture, form, and design are used purposefully and inclusively, they can contribute to the sustainable development of society and bridge growing economic, social, and geographical disparities (Winberry, 1983). A creative city combines heritage, public art, media, and useful creations to promote urban growth. This concept highlights the critical role of the creative class in the information economy, making their attraction and retention a key goal for cities aiming to foster innovation. Public spaces are an integral part of the city, physically and functionally integrated into the urban fabric. Public art plays a diverse range of societal roles, including enhancing interactions, promoting inclusion, combating prejudice and intolerance, and transforming the meanings of urban environments. Public art can convey symbolic meanings by presenting local history and identity, making it a valuable addition to the cultural landscape. It enhances national and local identity, fosters innovation, and provides educational benefits (Cudny & Appelblad, 2019).

Symbolic Function of Monuments and Tourism

Tourism is both a social and economic phenomenon. Monuments represent social relations, beliefs, powers, and identities, as well as collective memory, mirrored in urban space. The monument's placement in an open public location creates a visible morphological aspect that represents the local community's culture and heritage. Modern monuments serve as a guide, providing a spatial framework for visitors to explore[14]. They tend to create a dialogical relationship and mutual understanding between the artist and the people who look at and use the area surrounding, and sometimes within, monuments. Furthermore, monuments have an educational purpose, allowing visitors to learn about local and national history, heritage, and social issues. They influence tourists' behaviour, perceptions of destinations, and attitudes toward those areas.

Toponyms and Political Power

Place names have been incorporated into broader apparatuses of urban space (Mamvura, 2023). Places named after political icons serve as markers of collective memory. In such circumstances, the main purpose of naming is eclipsed by the memorial's politically charged role. The commemorative function is backgrounded. Place names also serve more direct political purposes. Critical

---

[14] Madakovic, J. et al., 2024. The interplay between Spatial layout and visitor paths in Modern Museums architecture. Building. 14(7)2147. https://doi.org/10.3390/buildings14072147.

studies of place-naming have explored the political issues surrounding place-naming (Wu & Young, 2023). These studies have explored contentious cultural politics, political economy, and the emotive aspects of naming and renaming, as well as the tensions between minority ethnic, class, and gender groups vying for visibility and recognition[15]. The critical toponymy literature has examined how names are inextricably linked to politics, power, and place.

In South Africa, official street names and the names of non-European immigrants coexisted in daily life, although the landscape is currently undergoing an intense, politically charged process of renaming. (Yeoh, 2018). Place names develop and retain an emotional connection to locations; hence, older, less frequently used place names can remain in everyday usage (Bigon & Njoh, 2018). Place naming acts as a tool for constructing, contesting, and replicating the symbolic and material order of a location. The act of naming places serves to normalize and solidify hegemonic power relations (Wu & Young, 2023). Changes in political regimes are frequently accompanied by attempts to reinforce hegemony through toponymic changes, particularly in post-colonial, post-socialist, and post-apartheid contexts (Wu & Young, 2023). Where the critical toponymy literature has investigated 'bottom-up' or public responses to such 'toponymic cleansing', it has concentrated on resistance to renaming. Most critical toponymy research suggests that opposing and rejecting a hegemonic place-naming system is common (Mamvura, 2023). Some recognise that urban municipal

[15] Soyer, F and Tunca, A.E. Political and cultural memory in urban space: Public naming practices in Northern Cyprus. Cities. 160, 105851.

government players, as low-level urban actors, can stymie the top-down naming process.

Post-independence, most countries in Southern Africa placed importance on a systematic, government-led transformation of place names, replacing colonial and apartheid-era names with indigenous, historical, or liberation-struggle-related names. Key changes include Pretoria (Tshwane Metropolitan Municipality), Durban (eThekwini Metropolitan Municipality), Gqeberha (Port Elizabeth), and many others. Several major streets and airports were renamed to reflect the new democratic cultural heritage. In Zimbabwe, after 1982, the government initiated a widespread renaming of cities, towns, and streets to eradicate British colonial-era white minority names. The English city names were replaced with indigenous Shona or Ndebele names. Key changes included Salisbury (Harare), Gwelo (Gweru), Umtali (Mutare), and Fort Victoria (Masvingo). This also applies to Namibia, which renamed cities, towns, and regions to remove colonial, German, and apartheid-era names. The major changes included renaming streets, rebranding the Caprivi Strip as the Zambezi Region, renaming Lüderitz (!Nami=Nüs), and changing Feld Street in Windhoek to Sir Seretse Khama Street, among other changes.

Conclusion

Toponymic politics in Southern Africa demonstrate how place-naming has become a battlefield for memory, power, and identity. Mythic history reflects the era's power dynamics, combining heritage, public art, media, and innovation to foster urban expansion by emphasising the role of creative class in the new information economy. Attracting and retaining the creative class is a significant challenge for cities seeking to foster creativity. Public spaces are then viewed as integral parts of the city, physically and functionally integrated into the urban fabric. Naming places is not always neutral, as it is a social process that shapes how space is understood and contested. It creates and reinforces a symbolic and material order that serves as a tool for normalising or legitimising dominant power structures. While critical toponymy literature often analyses how new political regimes use street renames to establish hegemony, particularly in post-colonial and post-apartheid contexts, it has largely overlooked the low-level actors who are responsible for implementing these decisions. Key toponymy research indicates that marginalised groups frequently oppose and reject dominant, hegemonic place-naming systems. Place names convey desires for belonging, reconciliation, and regional pride. However, the symbolic landscapes raise concerns about trauma, legitimacy, and accessibility to ordinary people.

Chapter 7
The Promotion of Cultural Heritage in Southern Africa

This chapter examines the significance of various cultural assets at a location. The chapter examines how international cultural tourism is promoted by describing the cultural tourism product. Roots tourism and visiting friends and relatives are discussed, focusing on tangible and intangible heritage, traditional villages, nostalgia, and critical engagement in cultural consumption. The different market segments for historical sites, national parks, archaeological sites, and museums are discussed. The chapter profiles the types of tourists who visit cultural heritage sites, distinguishing their behaviours from those of other travellers. The chapter discusses the supply and demand elements that attract cultural tourists. While different elements motivate tourists to visit cultural heritage sites, this chapter focuses on the characteristics and significance of cultural tourists in Southern Africa. The chapter examines how post-colonial artefacts are created and displayed, and demonstrates how the configuration of post-colonial transnational interests provides insights into the cultures of state and identity politics. It explores how collaboration with communities can create itineraries that reflect varied histories and contemporary narratives rather than a single origin tale. The chapter discusses museums and places that feature inclusive displays, oral history initiatives, and multilingual guides. It recommends developing policies that prioritise responsible interpretation to address memory politics, repatriation issues, and ethical representation.

Balancing Theory and Heritage Tourism

There are several theoretical frameworks (participatory, decolonial, and ethical tourism) that can help prevent heritage from being curated solely for profit. This calls for a balanced approach towards authenticity against commodification. Community participation involves empowering residents to make decisions about their heritage resources. This includes co-management and benefit-sharing to ensure that residents have a voice on what is exhibited, how stories are told, and the benefit. Communities need to balance preservation (conservation ethics) with community needs to promote the long-term viability of sites and livelihoods[1]. Balancing representation and memory helps prevent stereotyping and ensures that diverse, authentic views are heard. There is a need for risk-reduction frameworks for ethics, permissions, and intellectual property to prevent the exploitation of information and cultural manifestations. Balancing heritage tourism emphasises the importance of balance among various aspects, which can be effectively applied in culture and heritage tourism to enhance the experience. Involving local communities in tourism planning ensures that their culture and heritage are properly represented[2]. For example, in Botswana and Namibia, local artists and individual families showcase traditional crafts and ceremonies to tourists, thereby balancing tourism growth with cultural preservation.

---

[1] Nyumah S.D. and Branbilla, M. Balancing habitat conservation and community livelihoods: an evaluation of community based wetlands management in the lake Piso multiple-use nature reserve. Journal of Tourism Management, 386, 125740.

[2] Onnoghen, N.U. et al., Balancing livelihoods and conservation in protected areas: Insights from Forest Adjacent Communities. African Journal of Tourism and Leisure. 14(2)481-490.

The tourism policies in these countries ensure that tourist growth directly benefits local communities by producing jobs and opening economic opportunities.

The Community-Based Natural Resource Management (CBNRM) programs grant rural residents ownership or management rights over natural resources and wildlife. In Namibia, the key aspects of CBNRM include Joint Venture Partnerships (JVPs) with private operators, employment, local equity in tourism, and revenue sharing from photographic/hunting concessions (Kavita & Saarinen, 2016). Registered conservancies can earn income from tourism while conserving, reducing poverty, and boosting local livelihoods. In Botswana, the CBNRM policy focuses on diversifying tourism by promoting community-based cultural tourism, such as hand-painted textiles, handicrafts, and community-owned lodges (Nyakunu & Rogerson, 2014). In both countries, the emphasis is on promoting sustainable, low-impact tourism that links environmental conservation with rural development.

The South African Township and Village Tourism Association aggressively supports inclusive tourism, ensuring that local companies and communities are represented in the tourism industry. South Africa also has World Heritage Sites that are part of Transfrontier Conservation Areas (TFCAs) with neighbouring nations, which encourages community participation in tourism. Namibia's Community-Based Natural Resource Management (CBNRM) initiative establishes an institutional framework that empowers communities to manage wildlife and tourism resources, thereby giving them a stake in decision-making in the tourism industry[3]. Botswana, like other countries in the region, views tourism as a significant driver of economic development and employs it as a tool for nation-building. While Namibia, South Africa, and Botswana provide specific examples, other SADC member nations, such as Lesotho, Malawi, Mozambique, and Eswatini, have also employed community-based tourism initiatives in various ways. This method ensures that tourism benefits the local community while also promoting sustainable and ethical tourism practices.

Implementing eco-friendly measures at heritage sites benefits both the natural environment and cultural tourism. For example, Namibia is actively promoting sustainable tourism by educating visitors about the local ecosystem and indigenous traditions while balancing visitor effects with conservation initiatives[4]. The Namibian government has launched initiatives such as the Sustainable Travel Pledge and the 4 Africa Youth in Tourism Innovation Summit and Challenge to educate visitors about responsible activities. South Africa also prioritises sustainable tourism, particularly through its responsible tourism ethic and initiatives such as the Green Tourism Incentive Programme. Promoting tourism that emphasises both attractions and local culture can result in more respectful tourism[5]. Namibian tourism advertisements, for example, frequently highlight the country's

---

[3] Boudreaux, K. Community Based Natural Resource Management: A case study. SSRN Electronic Journal. https://doi.102139/ssrn.1336643.

[4] UNESCO. Educating visitors to enjoy Namibia's World heritage responsibly. 2022. World Heritage Convention.

[5] Asa, R.A. et al., The impact of Tourism development on local communities in Namibia. 2022. International Journal of operations Management. vol. 2(2), pages 7-16.

natural beauty and rich history, attracting travellers interested in both scenery and culture.

Promotion Of Culture and Heritage Tourism to Enhance the Tourism Experience

In the current highly competitive environment, Van Zyl (2005) notes that tourism promotion in most destinations generally focuses on one principle: conveying a positive image. Globally, the development of cultural and heritage tourism is facing increasing competition. As a result, destinations have continued to make efforts to attract more tourists through marketing initiatives and policies. Promotion is one of the most important elements, designed to inform current or prospective customers about the tourism product offered, highlighting attractive and innovative attributes, such as physical ambience and competitive pricing (Hasan, 2015). Promotion is also used for publicity to communicate selective and specific images of a place to a target audience, with the intention of influencing attitudes (Nelson, 2005; Hopkins, 1998).

Through information dissemination, Hasan (2015) and Baldemoro (2013) view tourism promotion as a means of encouraging or stimulating sales among actual and potential customers to travel to a destination. Put differently, promotion is recognised by many as one of the most critical and effective elements of the marketing mix for marketing a tourism product (Molina, Gomez and Martin-Consuegra, 2010). It is thus acknowledged as a marketing tool with strategic objectives to spread product information to potential target markets, obtain an increase in sales and profits, gain new customers, maintain customer loyalty, maintain stability in the event of a sluggish sales market, differentiate and favour products compared to competitors' products, and shape the image of the product in the eyes of consumers as desired (Rahayu & Hendro, 2014). Van Zyl (2005) points out that in many cases the promotion of cultural and heritage tourism has been used to revive or re-position a destination's image. Similarly, promotion plays a vital role in promoting a destination and can help modify tourist behaviour by strengthening the intention to revisit. Simply put, tourism promotion helps attract potential tourists, modify the behaviour of existing buyers, and influence them to visit a destination (Hasan, 2015; Mill & Morrison, 2009).

Van Zyl (2005) argues that for promotion to be effective, marketers need to analyse target markets and identify marketing opportunities. This includes assessing the characteristics of individual target markets and how external factors (e.g., marketing) would impact a promotion. Destination marketing organisations are charged with going the extra mile to ensure that the positive image tourists hold of a particular destination remains consistent.

Psychographic and Socio-Demographic Characteristics of Heritage Tourists

Cultural tourists are consumers who seek to visit tourism attractions and participate in cultural activities. Cultural tourists share an interest in culture, but their level of interest varies depending on the reason for their visit, which is largely determined by their educational background. Thus, psychographic segmentation variables (the degree of interest in culture and the resulting purpose of visit) and socio-demographic segmentation variables (level of education) can be used to characterize cultural tourists in general. These characteristics account for the disparities in perceptions, attitudes, and behaviours toward cultural tourism provision across the segments.

Culture seekers perceive culture as the primary reason they travel to a country. A classic archetype of the learning-oriented cultural tourist is an inner explorer who endlessly seeks new insights[6]. They visit unique monuments and museums to encounter unfamiliar cultures and ways of life, and to interact with the host community. The constant pursuit of new cultural knowledge and experiences transforms culture searchers into true culture vultures (Salazar & Zhang, 2013). A culture vulture is someone who is highly enthusiastic about the arts and culture, frequently seeking out museums, theatre, concerts, literary events, galleries, and festivals. They have a wealth of knowledge about places, people, and cultures as a result of their higher education. Driven by the desire to broaden their cultural knowledge as part of their ongoing education, culture seekers want to see and experience firsthand what they have learnt from books and travel literature, to broaden their perspective.

Culture players are generally interested in culture and view it as only one aspect of the tourism industry's appeal. They occasionally visit cultural attractions or events. For this sort of cultural tourist, the most important component is demographic, namely, family composition (Salazar, 2005). Culture enthusiasts

---

[6] Baltaci, M. and Cakici C.A. Serendipitous Cultural Tourist. Book Chapter. https://doi.10.4018/978-1-7998-8528-3.ch018.

are frequently young families with children. This is reflected in the psychographic factors and subsequent customer behaviour. The choice of a day trip or vacation site is determined by the availability of active entertainment options and cultural offerings that add value. As a result, people favour cultural cycling and walking routes, as well as museums, monuments, and events that encourage physical and educational visits.

Culture viewers have little to no affinity for or interest in culture. As a result, they require less background information about culture. They are vacationers seeking a mix of entertainment and relaxation. Cultural attractions have a modest influence on their vacation plans. If these tourists visit a monument, it is because of its impressive size or location, as well as its widespread recognition[7]. Architectural history is viewed only as extra entertainment for the cultural viewer: it merely creates an atmosphere for passive recreational activities, such as shopping, relaxing on a terrace, or attending a folk event. This attitude is typical of day visitors who do not stay long enough to fully immerse themselves in the destination's culture, instead focusing on leisurely sightseeing and enjoying a historic setting without placing a high value on cultural authenticity (Salazar, 2005). Culture fans do not want to feel disoriented while travelling abroad on vacation. When they are far from home, they do not want to be disrupted from their usual cultural patterns.

[7] Markina, E. et al. The correlation between Cultural Tourism motivation and Tourism Tolerance. Tourism and Hospitality. 5(4),

Marketing Cultural and Heritage Tourism Destinations

According to Moithy and Boyd (2003), heritage deliberately shapes the present through interpretation, using the past to powerfully market experiences to tourists. Ashworth and Larkham (1994) argue that heritage can become a conflicting resource when it comes to sensitive topics like memory politicization, tourism pressure, preservation and development. The heritage identity or attractiveness of a place is first advertised, allowing travellers to experience and appreciate the location[8]. Cultural heritage sites encompass a diverse range of human creations from throughout history. Destination marketing follows the conventional marketing policy phases: market analysis, policy development, policy implementation, and policy evaluation. In the first phase, the internal and external market environment is analysed. The second phase involves developing a marketing strategy based on external and internal analyses, starting with strategic marketing objectives such as increasing cultural tourism market share or establishing a new cultural tourism image. To attain these goals, necessary policy decisions are taken. On the demand side, target groups for cultural tourism are chosen and represented in personas.

As knowledge, mobility, and travel become more accessible, there is a growing desire to learn about and experience different cultures. Most cities, towns, villages, and settled landscapes host some form of tourism. Tourism and culture are leading the way

---

[8] Asa, R.A. et al., The impact of Tourism development on local communities in Namibia. 2022. International Journal of operations Management. vol. 2(2), pages 7-16

in revitalising old buildings and open spaces for modern use, preserving both historic and contemporary cultural values[9]. Abandoned historic buildings and open spaces pose a risk of physical decay or redevelopment and represent a missed chance to revitalise structures that reflect a community's identity and social customs. Hotels, restaurants, workplaces, shopping areas, and revitalised urban wastelands can complement art galleries, museums, and performance venues to create imaginative and appealing venues for tourists and locals. Twentieth-century buildings and urban ensembles are as popular as classical or medieval structures.

Due to their rich cultural traditions, host places provide diverse tourism experiences and provide a comprehensive portrayal of local social life. Traditions are celebrated through live performances, festivals, events, storytellers, and local markets, as well as through the daily activities of the host people[10]. Although heritage tourism is described in various ways, it is essential to remember that, ultimately, it is a consumer-driven practice. Tourists who wish to truly connect with a local place often seek to engage in local events and festivals rather than attend specialized cultural performances designed for visitors. Traditional and popular culture, such as language, literature, music, dance, festivals, food, oral traditions, and sports, are often complemented by physical heritage.

---

[9] Hassan, N. and Alamoudy, O.F. Promoting Tourism through sustainable adaptive Reuse of Heritage Buildings in Lower income counties. IOP Conference Series Earth and Environmental Science. 1530 (1), 012042.

[10] Shubbar, F. et al., Cultural heritage Tourism as a catalyst of urban regeneration: The case of the historic city of Manama Bahrain. 2025. Journal of Tourism and Cultural Change. 23(6) 619-661.

Promoting Tourism to Increase Benefits to the Destination

The increased flow of tourists into an area can help reduce hunger and poverty by stimulating local businesses and creating employment opportunities, thereby increasing the area's revenue. However, if tourism is not properly controlled, it can lead to a negative increase in the cost of living and the displacement of residents. One of the primary contributions of tourism is economic growth and advancement. According to the World Travel and Tourism Council (2020), tourism alone accounts for approximately 0.4% of global GDP and generates nearly 330 million jobs worldwide. This figure shows that tourism is a major global employer and contributes a significant component of the economy. The number of people employed in the sector suggests that heritage-specific tourism accounts for a modest share of global jobs and incomes.

In many developing countries, tourism is a significant economic activity that generates employment opportunities for residents. Revenues from employment opportunities and related services, such as hospitality, transportation, and retail, can help alleviate poverty for families[11]. For instance, countries such as Kenya and Tanzania rely heavily on ecotourism as a source of income, not only creating employment opportunities but also helping to preserve natural resources and wildlife, which can significantly contribute to the economy (Walpole & Goodwin, 2000). Thereafter, tourism revenues can be reinvested to advance the

---

[11] Shubbar, F. et al., Cultural heritage Tourism as a catalyst of urban regeneration: the case of the historic city of Manama Bahrain. 2025. Journal of Tourism and Cultural Change. 23(6) 619-661.

Sustainable Development Goals by funding local infrastructure and essential services (SDG 6, 9, 11). They can be used to create local employment and skills development (SDG 4, 8), support inclusive economic opportunities (SDG 1, 5, 10), and protect people and places (SDG 13, 14, 15). Tourism revenues can also help preserve culture and heritage (SDG 11, 16), promote sustainable transportation and energy (SDG 7, 9, 13), and strengthen governance, data, and planning (SDG 16, 17). By establishing a dedicated revenue-holding fund with a clear mandate to reinvest in SDG-aligned areas to encourage responsible nature-based tourism (SDG 12, 14, 15).

Tourism accelerates infrastructure development, directly benefiting citizens. An increase in the number of visitors leads to improvements in transportation, healthcare, and educational facilities, which, in turn, raise the standard of living in the region, depending on the availability of essential services and the degree to which they are utilised (UNWTO, 2019). Improvements in infrastructure may also enhance agricultural productivity by increasing market access for local farmers, thereby reducing hunger and food insecurity. Improving the accessibility of remote infrastructure can also enhance the transportation of rural agricultural products to urban centres. By promoting local culture, tourism can foster community social cohesion, pride, and empowerment, thereby enhancing the well-being of communities[12]. Local people can reap greater benefits and enjoy an equitable distribution of funds raised from tourism (Scheyvens, 2002). Initiatives that train local people in entrepreneurship,

---

[12] Hassan, N. and Alamoudy, O.F. Promoting Tourism through sustainable adaptive Reuse of Heritage Buildings in Lower income counties. IOP Conference Series Earth and Environmental Science. 1530 (1), 012042.

management and hospitality through tourism development empower community members, enabling them to actively engage in the tourism sector and reducing poverty.

A major concern is economic leakage, the outflow of spending from the host country's economy to foreign markets. The UN Environment Programme (UNEP) claims that developing countries, particularly in Africa, lose up to 80% of their earned tourism revenue due to leakages. This occurs when revenue leaves the local economy to fund foreign-owned airlines, hotels, and imported goods, and to finance the repatriation of profits by multinational firms (UNEP, 2011). For example, in several African countries, a substantial portion of tourism revenue is siphoned off by foreign enterprises, with local communities receiving a meagre share of the profits (Anderson & Juma, 2011). This situation limits the potential to alleviate poverty and improve food security.

Furthermore, the rising cost of living in major tourist attraction areas disproportionately affects the quality of life of low-income households. Because of increased demand for goods, services, and housing, these areas become more expensive for residents. Research in countries such as Kenya suggests that the development of high-end tourism facilities is associated with higher food and accommodation prices, displacing local people and increasing food insecurity (Akama & Kieti, 2020). Such economic changes can exacerbate existing inequalities by making it harder for vulnerable groups to access basic goods and services.

Low-paying jobs are often considered seasonal work and do not guarantee a steady income. Many in the tourism industry work on part-time, temporary, or informal contracts, receiving limited benefits and no job security. A World Bank report on tourism in Sub-Saharan Africa confirms that employment in this sector is basic and low-skilled, offers low wages, and offers minimal opportunities for advancement (World Bank, 2013). This does not generate economic stability for workers, who remain vulnerable to poverty and hunger, particularly during off-peak seasons.

Displacement of communities is another major problem associated with tourism. The development of land to support tourism—for example, by building hotels or designating land as natural reserves—can displace residents or restrict their access to essential resources. For example, in Tanzania, when land was allocated to national parks and developed for tourism, this resulted in the forced relocation of several indigenous people who depended on the land for agriculture and livestock (Nelson, 2010). In such cases, families not only lose their homes and land but also their means to sustain their lives. Thus, tourism development can devastate food systems and exacerbate the socio-economic hardships faced by rural populations that are heavily dependent on these resources, thereby increasing poverty.

Connecting Hunger, Poverty, and Tourism

While tourism promotes economic development and cultural exchange, it can also contribute to hunger and poverty. Poverty is a lack of resources to fulfil basic needs such as food, shelter, and health, whereas hunger is a direct result of food insecurity and extreme poverty. Poverty is a multidimensional condition in which individuals or households lack the financial resources to meet essential needs. Ramphoma (2014) states that poverty is

> the inability of individuals or households to attain sufficient resources to satisfy a socially acceptable minimum standard of living. Characteristics that determine poverty include individual, community, household, and regional factors. Lack of access to basic services such as dwelling, electricity, water and sanitation was found to aggravate poverty. Socio-economic factors such as unemployment, education level, gender, income and household size also affect poverty. Causes, determinants and types of poverty must first be understood before poverty can be alleviated. (p. 59)

Ramphoma (2014) identifies two approaches to poverty: absolute and relative. The absolute approach views poverty as the failure of needs fulfilment, which impairs the ability of the individual or the family to function adequately in society.

Increased tourism can improve local economies and help alleviate poverty by generating income; however, it can also exacerbate inequality and deplete resources, thereby increasing hunger for some groups (Gweshengwe & Hassan, 2020). Economic and food insecurity pose a potential challenge to the long-term development and growth of the tourism sector. Infrastructure, tourist perceptions, and community participation, all crucial to the growth of the area's tourism economy, can pose significant obstacles when affected by poverty or hunger (Odhiambo, 2021). Not only do these problems impede tourism development, but they also prevent it from realising its full potential for community members.

In many developing regions, tourists encounter inadequate transportation facilities, unreliable supply services, and communication systems. For example, Bayih and Singh (2022) emphasise that limited tourism infrastructure and peripheral amenities constrain poor communities' participation in the tourism economy. These communities struggle to tackle poverty and hunger due to reduced economic benefits, inequality, and lack of access to key services. In many cases, tourism cannot attract visitors or sustain operations without significant investment, thereby restricting the potential for economic opportunities that could benefit local communities.

The stigmas associated with hunger and poverty also hinder tourism promotion in some areas (ICOMOS, 1999). Communities experiencing poverty or food deprivation are likely to be perceived as unsafe or unappealing by potential tourists. This reduces the volume of visits, which could stimulate the economy and alleviate poverty. This creates a vicious circle: poverty hinders tourism, which could stimulate development and alleviate poverty. Scheyvens (2011) observes that while tourism has the potential to reduce poverty, careful management is required because tourists often hold negative perceptions of poverty. Inadequate infrastructure, negative community perception, and the unwillingness of local community members to volunteer limit the potential for tourism to effectively deliver benefits. Post-apartheid South Africa is a prime example of a country that promotes 'struggle' tourism, which involves visiting anti-apartheid sites and experiencing life in former African townships (Hlongwane & Ndlovu, 2019).

Sustainable Cultural Tourism Strategies

Studies have demonstrated the potential of sustainable tourism to alleviate poverty by creating job opportunities, supporting local businesses, and stimulating economic growth; however, this may have profound, multifaceted, and often contradictory effects on a destination's appeal to tourists. Although extreme poverty may discourage mainstream tourism, it can create opportunities for niche markets in slum tourism[13]. While slum tourism may be unpleasant, it may foster a sense of authentic experience. There is a need to remove these barriers through targeted funding for infrastructure, education, community-driven projects, and poverty-reduction and poverty-alleviation schemes, so that tourism can effectively contribute to poverty reduction and sustainable development (Scheyvens, 2011).

Sustainable tourism can help mitigate the negative impacts of poverty by economically uplifting targeted areas while conserving local culture and the environment. An example of this is community-based tourism (CBT), which empowers local people to take charge of their own tourism resources. This model involves face-to-face contact between tourists and locals, facilitating cultural exchange and a high level of local spending (Bramwell & Lane, 2011). Fair Trade Tourism promotes trade that fosters diverse relationships with local people and tourism operators and ensures fair payment and working conditions for staff. Not only does this improve the standard of living for people in low-income localities, but it also increases tourists' awareness

---

[13] Tamasan, M. Adaptive reuse of historic urban spaces: Challenges in interior Redesign for Tourism. In: Negrusa, A.L. Coros, M.M. (eds) Innovation, sustainability and growth in a VUCA Environment. Springer.

of ethical spending (Patterson, 2019). Eco-tourism is another form of sustainable tourism that can help reduce hunger and poverty. In line with nature conservation, eco-tourism offers eco-friendly travel experiences that benefit both nature and the local community (Weaver & Lawton, 2002).

Challenges and Opportunities for Sustainable Cultural Tourism

The creation of employment opportunities and the stimulation of local economies and food systems are ways in which sustainable tourism can significantly contribute to alleviating hunger and poverty. If well managed, tourism can economically empower local communities, particularly those in remote areas, which often have limited employment opportunities. For example, at Didima Resort in the KwaZulu-Natal province of South Africa, Zulu culture is integrated into the tourist experience, yielding increased economic benefits through local employment opportunities and enhanced social cohesion (Rogerson, 2011). Going beyond the use of the safari tourism model to integrate local cultural encounters bridges gaps among diverse groups, builds local pride, and creates shared value.

However, there is often an unequal distribution of the income generated through tourism. Many international companies cause economic leakage when wealth, capital, or resources generated in a host country are moved back to the company's home country or to another foreign organisation rather than being reinvested locally. This undermines the potential for tourism to relieve poverty in local communities (Telfer & Sharpley, 2015). While tourism can boost economic activity, it may also exacerbate economic inequality. Economically, there is a danger that tourism could cause the prices of food and other basic needs to rise, resulting in displacement and exacerbating poverty among marginalised groups. In South Africa, tourism-fuelled gentrification in areas such as Bo-Kaap and Green Point has led to higher living costs and reduced access to affordable food (Brown-Luthango et al., 2017). Residents risk displacement due to rising property values and high-end redevelopment. Neighbourhoods have shifted towards catering for visitors rather than locals, thereby increasing food insecurity.

In Mpumalanga, South Africa, the growth of private game reserves has restricted access to communal land for farming, thereby diminishing local food production and increasing food dependency in rural areas (Ashley & Tshona, 2003). Converting agricultural land into tourism infrastructure has altered access to water and driven local migration. The Okavango Delta safari lodge development displaced local residents from agricultural land, directly impacting local food production. In Southern Africa, a study by Mangwiro et al. (2025) concluded that the region needs to invest in developing clear policies, building infrastructure, establishing clear institutional and regulatory frameworks, encouraging collaboration among stakeholders, and developing monitoring and support mechanisms that ensure the sustainability of agritourism in the region.

On the other hand, tourism often promises significant opportunities for economic growth. Through community-based tourism frameworks, locals benefit directly from participation and stake ownership in the tourism value chain. On South Africa's Wild Coast, such frameworks help to sustain employment, conserve the environment, and preserve culture. Linking tourism to local farming through pro-poor policies also helps alleviate hunger. Lodges and hotels purchasing supplies from local farmers promote stable markets, which increases food security.

Local priorities should be integrated with tourism development to alleviate hunger and poverty. To foster a beneficial relationship between tourists and local communities, sustainable tourism efforts are crucial, as such approaches help transform tourism from an extractive to an enabling model through local empowerment, community participation, and cultural respect (ICOMOS, 1999). Tourists are not passive observers; their choices may either perpetuate or challenge prevailing injustices. There is a need to foster positive tourism outcomes for the host communities and mitigate any negative social, economic, and environmental repercussions of tourism. Supporting such options is not only an ethical choice but also actively contributes to a more just and fair global tourism system.

Conclusion

The promotion of cultural heritage in southern Africa requires a coordinated approach to link people's heritage to their livelihoods and development. To effectively promote cultural heritage, a combination of strategies must be employed, including education, creative industries, legal frameworks, tourism, and ancestral knowledge. The involvement of local communities is important for preserving tangible and intangible heritage. As custodians of traditions and communities' narratives, the use of concrete landmarks, digital platforms, festivals, and events can enhance authenticity. Stakeholder collaboration, including the business community, civic society, and government, is the cornerstone of any successful promotion. Funding should be made available to support festivals, historical events, and educational activities targeting both rural and urban students. Developing multi-country partnerships and regional cooperation for shared history, archives, and exhibitions across borders is vital to enhancing resilience against the eroding pressures of globalisation. The challenges of promoting cultural heritage in Southern Africa include unsustainable development, political pressures, and climate change. The immediate priority is to ensure that cultural heritage tourism benefits the disadvantaged/minority groups, such as women, youth, and people living with disabilities. Promoting heritage in Southern Africa offers opportunities to protect memories, strengthen communities, foster social cohesion and enhance economic diversification. The region should begin to advance research-led solutions that prioritise community-led projects, capacity building, and transparency in heritage conservation. Research should inform policy and encourage creativity to nurture a living culture that enables residents and visitors to share a proud, common story that celebrates the region's long-term prosperity.

Chapter 8
Climate Change, Heritage and Tourism

Cultural heritage sites are popular tourist destinations in Southern Africa. People who visit these sites are primarily drawn by their heritage, natural beauty, and culture. The increasing number of visitors to attractions means that the potential problems caused by tourism should be managed appropriately. As core products, cultural heritage sites should provide adequate accommodation, transport, and other ancillary services. Information and services on the sites should be disseminated to visitors to minimise the negative impacts. Several impacts can emanate from the management and promotion of cultural heritage sites. Conflicts between organisations and the government can arise over the ownership and management of sites, as well as the provision of appropriate behaviour, education, and interpretation services, when there is no proper planning in place.

Cultural Theory of Risk (CTR), Heritage Tourism, and Climate Change

Cognitive patterns and social contexts influence human behaviour, resulting in the development of numerous relevant theories and research paradigms. Quan et al (2025) note that "the existing research mainly analyses values and behavioural awareness but often overlooks the impact of social environments on individual behaviour. This helps analyse the choices individuals make when facing natural resource management issues, thereby providing valuable support for implementing natural resource conservation and cultural heritage policies.

Cultural theory of risk (CTR) holds that cultural values and social frameworks significantly shape people's perceptions of risk, particularly in relation to climate change. Cultural theory of risk (also known as cultural theory or grid-group theory) was developed by anthropologist Mary Douglas and later refined by political scientists such as Aaron Wildavsky and Michael Thomson (Quan et al., 2025). It provides a powerful framework for understanding why people see and prefer different responses to the same climate risk. Cultural theory explains social behaviour through four elementary types of cultural values: hierarchy, individualism, egalitarianism, and fatalism (Toorzani & Rassafi, 2022, p.291).

Hierarchists tend to rely on institutions and specialists to develop climate adaptation plans[1]. For example, they may favour government-led efforts to protect cultural heritage sites from rising sea levels, as they believe in the benefits of regulation and planning. Egalitarians value community involvement and environmental justice[2]. They may advocate for using local knowledge to adapt cultural activities to climate change, for example, by applying traditional ecological knowledge to enhance resilience in heritage conservation. Individualists value

---

[1] Toorzani, A. A & Rassafi, A. A. The effect of cultural values on pro-environmental attitude in the context of travel mode choice: A hierarchical approach. 2022. Transportation Research Part F. Traffic Psychology and Behaviour, 88, 291–308.

[2] Toorzani, A. A & Rassafi, A. A. The effect of cultural values on pro-environmental attitude in the context of travel mode choice: A hierarchical approach. 2022. Transportation Research Part F. Traffic Psychology and Behaviour, 88, 291–308.

personal choice and market solutions[3]. This viewpoint may lead to adaptive solutions that prioritise innovation and technology, such as the construction of smart infrastructure to protect cultural sites. Fatalists believe they have no control over climate change, which typically leads to apathy[4]. This mindset may lead to disregard for cultural heritage, as adaptation efforts are seen as hopeless.

Cultural theory of risk posits that to make the necessary adaptations to climate change to preserve cultural heritage, an awareness of these diverse cultural responses is needed. Quan et al. (2025) explain that risk highlights the possibility of crisis, indicating that cultural distortion is a real threat and that a trend of cultural crisis is emerging at heritage sites. Adaptive measures should address the values and beliefs of each group to encourage their support and effective action. For example, incorporating community members in the decision-making process for safeguarding a local historical site can help to bridge the divide between hierarchists and egalitarians, resulting in a more inclusive approach.

---

[3] Toorzani, A. A & Rassafi, A. A. The effect of cultural values on pro-environmental attitude in the context of travel mode choice: A hierarchical approach. 2022. Transportation Research Part F. Traffic Psychology and Behaviour, 88, 291–308.

[4] Toorzani, A. A & Rassafi, A. A. The effect of cultural values on pro-environmental attitude in the context of travel mode choice: A hierarchical approach. 2022. Transportation Research Part F. Traffic Psychology and Behaviour, 88, 291–308.

Policy Planning, Climate Change, and Heritage Sites in Southern Africa

Climate change, characterised by intense storms, rising sea levels, and changing weather patterns, poses significant threats to cultural and heritage sites across southern Africa. To address this challenge, it is crucial to develop effective policy planning and adaptation strategies that protect these sites, which are vital to the region's identity and hold substantial cultural and historical significance. Crowley et al. (2022) indicate that "to understand both risks and opportunities, consideration of the existing social, political, and cultural contexts in which communities operate is required, providing a clearer understanding of the threats to, and capacities of, cultural heritage" (p. 2). This section evaluates the current state of cultural and heritage sites in the region and the impacts of climate change on these sites. It reviews adaptation strategies to protect cultural and heritage sites and aims to inform policy decisions and actions for future generations.

Southern Africa boasts a diverse and vibrant cultural heritage, with numerous historical sites and monuments increasingly threatened by climate change. Several policies and frameworks have been established to address these challenges. In South Africa, the National Heritage Council has developed policies specifically designed to address the impact of climate change on heritage sites, providing guidelines for their protection and management (Chikodzi et al., 2022). The UNESCO World Heritage Convention (1972) and Climate Policy were ratified by all Southern African Development Community (SADC) countries. Its updated rules (such as the Policy Document on Climate Change's Impacts on World Heritage Properties) provide detailed guidance on identifying and preserving properties from flooding, heat, and structural damage. The SADC Protocol on Environmental Management for Sustainable Development serves as a regional framework for harmonising environmental laws. It is essential to maintain transboundary heritage monuments (such as the Maloti-Drakensberg Park) and to incorporate climate resilience into regional plans. The SADC Climate Change Strategy and Action Plan define strategic actions for climate change adaptation, such as recognising cultural landscape vulnerability and encouraging community-based adaptation.

Rising sea levels are threatening coastal cultural and heritage sites, such as the Robben Island Museum in South Africa, which is already experiencing erosion and flooding due to climate change (Dube, Nhamo and Chikodzi, 2021). Extreme weather events, such as floods and droughts, are also damaging cultural and heritage sites, including the Great Zimbabwe National Monument, which was severely affected by flooding (Nhamo, Dube, and Saurombe, 2021). Changing weather patterns are also altering the environmental conditions to which cultural and heritage sites are exposed, leading to degradation and damage[5]. For example, rising temperatures and changing rainfall patterns in South Africa's Western Cape province are affecting the preservation of rock art sites (Klostermann et al., 2018). To safeguard cultural and heritage sites in Southern Africa from the adverse effects of climate change, effective adaptation strategies must be developed.

---

[5] Pasikowska-Schnass, M. The impact of climate change on cultural heritage. 2024. European Parliamentary Research Service.

Quan et al. (2025, p. 8) note that some scholars argue that the 'intangibility' of culture poses a challenge to formulating effective principles and measurement indicators for tourism cultural sustainability. One approach is to adopt climate-resilient conservation techniques, such as using materials that withstand extreme weather conditions and developing site designs that endure climate-related stresses (Chikodzi, Hamo, Dube, and Chapungu, 2022). Another approach is ecosystem-based adaptation, which utilises natural landscapes to buffer the impacts of climate change. For instance, restoring wetlands and natural habitats can significantly reduce risks such as flooding and soil erosion that threaten heritage sites (Jigyasu et al., 2013). Local communities can play a key role in adaptation. Community-based strategies focus on involving residents in the preservation and management of cultural sites, as well as providing training and resources to help them address climate-related challenges effectively (Dodman & Mitlin, 2013). Using these approaches in combination is crucial for building resilience and safeguarding cultural and heritage sites against the impacts of climate change.

A policy framework for protecting cultural and heritage sites in Southern Africa from the impacts of climate change should be guided by key principles, including sustainability, community engagement, collaboration, and risk management. Sustainability is crucial to ensuring that cultural and heritage sites are managed in ways that consider the potential impacts of climate change (Daly, 2014). Community engagement is also essential, as it involves local communities in the development and implementation of adaptation strategies (Dodman & Mitlin, 2013). Collaboration among government agencies, international organisations, and local communities is necessary to address the impacts of climate change on cultural and heritage sites. Risk management is also crucial, as it involves identifying and managing risks associated with climate change to cultural and heritage sites (Nwauche, 2014).

A policy framework should have clear objectives, including conservation, adaptation, and capacity building. Conservation involves conserving cultural and heritage sites with cognisance of the projected impacts of climate change (ICOMOS, 2019). Adaptation involves developing and implementing adaptation strategies to protect cultural and heritage sites from the impacts of climate change (Klostermann et al., 2018). Capacity building involves strengthening stakeholders' capacity to mitigate the impacts of climate change on cultural and heritage sites (Jigyasu et al., 2013). Key stakeholders in the development and implementation of a policy framework for protecting cultural and heritage sites from climate change in Southern Africa include government agencies, local communities, and international organisations. Government agencies, including national and local government entities responsible for cultural heritage and environmental management, play a crucial role in developing and implementing adaptation strategies (Chikodzi et al., 2022). Local communities living in and around cultural and heritage sites are also essential stakeholders, as they are often the primary beneficiaries of these sites (Dodman & Mitlin, 2013). International organisations, such as UNESCO, ICOMOS, and the African World Heritage Fund, provide technical and financial support for the conservation and management of cultural and heritage sites (Ndoro, 2017).

Implementation strategies for the policy framework should include funding, capacity building, and community engagement. Funding is essential for supporting the development and implementation of adaptation strategies (ICOMOS, 2019). Capacity building involves providing training and programs to help stakeholders manage the impacts of climate change on cultural and heritage sites (Jigyasu et al., 2013). Community engagement involves working with local communities to develop and implement adaptation strategies (Dodman & Mitlin, 2013). For example, the South African National Heritage Council's (SANHC) community engagement program offers training and capacity-building initiatives to help local communities manage cultural and heritage sites (Chikodzi et al., 2022).

Crowley et al. (2022) argue that "beyond the built environment and portable objects that dominate cultural heritage literature, traditional knowledge, beliefs, symbols, and practices constitute group identity and convey important information across generations about how to observe and respond to environmental change" (p. 2). Creating effective adaptation measures is crucial for safeguarding cultural and heritage sites in Southern Africa against the adverse effects of climate change. Strategies such as relocating vulnerable structures, implementing flood defences, or modifying buildings to withstand flooding are practical ways to reduce the risks associated with sea-level rise (Dube et al., 2021). For instance, Cape Town has adopted a flood protection plan to shield its historic city centre from rising waters and storm surges (Dube et al., 2021).

Another vital approach is preparing for extreme weather phenomena, such as floods, droughts, and storms. Developing comprehensive emergency response plans, evacuation procedures, and damage assessment systems enables site managers and stakeholders to respond swiftly during crises, thereby limiting damage to cultural heritage (Nhamo et al., 2021). This requires collaboration among key stakeholders, including the host community and the local government, to craft tailored emergency strategies that address the unique vulnerabilities of each site.

A notable example of an adaptation strategy is the emergency preparedness plan developed by the National Museum of South Africa to respond to floods and other extreme weather events (Vollgraaff, 2015). This plan includes measures such as evacuation procedures, damage assessment protocols, and emergency response teams, all of which are designed to minimize the impacts of extreme weather events on the museum's collections and facilities. By adopting this proactive approach, the National Museum of South Africa is helping ensure the long-term management and conservation of its cultural and heritage resources, even in the face of a changing climate. This example highlights the importance of emergency preparedness and planning in protecting cultural and heritage sites from the impacts of extreme weather events, underscoring the need to implement similar initiatives at other sites across southern Africa.

Changing weather patterns, such as increased temperatures and altered rainfall, pose a significant threat to cultural and heritage sites, requiring the development and implementation of effective adaptation strategies[6]. Monitoring, prediction, and mitigation

[6] Pasikowska-Schnass, M. The impact of climate change on cultural heritage. 2024. European Parliamentary Research Service.

strategies are essential components of this approach, as they enable site managers and stakeholders to anticipate and respond to changing weather patterns, thereby minimizing the impacts on cultural and heritage sites (Klostermann et al., 2018). This may involve using climate modelling and forecasting tools, as well as developing early warning systems, to provide advance notice of potential climate-related hazards.

By adopting a proactive approach to managing the impacts of changing weather patterns, cultural and heritage sites can be safeguarded from the effects of climate change, such as increased flooding, erosion, and damage to buildings and infrastructure[7]. A key example is the South African Weather Service (SAWS), which provides critical support for the conservation and management of cultural and heritage sites amid changing weather patterns. As a strategic partner, the SAWS provides scientific monitoring, early warning systems, and strategic climate data to site managers, allowing them to protect valuable assets.

Similar initiatives can benefit other Southern African heritage sites, such as Zimbabwe's Great Zimbabwe National Monument, where climate monitoring can help protect the ancient city's stone structures from erosion (Mushandu & Zhang, 2024). In Botswana, the delicate rock art of Tsodilo Hills can be preserved through informed conservation strategies (Segadika, 2006). Mozambique's Island of Mozambique can benefit from early warning systems to mitigate the impacts of storms and sea-level rise (Palalane et al., 2016). The Maloti-Drakensberg Park, shared by Lesotho and

---

[7] Chikodzi, D. et al., Climate change risk assessment of heritage tourism sites within South African national parks. International Journal of Geo-heritage and Parks. 10(3) 417-434.

South Africa, requires climate-informed management to protect its unique biodiversity and cultural heritage (Zunckel, 2007). Namibia's Twyfelfontein, with its ancient rock engravings, also needs climate resilience strategies (Malwa, 2018).

By providing accurate and reliable climate information, organisations such as the South African Weather Service enable site managers and stakeholders to make informed decisions about the conservation and management of cultural and heritage sites and develop effective adaptation strategies to mitigate the impacts of changing weather patterns (Meque et al., 2021). This highlights the importance of collaboration and partnership between climate service providers, site managers, and other stakeholders in protecting cultural and heritage sites from the impacts of climate change (Orr et al., 2021).

Several case studies and examples of successful adaptation strategies can be found across Southern Africa and other regions. For example, the city of Durban, South Africa, has implemented a climate change adaptation strategy that includes measures to protect cultural and heritage sites from the impacts of rising sea levels and floods (Mgadle, 2022). The strategy includes relocating buildings and infrastructure and implementing flood protection measures. Another example is the adaptation strategy implemented by the National Parks Board of South Africa to protect the cultural and heritage sites within national parks from the effects of climate change (Loftus, 2013). The strategy includes measures to monitor and predict the impacts of climate change, as well as to develop and implement adaptation plans for each national park[8]. In other regions, there are also examples of successful adaptation strategies. For instance, the city of Venice, Italy, has implemented a flood protection strategy to safeguard its cultural and heritage sites from floods and rising sea levels (Munaretto, Vellinga, & Tobi, 2012). The strategy includes the construction of floodgates and other measures to protect the city from flooding.

A detailed implementation plan is crucial for the successful implementation of a policy framework and adaptation strategies to protect cultural and heritage sites in southern Africa from the impacts of climate change. The implementation plan should include timelines, budgets, and responsible stakeholders (UNESCO, 2016). For example, the South African National Heritage Council (SANHC) could be responsible for implementing the policy framework within a particular timeframe (Chikodzi et al., 2022). The implementation plan should also include specific activities, such as conducting vulnerability assessments, developing adaptation strategies, and providing training and capacity-building for stakeholders (Nhamo et al., 2021). An evaluation and monitoring framework is necessary to assess the effectiveness of the adaptation strategies and policy framework (Klostermann et al., 2018). The framework should include indicators, such as the number of cultural and heritage sites protected, the number of stakeholders trained, and the amount of funding allocated (ICOMOS, 2019). For example, the region could develop a monitoring and evaluation framework that includes indicators such as the number of cultural and

---

[8] Fatoric S. and Biesbroek, R. Adapting cultural heritage to climate change impacts in the Netherlands: barriers, interdependences and strategies for overcoming them. Climate change 162(10.

heritage sites protected from flooding and rising sea levels (Chikodzi et al., 2022). The framework could also include timeframes for monitoring and evaluation (Jigyasu et al., 2013).

The Relationship Between Tourism, Culture, and Livelihoods

The relationship between culture and tourism is complex and not self-evident because, in the first instance, culture has not been created to serve as a tourist attraction[9]. In this way, heritage transmits meanings and values from one generation to the next by preserving material substance. Understanding and interpreting these values is crucial to the true meaning of assets, their appropriate use, and their authenticity. This includes preserving both material and intangible components, such as functions, vocations, and traditions (Conti, 2011). For example, monuments that have been classified for preservation may be detrimentally affected by tourism. Thus, tension exists between the tourism sector and the parties tasked with preserving the cultural resources. The commercialization of cultural resources through tourism product development and their preservation by means of protective measures appear to be contradictory and incompatible objectives. Park visibility and tourist flows can be affected by drought, heat stress, cyclones/floods, and wildlife shifts.

Cultural heritage attracts visitors and provides a stable source of income during slow tourism periods. To distribute risk, communities mix tourism with farming, crafts, and conservation.

[9] Singh, A. Culture and Tourism: Issues and challenges. 2025. International Journal of Applied Research. 2(10). 230-234.

Ecosystem changes, biodiversity loss, altered wildlife patterns, water scarcity, and habitat loss can lower safari appeal while increasing management costs. Many historic centres or old quarters may be well-preserved, but some buildings and public spaces are not receiving proper maintenance (ICOMOS, 1999). Wuet al. (2025) note that

> "Cultural distortion undermines the authenticity of heritage by simplifying cultural expressions for commercial purposes, thereby directly reducing tourists' perceptions of value. Cultural distortion, stemming from modernization, globalization, and inadequate conservation, erodes the authenticity of heritage sites, thereby diminishing public cultural identification and support" (p. 2).

Tourism and livelihood diversification are deeply interconnected, particularly in regions where local economies rely heavily on visitor arrivals[10]. As global travel trends evolve, understanding the nuances of this relationship is crucial for fostering sustainable development and resilience among communities. Tourism can serve as a catalyst for diversification, creating new income opportunities and broadening local communities' income streams[11]. However, challenges remain, including uneven benefit distribution, environmental impacts, and the potential to disrupt traditional livelihoods. Heritage and tourism development have a dynamic and interactive

---

[10] Bires, Z and Raj, S. Tourism as a pathway to livelihood diversification: Evidence from the biosphere reserves, Ethiopia. Tourism Management. 81(1), 104159.

[11] Agboola, M.T. and Yotsumoto, Y. The interplay Between Tourism development Quality of life, and Local support for growth. African Journal of Hospitality Tourism and Leisure. 13(30615-623.

relationship. Tourism protects and revitalizes the physical and intangible heritage of destinations, sites, and local communities, while tourists and visitors benefit from cultural, emotional, and intellectual exchanges. Wu et al. (2025) explain that "when tourists perceive cultural distortion risk, there are three critical satisfaction pathways that are disrupted:

a) Authenticity Deprivation: Tourists inherently value genuine cultural encounters. Commercialization and contrived representations dissociate visitors from authentic experiences, triggering negative appraisals.
b) Emotional Disconnection: Distorted cultural narratives inhibit affective bonding with the heritage setting, directly reducing enjoyment.
c) Educational Value Erosion: Trivialization or misinterpretation of cultural practices compromises pedagogical efficacy, propagating misinformation and frustration" (p.4).

Heritage protection and tourism thus coexist in proximity, not in separate spheres. Effective tourism programs are crucial for preserving and communicating heritage. Many communities, especially in developing countries, rely on tourism as a primary source of income, and it has created economic dependency[12]. This reliance can leave the sector vulnerable if tourism fluctuates due to economic downturns, natural disasters, or global crises such as pandemics. For instance, the COVID-19 pandemic severely

[12] Gayo, L. and Katonge, J. The impact of community-based tourism on local livelihoods in communities adjacent to national parks in Northen Tanzanian. Cogent Social sciences 11(10.

impacted tourism-dependent economies, highlighting the need for diversification.

Custodians of culture, ranging from administrators of monuments to practitioners of traditions, primarily focus on preserving the cultural resource. The tourism service providers, ranging from tourism organisations to tour operators, primarily aim to commercialise the same cultural resource as a tourist attraction or event. Livelihood diversification involves individuals or communities expanding their income-generating activities. This can include developing complementary enterprises, such as local crafts, agriculture, or service sectors, to reduce dependence on tourism. For example, in South Africa, grape farmers have started offering wine route eco-tourism experiences, blending traditional farming with tourism.

Tourists' visits cause material damage to cultural resources. There are numerous examples of material damage to vulnerable monuments, whether deliberate or not, resulting from tourism. Climate change reshapes where and how tourists travel. Over-reliance on tourism poses significant risks to local communities and developing economies, as they are vulnerable to economic shocks, infrastructure strain, and cultural dilution[13]. For example, Zimbabwe experienced significant foreign currency shortages during the 2008 political instability. While tourism can generate income, the benefits are not always distributed equitably. Large-scale tourism projects can disproportionately benefit large companies or individuals, leaving local communities with limited opportunities (Amarilla &Conti, 2012). Tourism often

[13] Baloch, Q.B et al. Impact of tourism development upon environmental sustainability: a suggested framework for sustainable tourism. 30(30 5917-5930.

experiences seasonal fluctuations, resulting in unstable income for local businesses. This seasonality can create challenges to maintaining year-round employment opportunities. In places like Cape Town, South Africa, the tourism season impacts local economies, forcing many small businesses to close during off-peak months. Developing a successful tourism sector requires significant infrastructure, including roads, communication networks, and tourism-related facilities. Local communities may lack the necessary resources and expertise to develop and manage these infrastructure projects effectively (Conti, 2011).

Tourism involves the commodification of tangible and intangible culture. The exploitation of tangible and intangible cultural heritage for commercial gain can have negative environmental impacts, such as resource depletion, pollution, and habitat destruction[14]. This degradation can adversely affect livelihoods tied to agriculture or fishing, creating a paradox where tourism, intended to provide economic opportunities, undermines other local industries (ICOMOS, 1999). Visitors and local communities may face social and economic inequalities, which can pose additional challenges. In developing nations, local populations may feel alienated by visitors' expectations and wishes, which can threaten authenticity. These impacts can undermine sustainable livelihoods, particularly those that depend on natural resources. Opponents of the commercialization of culture argue that cultural value is lost when traditions and art crafts are adapted to the needs and wants of tourists.

---

[14] Matanzima J. and Loginova, J. Sociocultural risks of resource extraction for the low carbon energy transition: Evidence from the Global South. The Extractive Industries and Society. 18, 101478.

While tourism can promote cultural exchange, it can also lead to the commercialisation of local traditions. Authentic practices may be altered or staged for tourists, potentially alienating local communities (Conti, 2011). In places like Thailand, the commercialisation of traditional festivals has sparked debate over cultural authenticity and integrity. The production of souvenirs for the tourist market is a prime example of the commodification of tangible culture. Kalla and Metaxas (2024) indicate that the extensive promotion of tourism to generate economic profits may negatively affect cultural heritage, leading to problems such as the commercialisation of traditional folk festivals, the illegal trade in historical artefacts, illegal archaeological excavations, degradation, and, in some cases, the elimination of traditional crafts. In fact, souvenirs are commercialised practical artefacts (clothing, pottery) or artisanal products (wall hangings, dolls), that have been adapted in size, design, material, and colour to the preferences and expenditure patterns of the tourist consumer[15].

Tourism can sometimes disrupt traditional livelihoods, particularly in areas where tourism development is rapid or poorly planned. Research suggests that travellers are primarily motivated by pleasure experiences, such as visiting historical sites, rather than by seeking to enhance their knowledge or engage with diverse cultures (Amarilla & Conti, 2012). The most promising way forward is the use of sustainable, climate-smart, community-led tourism to protect and improve the local livelihoods.

---

[15] Chaturvedi, P. et al., The role of Souvenir marketing in Sustainable handmade Craftsmanship. Shodhkosh: Journal of Visual and Performing Arts. 5(30.

Positive Effects of Cultural Tourism on the Advent of Climate Change

Tourism can be a key driver of the local economy. In Southern Africa, climate change has reshaped how tourists travel and has encouraged the preservation of enduring cultures for visitor interest. Tourism can stimulate entrepreneurial opportunities, resulting in the growth of small and medium-sized enterprises that provide employment for residents[16]. Tourism can generate income from various sources, including accommodation, food and beverages, transportation, handicrafts, and guided tours. Visitors are drawn to historic centres for their tangible features (Amarilla &Conti, 2012). This can significantly diversify livelihood options, particularly in areas where traditional livelihoods are declining or unsustainable. Tourism can generate significant revenue for the preservation of cultural resources. Despite the destructive impact of mass tourism, visitor entrance fees are indispensable for the restoration of heritage sites and monuments.

While both locals and visitors benefit from improved public spaces, some economic, cultural, and entertainment facilities are inaccessible to the local community. Public investment prioritises visitor-friendly locations, while private investment prioritises revenue-generating projects (Amarilla &Conti, 2012). Increased tourism often leads to improved infrastructure, including roads, hospitals, and schools, which benefits local populations and

---

[16] Ramukumba, T. Tourism and Entrepreneurship: A South African Literature. African Journal of Hospitality, Tourism, and Leisure. 12(2), 535-554.

creates opportunities for new businesses[17]. In Namibia, conservancies have led the establishment of community-based tourism, thereby promoting infrastructure development and allowing locals to engage in various sectors beyond traditional tourism. Thus, empowering local communities to control their natural resources, cultural heritage, and tourism development processes, as evidenced by the number of conservancies established.

Tourism promotes cultural exchange, allowing local communities to showcase their heritage while creating income opportunities. This exchange often leads to the development of new businesses, such as arts and crafts, culinary experiences, and guided tours, thereby diversifying livelihoods[18]. The Maasai people in Kenya, for instance, have capitalised on cultural tourism by offering village tours and traditional performances (ICOMOS,1999). Tourism can also contribute to the preservation of culture for future generations by making it more accessible to a wider audience. Tourism stimulates cultural participation and, in turn, fosters historical awareness. Both are prerequisites for creating public support for the preservation of monuments and for subsidising museums. Kalla and Metaxas (2024) comment that "to reduce the risk and impact of threats, cities and communities must be more resilient and better prepared to address risks head-on. If they are not, their urban communities will be constantly threatened and become increasingly vulnerable to risk" (p. 2). In

---

[17] Godovykh, M et al., Exploring the impacts of tourism on the wellbeing of local communities. Sustainability. 17(13), 5849.

[18] Gayo, L. and Katonge, J. The impact of community-based tourism on local livelihoods in communities adjacent to national parks in Northen Tanzanian. Cogent Social sciences 11(10.

Namibia, rock-art routes and Himba cultural stays leverage low water to enhance dry-season wildlife visibility while offering offline, low-water experiences.

Conclusion

Climate change poses a significant threat to Southern Africa's cultural and heritage sites, with intense storms, rising sea levels, and shifting weather patterns putting the region's priceless cultural and heritage sites at risk. To combat this challenge, effective policy planning and adaptation strategies are crucial to protect these sites, which are essential to the region's identity and hold significant cultural and historical value. A policy framework for safeguarding cultural and heritage sites in Southern Africa from the impacts of climate change should be guided by principles such as sustainability, community engagement, collaboration, and risk management, with clear objectives including conservation, adaptation, and capacity building. The symbiosis between culture and tourism is complex and not self-evident because, in the first instance, culture has not been created to serve as a tourist attraction. Tourism can become a threat to both tangible and intangible cultural heritage when exploited for commercial gain. Hence, it can have negative environmental impacts, such as resource depletion, pollution, and habitat destruction. Conflicts between organisations and the government can arise over the ownership and management of sites, as well as the provision of appropriate behaviour, education, and interpretation services, when there is no proper planning in place. Information and services on the sites should be disseminated to visitors to minimise the negative impacts.

Chapter 9
The Sustainability of Cultural Heritage in Southern Africa

There is a growing demand for cultural heritage sites in Southern African tourism. Cultural tourism has been perceived as a field of conflict due to the failure to strike a balance between conservation and commodification. Visiting cultural heritage sites has generated significant revenue for the regions where they are located. Governments in the SADC region have benefited substantially from tourism. However, the sustainability of cultural heritage depends on the government allocating resources towards the conservation of cultural assets. The value placed on culture can encourage local communities to take pride in their own culture and increase their efforts to conserve and protect it. Although most tourists visiting the region go to national parks, there has been a steady increase in visits to cultural heritage attractions. Therefore, it is essential to develop strategies to attract cultural tourists to diversify tourism products. The chapter concludes that the sustainability of culture and heritage can serve as a gateway to local communities and facilitate product diversification.

Cultural Sustainability

Southern African heritage tourism seeks to prioritise cultural sustainability by preserving living cultures, landscapes, and history to anchor economic growth in locally owned, community assets. UNESCO has supported initiatives that promote community-based, eco-friendly tourism to safeguard cultural identity and create jobs in rural areas. As a result, this has helped move away from safari-style experiences toward more diverse, authentic cultural exchange. Cultural sustainability plays a crucial role in sustainable development by safeguarding cultural identity, traditions, heritage, and values for current and future generations[1]. It emphasises the importance of maintaining cultural diversity, traditional knowledge systems, languages, and collective memory as essential to societal well-being and resilience. Cultural sustainability supports communities' ability to retain their distinctiveness and cohesion in the face of globalisation, modernisation, and social change[2]. It builds a sense of belonging, continuity, and purpose, which are crucial to overall human development.

The promotion of cultural sustainability involves inclusive education, supportive policy frameworks, community engagement, and institutional protection of heritage and creative expressions. Without cultural sustainability, there is a risk that development will become detached from the values and identities of the people it seeks to serve. As highlighted by Soini and Birkeland (2014), integrating culture into the sustainability discourse enhances social cohesion and ensures that development is rooted in the local context and meaning. For instance, the UNESCO Convention on the Protection and Promotion of the Diversity of Cultural Expressions (2005)

---

[1] Giliberto, F. and Labadi S. Harnessing cultural heritage for sustainable development: an analysis of three internationally funded projects in MENA countries. 2022. International Journal of Heritage Studies. 28(20 133-146.
[2] Tang, Y. The effect of globalisation on social sustainability in local communities. 2025. Journal of lifestyle and SDGs Review. 5(5)e06592.

underscores the need to support cultural diversity as a driver and enabler of sustainable development.

Sustainable Cultural Festivals and Events

Sustainable cultural festivals and events are one way to harness cultural sustainability for sustainable development. This involves promoting environmentally friendly, socially responsible cultural festivals and events. According to Quinn (2017), sustainable cultural festivals and events can contribute to local economic development and community engagement. For example, the town can establish a sustainable cultural festival that promotes traditional music, dance, and handicrafts.

Cultural Heritage Conservation

Cultural heritage conservation is another way to harness cultural sustainability for sustainable development. This involves preserving cultural heritage sites, traditions, and practices for future generations. According to Mitchell (2018), cultural heritage conservation can contribute to the preservation of cultural heritage and community development. For example, the town can establish a cultural heritage conservation program that preserves traditional music, dance, and handicrafts.

Cultural Tourism Development

Cultural tourism development is a way to harness cultural sustainability for sustainable development. This involves promoting cultural heritage sites, traditions, and practices to attract tourists and generate income for local communities. According to Richards (2018), cultural tourism can contribute to local economic development and community engagement. For example, the town can develop guided tours of its cultural heritage sites, including traditional music and dance performances and handicraft demonstrations.

Community-Based Cultural Initiatives

Community-based cultural initiatives are another way to harness cultural sustainability for sustainable development. This involves empowering local communities to take ownership of their cultural heritage and develop initiatives that promote cultural preservation and exchange. According to Klamer (2016), community-based cultural initiatives can contribute to the preservation of cultural heritage and community development. For example, the town can establish a community-based cultural initiative that promotes traditional music, dance, and handicrafts.

Cultural Education and Training

Cultural education and training are ways to harness cultural sustainability for sustainable development. This involves providing education and training programs that promote cultural awareness and preservation. According to Stefano (2018), cultural education and training can contribute to the preservation of cultural heritage and community development. For example, the town can establish a cultural education and training program that teaches young people traditional music, dance, and handicrafts.

Existing studies on sustainability largely focus on the cultural practices and behaviours that contribute to environmental sustainability within tourism. Yet there remains a gap in understanding how culture-driven customs can promote sustainability in tourist contexts. Investigating these culturally embedded practices could yield important insights into more comprehensive ecologically sound tourism strategies (Zhou & Edelheim, 2021; Rastegar & Ruhanen, 2023).

Intersectional Ecofeminism and the Sustainability of Heritage Tourism

Intersectional ecofeminism is a useful theoretical framework for addressing gender, climate change, and tourism. It acknowledges that multiple forms of inequality, such as gender, racism, class, and ability, overlap and compound each other, influencing how people perceive and respond to climate change and tourism[3]. This lens highlights how climate change and tourism disproportionately impact women, particularly Indigenous and Afro-descendant women, and emphasises the importance of incorporating women's perspectives and traditional knowledge into sustainable tourism practices. Intersectional ecofeminism goes beyond green sustainability to embrace regenerative and equitable methods that support and empower women and marginalised groups who care for heritage preservation.

The focus of traditional heritage tourism is to highlight the deeds of great men while overlooking the contributions of women, indigenous peoples, and the environment[4]. In intersectional ecofeminism, this view is deconstructed by including intangible

---

[3] Amorim-Maia, T.A. et al., Intersectional climate justice: A conceptual pathway for bridging adaptation planning, transformative action and social equity. Urban Climate. 41, 101053.

[4] Godovykh, M et al., Exploring the impacts of tourism on the wellbeing of Local communities. Sustainability. 17(13), 5849.

cultural heritage that emphasises traditions frequently preserved by women, including stories, foodways, and crafts. Ecofeminism promotes sustainability as a more inclusive, diverse, and authentic portrayal of the past, preventing culture from becoming fossilised through a tourist gaze.

Intersectional Ecofeminism and Entrepreneurship

Intersectional analysis examines how multiple forms of inequality intersect, such as gender and climate change, leading to distinct vulnerabilities and disparities in access to resources and opportunities. Ecofeminism promotes care ethics over consumption by presenting a 'care ethic' that contends that the environment and local communities are not merely resources but entities that must be protected. Mainstream tourism often views heritage sites as mere products for consumption. By advocating for slow tourism, ecofeminism emphasises the development of relationships between hosts and visitors rather than quick turnover and profitability. The sustainability of heritage is based on safeguarding heritage places from overtourism and physical damage by promoting a respectful rather than exploitative or extraction-based experience. Intersectional ecofeminism focuses on economic justice and empowerment by advocating for feminist alternative tourist economics (FATE), paying fair wages, and ensuring that tourism is led and controlled by women tourism entrepreneurs. Heritage is more sustainable when women benefit economically from heritage. They are more likely to safeguard the natural and cultural resources on which tourism depends, thereby sustaining the system in the long term.

The use of intersectional ecofeminism makes people aware that the interconnected oppressions (intersectionality) resulting from the exploitation of the environment are linked to women's oppression, economic struggles, and colonial legacies. It argues that sustainability measures should not only address environmental concerns (such as carbon footprints), but also focus on racial disparities, class and gender imbalances in accessibility, and the benefits of heritage. As a result, sustainability should avoid greenwashing by tackling systemic inequities and ensuring that communities in community-based tourism include minority and marginalised people. Intersectional ecofeminism advocates for the stewardship of Indigenous and local knowledge, with women as the genuine caretakers of local ecosystems and cultural traditions. Women play an important role in advancing indigenous knowledge and traditional environmental conservation practices of natural and cultural heritage sites. Therefore, to achieve higher success rates in environmental preservation, conservation initiatives should be community-led rather than imposed by outside patriarchal institutions.

Brush et al. (2006) state that the environment in which entrepreneurship occurs is linked to the recognition of opportunities. For instance, women entrepreneurs' ability to identify opportunities largely depends on how society defines their role. If society defines women's role in terms of family responsibilities, it means that society attaches less importance to their engaging in entrepreneurship. Women entrepreneurs in this kind of society may be constrained in their ability to recognize and fully exploit those opportunities in the marketplace. Men may gain an advantage in recognizing opportunities through their positions in society and work experience. Gender differences in entrepreneurship can be broadly categorised into education, experience, networks, access to capital, and culture (Henry et al., 2017). Stereotypes, labelling, societal norms, and organisational practices affect decision-making and work-life balance. Men are frequently given leadership roles with experience in specific industries, thereby influencing risk-taking and hiring practices. Cultural expectations regarding caregiving affect women's personal development, networking, and fundraising. Extensive networks in certain areas can lead to new opportunities, partnerships, and financing for men. Sometimes, women experience higher rejection rates for loan applications and are more likely to rely on personal resources or self-employment.

Various studies have reported that women tourism entrepreneurs lack business knowledge and skills (Panta & Thapa, 2018), have limited access to collateral and financial resources to start and grow their businesses (Moswete & Lacey, 2015; Ngoasong & Kimbu, 2019), and need collaborative networks (Adu-Ampong & Kimbu, 2019). Culture also shapes the social and structural impediments women face in tourism entrepreneurship. In some cultures, interactions between women entrepreneurs and male customers are scrutinised and viewed unfavourably by the community (Panta & Thapa, 2018). In countries where patriarchal culture prevails, such as Rwanda, India, Pakistan, and South Africa, empirical evidence suggests that female entrepreneurship is often discouraged or limited unless the entrepreneurial activities resemble those of domestic responsibilities (Kamberidou, 2020).

Women-focused entrepreneurship policies play a crucial role in empowering women, increasing the number of start-ups, and fostering the growth of businesses owned by women (Halabisky, 2018; Henry et al., 2017; Piacentini, 2013). Some examples of government interventions for women entrepreneurs include raising awareness of entrepreneurial opportunities, providing skills and information, facilitating access to capital and networks, and increasing the provision of affordable child and elderly care services (Halabisky, 2018; Henry et al., 2017; Piacentini, 2013). However, these policies and interventions are uncommon and are only available in a few countries. Henry et al. (2017) compared women's entrepreneurship policies across 13 countries and identified significant gaps between policies and actual practices, as well as between advanced Western economies and the rest of the world. Policy statements addressing women entrepreneurs often broadly state the importance of equal opportunities and lack clear targets, strong policy commitments, and consultation mechanisms (Piacentini, 2013). Furthermore, gender-focused entrepreneurship policies have tended to focus on individual challenges; few have addressed cultural and normative challenges and provided institutional interventions (Henry et al., 2017).

Experiences of Women Entrepreneurs in Tourism

Women entrepreneurs in the tourism industry often face challenges accessing the resources and inputs necessary for their businesses. This includes difficulties in obtaining funding, accessing technology and equipment, and securing reliable suppliers (Scheyvens et al., 2018). In the product development and marketing stages of the tourism value chain, women entrepreneurs face opportunities to differentiate their offerings and target niche markets. However, they also encounter barriers such as limited access to market information, skills gaps in marketing and branding, and gender biases in consumer preferences (Schneider & Singh, 2017). Distribution and sales channels present both opportunities and challenges for women entrepreneurs in the tourism industry. While online platforms and digital marketing offer new avenues for reaching customers, women face barriers such as limited access to technology, lack of infrastructure, and gender-based constraints on mobility (Kizito & Ito, 2019). In the service delivery stage, women entrepreneurs can differentiate themselves through quality service and personalized experiences. However, they face challenges in workforce management, training, and cultural norms that affect customer interactions (Mbaiwa & Stronza, 2018).

Strategies Employed by Women Entrepreneurs in Tourism for Sustainability

Diversification is a common strategy adopted by women entrepreneurs to sustain their businesses. By offering a range of products or services, women cater to diverse market segments, thereby mitigating the risks associated with seasonality and demand fluctuations (Mkono & Tribe, 2019). Collaboration and networking are crucial to the sustainability of women entrepreneurs in the tourism industry. By forming partnerships with other businesses, associations, and community organizations, women access resources, share knowledge, and create synergies that enhance their competitiveness (Hall & Jenkins, 2004). Innovation and adaptation are key strategies for women entrepreneurs to stay relevant in the dynamic tourism industry.

This may involve introducing new technologies, processes, or experiences that differentiate their offerings and meet evolving customer preferences (Hall & Williams, 2008). By actively participating in community development initiatives, supporting local suppliers, and promoting responsible tourism practices, women entrepreneurs enhance their reputation and contribute to the well-being of the destinations in which they operate (Dredge & Gyimóthy, 2015). Investing in education, training, and mentorship programs enables women to develop the skills, knowledge, and confidence necessary to succeed in a competitive business environment (Gretzel et al., 2019).

Systems and Initiatives Supporting Women in the Tourism Industry

Women-centric microfinance programs specifically tailored to women in the tourism industry provide access to capital for business start-ups, expansions, and operational needs. These programs often offer favourable terms and flexible repayment options to accommodate the needs of women entrepreneurs (Bhatt & Bhatt, 2019). Capacity-building and training workshops focus on equipping women entrepreneurs with the skills and knowledge needed to thrive in the tourism sector (Airey & Johnson, 1999). Mentorship and networking initiatives connect women entrepreneurs with experienced industry professionals who can offer guidance, support, and valuable business connections. These initiatives facilitate knowledge sharing, collaboration, and opportunities for professional growth (Araujo & Bramwell, 2019). Women-owned business certification programs provide recognition and visibility to women entrepreneurs in the tourism sector. Certification helps to build trust with customers, access procurement opportunities, and participate in supplier diversity initiatives (Pizam & Fleischer, 2002).

Environmental Sustainability

The environmental aspect of sustainability is a fundamental element in the broader discussion of sustainable development, underscoring the crucial need to maintain a harmonious balance between ecological preservation and development (Wanamaker, 2018; Mensah, 2019). Grounded in principles of preservation and equitable distribution across generations, it aims to safeguard natural ecosystems for the benefit of present and future generations. Key to this principle are the ideas of safeguarding biodiversity, promoting efficient resource utilisation, minimising waste, and mitigating the impacts of climate change, all of which intersect with societal and economic factors while maintaining a primary focus on ecological well-being (Goodland, 1995; Sutton, 2004; Little et al., 2016; Ekins, 2011; Giovannoni & Fabietti, 2013; Elkington, 1998). The underlying implication is that natural resources should be harvested only at a sustainable rate that allows for regeneration, and waste should be discharged at a rate that the environment can effectively absorb.

Organizations must prioritize the advancement of technology in a manner that enhances efficiency for sustainable progress, rather than focusing solely on increasing output (Oláh et al,.2020). The relentless pursuit of growth is placing immense pressure on the planet's resources, as technological innovation may not always align with the need for exponential expansion. Numerous studies have presented compelling evidence highlighting the escalating environmental impacts (Kirikkaleli & Adebayo, 2021; Amankwah-Amoah, 2020; Dube et al., 2024). This trend is especially noticeable in situations where conflicting social and economic interests overshadow ecological goals, potentially hampering endeavours to promote environmental sustainability (Mihalic, 2020). As a result, environmental justice movements highlight the unequal impacts of environmental damage on disadvantaged communities (McGregor et al., 2020). In Africa, researchers such as Happy (2023) support community-based conservation strategies that incorporate traditional ecological knowledge, emphasising the importance of comprehensive and culturally sensitive solutions. This approach promotes environmental sustainability by valuing and leveraging indigenous knowledge systems to maintain ecological balance.

The preservation and promotion of cultural and heritage resources are crucial to the well-being of communities. By empowering and encouraging communities to utilize their own strategies, they can better preserve their unique traditions (Happy, 2023). Therefore, it can be argued that valuing indigenous knowledge systems, which encompass cultural practices and behaviours towards the environment, can lead to greater sustainability for local communities. The link between environmental sustainability and cultural and heritage resources underscores the importance of ecological well-being in maintaining the integrity of these valuable assets (Lemy & Pramono, 2022).

Gendered Impacts of Climate Change

Women frequently bear the brunt of climate change impacts due to their social roles, obligations, and more limited access to resources. Climate change is one of the major challenges to sustainable development, especially in vulnerable regions of the Global South. The impacts of rising temperatures, extreme weather events, sea-level rise, and environmental degradation are inherently linked to problems such as food insecurity, water scarcity, biodiversity loss, and community displacement (IPCC, 2023). These environmental challenges threaten to undo development gains and deepen inequalities, with those 197ommercializ having the least resources to adapt. For example, erratic rainfall and prolonged droughts are driving declining crop yields, undermining local economies and threatening the livelihoods of subsistence farmers in sub-Saharan Africa (Sharma, Taheri, Chopra, and Parihar, 2025). However, with the right strategies and policies in place, tourism can also be a powerful tool for promoting sustainable development and combating climate change.

Initially, tourism was considered part of the broader sustainability discussion, but over the last two decades it has come into its own as a distinct sector. Earlier studies focused on sustainable development, but with time, researchers shifted their attention to sustainable tourism and its growth (Mtapuri et al., 2024). One of the key ways tourism contributes to sustainable development is by promoting eco-friendly practices and initiatives. This can include measures such as reducing energy consumption, promoting waste reduction and recycling, and supporting local conservation efforts (Oloso, 2025). By implementing these practices, tourism operators can minimize their environmental impact and help to preserve the natural resources that are essential for their industry (Scott, 2021). The growth in tourism poses new challenges for communities and destinations.

Heritage Tourism, Gender, and Climate Change

In South Africa, rural areas face multiple development challenges, including unsustainable use of natural resources, limited access to socio-economic and cultural services, water scarcity, low literacy and skills levels, migratory labour patterns, social decay, and missed economic opportunities (Phori, Hermann & Grobbelaar, 2024, p.555). Beyond simply protecting the environment, sustainable development necessitates an inclusive strategy that considers social justice and cultural integrity. Three interrelated components, gender equality, climate change, and cultural sustainability, are at the centre of this endeavour. Although they continue to be underrepresented in decision-making processes, women are frequently the group most impacted by environmental degradation, especially in marginalized and indigenous communities. At the same time, traditional lifestyles that contain centuries' worth of sustainable knowledge are also in danger due to climate change. Ignoring these processes may result in development initiatives that are too shortsighted, worsen inequality, and undermine cultural heritage.

Recognising that gender equality is both a goal and a catalyst for greater advancement is necessary to harness sustainable development through gender. Gender inequality must be addressed to achieve sustainable development, which is defined as providing current needs without endangering future generations (WCED, 1987). National and international development initiatives are slowed by gender inequality, which limits access to economic, healthcare, and educational opportunities, particularly for women and girls (Women, 2020). Gender inclusion, on the other hand, promotes creativity, raises living standards, and fortifies community resilience. In sectors such as agriculture, water management, and healthcare, which are essential to sustainable development, women and other 199ommercializ gender groups play crucial roles. Nonetheless, they are frequently underrepresented in leadership and policymaking positions (UNDP, 2020). More effective solutions to global issues like poverty and climate change are made possible by providing these groups with equitable access to resources, decision-making authority, and education. For example, research indicates that inclusive and community-centred strategies increase the likelihood of success for women-led climate projects.

The divergent cultural and commercial interests in cultural resources create tension in heritage tourism. Various approaches have been developed and implemented within the framework of sustainable cultural tourism policies to address the tension between cultural heritage and commercialization[5]. Museums, which function both as cultural institutions and as commercial businesses, increasingly consider themselves to be cultural enterprises. Many have replaced static, one-way presentations with dynamic interactions that shift the focus from the collection

---

[5] Sharma, GD, Taheri, B, Chopra, R, & Parihar, JS. Relationship between climate change and tourism: An integrative review'. 2025. The Service Industries Journal, vol. 45, no. 3-4, pp.426-453

to the visitor, creating a more lasting impact. Sustainable cultural tourism should focus on achieving a stable balance among the divergent goals, interests, and motivations of the various parties that constantly interact.

Optimization of Conservation and Preservation of Cultural Resources

Sustainable cultural tourism is culture-friendly because it guarantees the preservation and development of cultural resources, whether it concerns the original state of a monument, the conservation of a unique museum collection or the authentic character of an event. At the local, regional, and national levels, custodians of culture are placed in departments for monument preservation, in curatorial departments of museums, and in heritage conservation associations. For intangible culture, custodians can coincide with practitioners of traditions, rituals and customs who, as residents, are often members of a heritage community. Ideally, the quality of the experience and the memory value of the visit should be so high that the tourist becomes aware and convinced of the importance of cultural preservation. Sustainable cultural tourism also includes respect for the cultural identity, everyday life, and the living environment of the host community. That is why local residents should be involved in tourism development and benefit from it, whether through work and income or the shared use of tourism facilities.

Optimisation of Policy Support for the Sustainable Development of Cultural Tourism

The sustainable development of cultural tourism can be further stimulated through contributions from governments—specifically, policymakers. To optimise policy support, Southern Africa needs to move towards localised implementation, with tight enforcement of current regulations and community participation in cultural heritage tourism (UNWTO, 2025). The region needs to promote public-private partnerships by integrating economic incentives in cultural conservation. Investing in capacity building and the adoption of UNESCO-backed programmes for heritage asset protection will ensure that policies go beyond top-down directives to ensure local communities' voices are heard. Since current policies are often fragmented, they need to be better implemented and consistently enforced across the tourism value chain (DEAT, 2002). Dias et al. (2026) argue that

> some of the most common barriers to implementing sustainable tourism policies include low awareness and education about sustainable tourism, limited stakeholder involvement, and inadequate funding. In addition, sustainable tourism policies are often misunderstood or ignored by the main actors involved in tourism development, such as governments, businesses and local communities (p. 185).

Therefore, regional collaboration and investment in infrastructure and skills are required to sustain cultural heritage sites (Mollel, 2024). Instead of imposing sanctions, policies should provide financial incentives (grants, tax breaks for eco-certification), regulatory measures (stricter environmental standards), and capacity-building (training, technical assistance) to help tourism businesses adopt sustainable and ethical practices that reduce waste and support local livelihoods.

Conclusion

Southern Africa's sustainable heritage tourism is an important instrument for conservation and economic development, but it faces challenges in fair, local implementation. The link between ecological sustainability and cultural heritage highlights the importance of safeguarding these ecological resources for future generations. Tensions between cultural and commercial approaches reveal competing interests. Pragmatic solutions embedded in sustainable cultural tourism policies can harmonise preservation with economic viability. Cultural heritage sites are increasingly positioning themselves as cultural enterprises, balancing public value with commercial realities. The major challenge is to communicate effectively with residents about the benefits, infrastructure, and environmental degradation risks associated with inadequate tourism management. While cultural heritage can create jobs, reduce poverty, and preserve culture, its success requires active community involvement, infrastructure development, and a move away from top-down management. The success of heritage tourism lies in building, maintaining, and selling rural, distinct cultural experiences that go beyond high-profile places. To attract cultural tourists and diversify offerings, it is essential to craft strategies that amplify authentic cultural experiences, support community-led stewardship, and integrate inclusive governance. To maximise its potential, heritage tourism must be better integrated with other types, such as eco-tourism and nature-based tourism. These approaches can foster resilient, equitable, and enduring cultural tourism that respects people, place, and planet.

Chapter 10
The Governance of Heritage Conservation in Southern Africa

Preserving Southern Africa's natural heritage is crucial due to its rich biodiversity, diverse ecosystems, and cultural significance. The chapter presents diverse perspectives in the conservation debate, as well as anticipated future challenges and advancements. Recent years have seen a growing appreciation for the critical role that local communities play in biodiversity protection. Programs like community-based natural resource management are gaining popularity. These involve local communities in decision-making and management processes, giving them a stake in the health of their environment. Southern Africa's biodiversity protection faces various obstacles, including habitat loss, climate change, and poaching. The rise in the human population and agricultural expansion has put notable strain on natural environments. Urbanisation worsens these problems. This chapter discusses how tourism may simultaneously support and subvert power relations, particularly in the context of gender inequality. Tourism can promote gender equality by providing women with training, education, and employment opportunities. Women working in the tourism industry can gain capabilities that enable them to break gender stereotypes and transform their social roles.

Socio-ecological Systems and Heritage Tourism

Socio-ecological systems (SES) in the heritage sector are interconnected, complex, and adaptable systems in which humans (and their cultures, institutions, and knowledge systems) are closely linked to nature (Dondolo, 2005). Social ecology examines the relationships between individuals, groups, and their environments, with a focus on how cultural practices and legacies are interconnected with social structures and ecological contexts. In this perspective, legacy is viewed as a living, dynamic, and co-evolving phenomenon in which local communities and their surrounding ecosystems rely on and shape each other (Katapidi, 2026). For example, in Mavuradonga, Zimbabwe, community-led projects preserve cultural heritage while benefiting tourists, ensuring that locals have a stake in their own heritage. Community heritage management in Masvingo, Zimbabwe, notably around the Great Zimbabwe World Heritage Site, involves complex collaboration between local communities, government agencies, and international organisations to protect and enhance the site's cultural and historical importance. This involves integrating indigenous knowledge systems with modern conservation approaches to preserve and empower local communities, while promoting and strengthening community-led projects that foster sustainable tourism. Social ecology advocates for eco-friendly tourist practices that protect both the environment and cultural heritage. Eco-tourism programs in Zimbabwe include indigenous customs and ecological practices, thereby maintaining both the land and cultural identity. It emphasises the importance of evaluating tourism's social and environmental impacts. In Zimbabwe, discussion has arisen over how to manage tourist numbers at Victoria Falls to safeguard both the site and the local community's way of life.

Social ecology highlights the importance of balancing economic tourism development with the conservation of cultural and environmental values. The natural environment frequently shapes cultural practices, customs, and even religious beliefs, making the preservation of natural heritage essential to safeguarding culture. By preserving natural resources and ecosystems, we conserve the livelihoods, cultural contexts, and ecosystems that support cultural heritage. Some mountains, rivers, and forests, for example, are revered and used in customary ceremonies and rituals that are essential to the cultural identities of these groups. Both biodiversity preservation and the preservation of the customs and cultural practices closely associated with these settings depend on the conservation of these natural heritage sites (Hutton, 2005). In Southern Africa, the mandate to preserve and present the archaeological heritage is entrusted to national museums (Ndoro & Pwiti, 2001). Museums that are publicly funded or state-sponsored receive mandates from various national, provincial, and municipal governments. SAHRA (2021) reports that many museums are members of organisations such as the South African Museums Association (SAMA) and the International Council of Museums (ICOM) and function under the guidance of the International Centre for the Study of the Preservation and Restoration of Cultural Property (ICCROM). Southern African countries have World Heritage status, which is a designation higher than that of a National Monument. All the countries in southern Africa have ratified the 1972 World Heritage Convention.

Policy, Heritage Conservation and Governance

Conservation governance concerns decision-making processes, the distribution of authority, and accountability to safeguard natural resources. Effective frameworks integrate social and ecological processes, generally emphasising egalitarian, community-led, or co-managed systems, which, according to studies, produce better conservation and social outcomes than top-down approaches. Ndoro and Pwiti (2001) observe that "national legislation in southern Africa is similar in many ways in its objectives, definitions, forms of ownership, permitted or prohibited actions or practices, and sanctions. The focus is on protecting the structures and objects" (p.24).

Cultural heritage conservation is a way to harness cultural sustainability for sustainable development. This involves preserving cultural heritage sites, traditions, and practices for future generations. According to Mitchell (2018), cultural heritage conservation can contribute to the preservation of cultural heritage and community development. Conservation activities help to preserve Southern Africa's rich cultural and environmental legacy for future generations, encourage sustainable development, and enhance community well-being by protecting these regions[1]. Because natural and cultural assets are interdependent, this holistic approach to conservation emphasises the need for inclusive, cooperative measures that benefit both local populations and the environment.

Governments can facilitate livelihood diversification by implementing policies that support small businesses and sustainable practices. This could include training programs in hospitality, agriculture, or crafts, as well as financial support for local entrepreneurs. Countries like Namibia have successfully implemented such policies to enhance local engagement in

---

[1] Amorim-Maia, T.A. et al., Intersectional climate justice: A conceptual pathway for bridging adaptation planning, transformative action and social equity. Urban Climate. 41, 101053.

tourism. Natural heritage sites are essential to the cultural identities of many people in Southern Africa, serving as sacred sites for customary rites, ceremonies, and religious activities. The preservation of the customs and cultural practices associated with these ecosystems depends on maintaining these locations (Kolawole, 2013). Building local capacity is essential for ensuring communities can engage effectively in tourism and diversify their livelihoods (Sethaba & Scholes, 2021). Training programs in management, marketing, and customer service empower locals to compete in the tourism market. For example, community workshops in rural villages in Namibia have improved local skills and enhanced tourism offerings.

To ensure that future generations can enjoy and profit from heritage sites, they must be conserved. Conserving Southern Africa's natural heritage requires an inclusive, cooperative strategy that recognises the interconnection between cultural and natural heritage. Safeguarding the area's natural and cultural assets requires collaboration between local authorities, communities, and conservation groups. In addition to supporting sustainable development and the welfare of communities for future generations, collaborative strategies may help to preserve Southern Africa's distinctive cultural and environmental heritage. (Olarewaju, 2023). Encouraging collaboration between local stakeholders, the government, and the private sector can also create a more resilient tourism ecosystem. Partnerships can lead to innovative solutions to the challenges faced by both tourism and local communities. In Zimbabwe, collaborations between tour operators and local communities have created opportunities for Mavuradona Wilderness and Gairezi Eco-Tourism to lead tourism ventures. Through the Zimbabwe Sun

Hotels, a high-end tourism initiative was developed in the 1990s. The initiative involved establishing high-cost, low-volume game lodges on communal lands, primarily adjacent to National parks in the Zambezi valley and the southeast Lowveld.

Preserving natural heritage also yields economic benefits, including job creation, tourism, and sustainable development. Diamonds are Botswana's second-largest source of foreign exchange, contributing significantly to the economy (van Staden, 2023). Foreign exchange is also generated through crafts, souvenirs and the marketplace. Conservation usually generates direct and indirect employment. Direct employment includes tour guides, conservation scientists, and park rangers. Indirect employment is generated by hotels, transportation and souvenir sales.

Sectors such as agriculture are more vulnerable to climate change, have lower yields, and incur higher production costs. According to Turpie et al. (2008), the short-term financial benefits of using natural resources are significantly outweighed by the long-term economic losses resulting from ecosystem degradation. This illustrates the financial risks associated with inadequate conservation efforts. Environmental harm can also deter investment and raise government expenditures for infrastructure repair and disaster response. Water shortages, coastal erosion, and deforestation harm infrastructure, increase repair costs, and negatively impact livelihoods. For instance, flooding and costly infrastructure damage have occurred in some areas of South Africa because of urban growth that disregarded natural heritage (DEA, 2016). Conservation is an essential aspect of economic approaches because it preserves resources that future generations will rely on, thereby guaranteeing long-term economic stability.

Human-wildlife conflicts (HWCs) occur when humans and wildlife interact in ways that result in negative impacts on both humans and wildlife. These conflicts can arise from various factors such as habitat encroachment, where human activities such as deforestation, urbanisation, and agriculture, encroach on wildlife habitats (Konig, 2020). Humans and wildlife may also compete for resources such as water or food. Wildlife escapes from parks, damaging crops and leading to economic losses for farmers. Conflict can lead to physical harm or even death for both humans and wildlife (Murombedzi, 20 I 0). Protecting the natural heritage of Southern Africa is essential to maintaining ecological balance, biodiversity, and sustainable development.

Diversifying the types of tourism offered can stabilize the earnings of tourism providers. Promoting niche markets such as adventure, cultural, or culinary tourism can attract a broader range of demographics and visitors more evenly throughout the year. For instance, in Botswana, the Kalahari and Okavango Delta offer a unique landscape and wildlife experience that attracts visitors year-round, supporting local economies. The area includes diverse ecosystems, including coastal regions, marshes, and savannas, which provide habitats for rare plants and animals. Conservation initiatives support local communities that rely on natural resources, promote ecotourism, and help save endangered species. The cultural significance, economic benefits, and biodiversity conservation of Southern Africa thus depend on the preservation of its natural heritage. In addition to providing jobs for local populations, the wildlife tourist sector contributes significantly to local economies and conservation initiatives (Brockington, 2002).

As indigenous populations frequently attach spiritual and cultural significance to natural heritage sites, conservation efforts are crucial for sustaining their customs and lifestyles. Involving local communities in decision-making processes ensures that tourism development aligns with their needs and aspirations. This can foster ownership and pride in local culture and heritage, leading to a more sustainable tourism model. In Namibia, community-led eco-tourism initiatives have empowered local communities, enabling them to control their own tourism narrative. However, when local communities have been excluded from conservation efforts, conflicts have arisen. In South Africa, some conservation programs have forced indigenous populations to relocate or limited their access to traditional land-use rights. Due to its historical significance, the Mapungubwe Cultural Landscape has been protected and is designated as a World Heritage Site, showcasing the rich heritage of the former Kingdom of Mapungubwe. However, residents have not been included in decision-making processes, and mining operations in the region have sparked worries about environmental damage (Sebelebele, 2025).

In cases where a fortress conservation' strategy has been used and human populations are not permitted to live with the conservation area, Indigenous populations have been uprooted and relocated, destroying their historical and cultural connections to the land and depriving them of access to their natural resources. Community-led conservation efforts, on the other hand, have demonstrated potential to advance both community development and conservation in tandem. Both economic benefits and conservation have been achieved through community-based tourism initiatives where local groups oversee and benefit from tourism. Local residents are increasingly involved in employment and conservation activities in parks, with outreach programs sensitizing communities towards environmental protection and teaching them skills related to tourism (Khumalo, 2015; Nyawo and Mubangizi, 20I5). For widespread benefits to communities that catalyse inclusive, sustainable development, such initiatives must be scaled and supported with stronger institutional involvement (ICOMOS, 1999).

The example of Mtubatuba illustrates the potential and limitations of tourism for livelihood diversification. For local communities like Mtubatuba to benefit meaningfully from proximity to top tourist destinations, strategic planning is needed to incorporate informal traders into broader tourism value chains, improve infrastructure, and enhance community participation in tourism planning and conservation. Without these, the tourist economy may still exclude the very communities that reside around and serve it. In Eshowe, which is also rich in cultural heritage and rural landscapes, community-led initiatives— particularly those led by women—have resulted in new models of livelihood diversification. Local residents run small entrepreneurial ventures that could be enhanced by tourism (Linda, 2023). Women's self-help groups in Eshowe produce traditional clothing, grow gardens, and engage in other forms of home-based entrepreneurship. These activities are supported by group savings models. These activities have the potential to add value to tourism craft outlets, local tourism, and cultural events. Despite these initiatives, Eshowe is constrained in fully utilising tourism as a diversification strategy for livelihoods by structural factors, including limited market access, inadequate investment in rural infrastructure, and insufficient support from the local government. Rural places need to be valued as active agents of development, with their own configurations of sustainability and resilience, not as passive objects of aid, but as.

The community of Inanda, near Durban, provides insight into an environmental perspective on the tourism-livelihood interface. The local population has traditionally derived subsistence and income from forest products, including timber, medicinal plants, and bush foods. Contemporary tourism initiatives (introduced by the Wildlands Conservation Trust), such as eco-tourism and seed-harvesting activities, create additional income opportunities (Wale, Nkoana, & Mkuna, 2022). However, as Inanda's natural resource-based economy is sensitive to climate change, it faces increasing threats. Variable rainfall and changing temperatures have begun to affect forest product supplies, forcing local residents to seek new sources of income through home gardening, off-farm work, and microenterprises. While there are untapped tourism opportunities, the available financial resources, infrastructure, and institutions do not provide adequate support (ICOMOS, 1999).

The case of Inanda emphasises the need for integrated mechanisms that promote resilience to climate change, combined with economic diversification and effective environmental management, to overcome the limitations of ecologically sensitive sites. Without such integration, tourism may not be economically feasible. Comparing the examples of Mtubatuba, Eshowe and Inanda highlights both broader challenges and context-specific vulnerabilities. In Mtubatuba and Inanda, the informal economy serves as a livelihood diversification strategy. Eshowe demonstrates how neighbourhood agency, particularly by women, can propel pioneering and collective livelihood projects that could be expanded through targeted tourism development. Inanda illustrates how climate change directly affects livelihoods based on forest products and, consequently, the tourism value of forestland. This underscores the need to integrate climate adaptation into tourism planning. All three communities lack adequate support from their local governments as well as robust tourism or economic development policies that reflect local perspectives and capacities. Co-management strategies that engage residents in decision-making processes can enable the addressing of historical injustices and the adoption of more equitable conservation practices (Duval, 2011; 2012).

While this can yield positive effects, such as generating revenue for conservation and creating job opportunities, it also introduces significant contradictions and challenges. In Ukhahlamba, a South African region renowned for its dramatic landscape and rich history, local communities have developed tourism as a means to diversify their incomes and drive the area's economic development. The natural beauty, rich culture, and diverse ecosystems of the area attract tourists from all over the world. Tourist activities include community-led excursions and local arts and crafts markets. These have enabled resident who traditionally relied on agricultural activities to diversify their income streams through activities such as selling handcrafted products or offering accommodation (Sibanda, 2021). One of the greatest challenges in natural heritage conservation in Southern Africa lies in the commercialisation of protected areas, where the natural environment is increasingly treated as a commodity. Tourism enterprises such as luxury lodges, trophy hunting, and mass tourism may prioritise profit over genuine ecological preservation. While such ventures are often justified as a means of generating income for conservation and local development, the reality is more complex.

In South Africa, a clear example of this challenge is the management of the Kruger National Park, one of Africa's most iconic conservation areas. Portions of the park are leased to private operators who provide high-end safari experiences for affluent tourists. This model of public-private partnership has generated significant revenue, which is reinvested in park maintenance, anti-poaching initiatives, and employment opportunities for surrounding communities (Hutton & Adams, 2005). However, this relationship also presents challenges. One of the primary concerns is that tourism benefits are not evenly distributed. Tourism revenues tend to be concentrated in the hands of a few firms. For example, while some smaller enterprises will successfully operate guest lodges, others will be forced out of business by competition with large companies that dominate the market (Moyo, 2022). Tourism can increase tensions it generates. In addition, the impacts of external factors, such as climate change and global pandemics, may hinder tourist flow and, subsequently, affect livelihoods. The global COVID-19 pandemic significantly hindered mobility, leading to the shutdown of various tourism enterprises in Ukhahlamba and negatively impacting residents who relied on this sector for their livelihoods (Ndlovu, 2023). This highlights the importance of communities adopting integrated approaches to livelihood diversification rather than relying solely on tourism.

Tourism that features cultural exchange, enabling local residents to showcase their traditions and heritage and generating income. The commercialisation of natural resources such as indigenous plants (e.g., rooibos, marula, and devil's claw) for global markets encourages sustainable harvesting and land stewardship. When local communities are involved in and benefit financially from these practices, conservation becomes integrated into their livelihoods, thereby reducing their reliance on destructive activities such as poaching or deforestation (Wynberg et al., 2009). However, commercialization must be approached cautiously to avoid overexploitation. Without proper regulation and benefit-sharing mechanisms, commercial activities can harm ecosystems and marginalise local people. Therefore, conservation-based commercial models must emphasise sustainability, community participation, and fair economic returns.

Women, Access Rights, and Equity in Tourism Access

Power, gender equality, and tourism exist in complex, multifaceted relationships. Women can be empowered or disempowered by tourism, depending on the situation and travel method (Scheyvens, 2000). In economic terms, women can benefit from tourism through employment within the industry or by starting their own enterprises (Kinnaird & Hall, 1994). Women have established tourism-related enterprises, such as crafting and selling goods, thereby enhancing their economic independence (Manyara & Jones, 2007). However, gender equality can be greatly improved through tourism policy and planning. In the tourism sector, for instance, policies encouraging women to assume leadership roles and engage in entrepreneurship can empower them and ensure an equitable sharing of benefits (UNWTO, 2019).

Women may find employment across a range of industries in the tourism sector, such as hospitality, transportation, and crafts (Mbaiwa, 2005). Women may also establish their own enterprises in industries such as tour guiding, accommodation, and souvenir-making (Kinnaird & Hall, 1994). Women-owned enterprises or women-only tours are among the tourism activities done by women that can enhance women's leadership and empowerment (WTO, 2019). Women can improve their employability and career prospects by learning new languages through their involvement in tourism (Cukier & Orris, 2017). Tourism may also create new leadership opportunities for women (Gaenther, 2015). It can empower women to control their own lives and livelihoods (Mbaiwa, 2005). Through tourism, women can network with other women, building relationships that can contribute to their professional and personal growth (Sinclair, 1997). Women can also contribute to the growth of their communities through community-based tourism activity enabled through tourism (Manyana & Jones, 2007). Additionally, tourism can offer women an opportunity to preserve and promote their cultural heritage, affirming their sense of identity and belonging (Rogerson, 2006).

Women's professional and personal development is enhanced by the additional skills and knowledge offered by tourism (Apostolopoulos et al., 2001). Additionally, women can be employed in various tourism industries, including restaurants, hotels, and tour operators (Kinnaird & Hall, 1994). Women can establish their own tourism-related enterprises, including tour guiding, homestays, and handicrafts production (Manyara & Jones, 2007). Women can achieve economic independence by earning income from tourism (Scheyvens, 2000). Additionally, beyond revenue generation, the production of handicrafts by women for tourists has promoted cultural preservation (Ehlers & Main, 1998). Women's empowerment and local development have been boosted through tourism projects initiated by women (UNWTO, 2019). Women may engage with stakeholders and other women through tourism.

Despite the potential benefits the tourism industry can offer women, the industry remains embedded in a larger system that tends to normalise gender hierarchies. Even when efforts to empower women through tourism are made, the empowerment may yield superficial or temporary outcomes, as it is often supported by the general public due to the persistent economic inequalities inherent in the tourism economy. A transition from patriarchal gender roles towards more empowering roles for women is thus usually constrained by the broader economic structure.

Due to regional cultural and social constructs, tourism has different effects on gender equality in different places[2]. For instance, in some nations, tourism has helped challenge gender stereotypes by enabling women to gain respect and prominence

---

[2] Thomas, A. The Role of Women's Entrepreneurship in Achieving Sustainable Development Goals (SDGs): A Comprehensive Review. 2024. Journal of Biotechnology & Bioinformatics Research 6(2):1–11. DOI:10.47363/JBBR/2024(6)174

in roles traditionally occupied by men. In other instances, the commercialisation of women as caregivers, caretakers, or sex objects may serve to further perpetuate gendered stereotypes. In sex tourism, when women's bodies are commodified and sold, and they are portrayed as passive and submissive, an oppressive power relationship may be aggravated (Goss, 1993). Such tourism activities may exploit women and deepen gender inequality. On the other hand, tourism has created opportunities for feminist activism and women's rights advocacy in some regions. Women have used women-owned community-based tourism to reclaim space and power in society (Binns, 2002). Tourism targeting women tourists represents a move towards more diversified tourism strategies that specifically address the interests and needs of women. Feminist tourism can also be a way through which women resist patriarchal domination of their leisure and preferences. Tourism can thus serve as a tool of empowerment in some instances, mediating the traditional power structures that exclude women[3]. However, these tend to be localised and exceptional cases.

The tourism industry is a global economic force that fuels the growth of many economies, particularly in the Global South. The tourism industry may also replicate the power dynamics of the past in countries that were previously colonised, where tourists from developed countries, primarily the Global North, exert influence over host communities in the Global South (Sharp, 2009). For instance, tourists may prefer certifications or coopera-

---

[3] Thomas, A. The Role of Women's Entrepreneurship in Achieving Sustainable Development Goals (SDGs): A Comprehensive Review. 2024. Journal of Biotechnology & Bioinformatics Research 6(2):1–11. DOI:10.47363/JBBR/2024(6)174

tives that prioritise fair wages, labour rights, and community benefits. Furthermore, this power dynamic not only shapes the social and economic conditions of the destination but also influences how gender roles are perceived and enacted. Women, particularly those from postcolonial contexts, become vulnerable to wider commodification within the tourism economy, which reinscribes passive stereotypes and reinforces traditional gender roles by positioning women as the object of the gaze, to be watched, admired, or consumed (Mowforth & Munt, 2016).

The industry also accentuates prevailing gender divisions and imbalances. Sex tourism exploits and objectifies women, perpetuating gender imbalances and inequality (Enloe, 1989). Another issue is violence related to tourism, such as harassment and assault, which frequently targets women and promotes gender discrimination (Sinclair, 1997). Thus, tourism may either reinforce or challenge gender inequality. When tourism perpetuates traditional gender roles and commodifies women, it reinforces gender inequality. Tourism also has the potential to challenge patriarchal norms and create opportunities for women to become economically and socially empowered. Ultimately, the relationship between gender equality, power, and tourism is complex, influenced by both local and international forces. This requires changing tourism's policies and practices to ensure equality and empower marginalised voices.

The Complex Relationship Between Tourism, Health and Well-Being

Tourism has been touted as a powerful driver of economic development, cultural exchange, and personal enrichment. This is becoming increasingly evident in light of environmental degradation, social disruption, and public health crises. There is thus a complex interplay between tourism, health, and well-being. Tourism may offer opportunities for social interaction and physical activity, which can enhance tourists' well-being. Outdoor tourism encourages physical activity, enhancing cardiovascular health and general fitness, according to a study by Lee and Scott (2016). The capacity of tourism to enhance mental health and reduce stress levels is among its most notable benefits. According to Smith (2017), travel can enhance mood and life satisfaction while lowering cortisol levels, the body's main stress hormone. Exposure to new and exciting surroundings can lower stress and anxiety while enhancing mood and cognitive abilities (Maller et al., 2008). Nature-based tourism has been connected to a lower incidence of depression and improved emotional well-being. Furthermore, tourism fosters community involvement and social ties, both of which are crucial for maintaining mental and emotional well-being. Social bonds and a sense of belonging are crucial components of mental health (Hawkins & Mowatt, 2019). For host communities, tourism may boost local economies by strengthening infrastructure and generating jobs, while also indirectly enhancing social services and health for locals.

While tourism benefits the economy, it can negatively impact the health and well-being of local populations in various ways. One of the most pressing issues is environmental degradation.

Tourism may pollute the air, water, and soil, thereby impacting public health. Overcrowding is a common issue in popular tourist destinations, straining local infrastructure and leading to the exploitation of natural resources. Additionally, improper waste management in many tourism areas contaminates local water bodies with litter, sewage, and other pollutants, posing significant health risks through the spread of waterborne illnesses and other diseases. Increased traffic congestion and transporttation emissions contribute to higher air pollution levels, which, in turn, increase respiratory problems and long-term health disorders among people (Gossling, 2002).

The tourism sector may employ local residents in exploitative working circumstances, particularly in developing countries where labour laws are weak or poorly implemented. Tourism jobs may involve long working hours, low income, seasonal or unstable employment, and exposure to risks such as extreme weather, unsafe equipment, or uncomfortable encounters with visitors. These working conditions not only harm workers' physical health but also cause mental exhaustion, anxiety, and burnout (Baum, 2015). Local residents may feel compelled to accept unfair working conditions if there are inadequate alternative employment opportunities. Furthermore, the psychological stress caused by tourism among residents is a growing concern. Rapid tourism development can lead to gentrification, pushing up housing prices and the cost of living, making it difficult for locals to afford to stay in their own neighbourhoods. The influx of tourists may also disrupt daily life, erode cultural traditions, and create a sense of alienation among long-time residents. Limited access to public services, as resources are diverted to cater to tourists, can further compound feelings of exclusion and diminished well-being (Kim, Uysal, & Sirgy, 2013).

The spread of infectious illnesses is one of the most obvious and direct tensions between tourism and health. The cross-border movement of travellers facilitates the spread of communicable diseases. The COVID-19 pandemic demonstrated how rapidly a virus can spread globally through international travel (Godovykh, 2022). According to Godovykh, popular tourist locations, including Italy, Spain, and the US, experienced a spike in cases in the early stages of the epidemic that was mostly ascribed to foreign visitors. Tourism has also contributed to the spread of illnesses like dengue fever in Southeast Asia and the Zika virus in South America (Faria, 2016). The spread of illness at tourist destinations may strain medical services that are ill-equipped to handle the demands of both visitors and residents simultaneously. As a result, during periods of high tourism, residents may have to wait longer and receive lower-quality care, which contributes to their discontent with tourism (Smith, 2017). The effects of tourism go beyond the obvious problems with access to healthcare. Additionally, the burden on local health services might worsen the situation for groups disproportionately affected by the strain tourism places on these services (Marmion, 2020). Strategic planning is needed so that health services have adequate capacity during peak tourist seasons.

Tourism Planning and Development

The tourism planning approach aims to balance socio-economic benefits to society, prioritising environmental protection, culture, and sustainable tourism planning to connect the triple bottom line by minimising negative impacts and maximising positive effects across these three dimensions. Finding the balance between them ensures the long-term sustainability of the tourism business. Another factor is the social values that influence environmental conservation and the prioritisation of other needs for sustainable development, which can be shaped by the government and planners (Padin, 2012). Tourism expansion has been a significant factor in both social and economic growth, mostly in developing countries. The COVID-19 pandemic highlighted the susceptibility of both visitors and host communities, as human movement facilitated the rapid global spread of the virus (Gossling, Scott, & Hall, 2020). The COVID-19 pandemic has driven widespread interest among policy-makers and academics to explore strategies to sustain the tourism industry (Xiong & Tang, 2023).

Higher volumes of waste and resource depletion in tourism hotspots may harm ecosystems crucial to human well-being (UNEP, 2019). Sustainable tourism offers a viable solution by promoting responsible travel practices that prioritise environmental preservation, community well-being, and cultural integrity[4]. Strategies such as controlling tourist numbers, increasing off-season travel, and supporting local health infrastructure can help balance visitor and resident needs while ensuring long-term benefits (UNWTO, 2020). Thus, while tourism can enhance cultural understanding and economic

---

[4] Berdej, S., D. Armitage & A. Charles. Governance and Community Conservation. 2015. Community Conservation Research Network. Halifax, Nova Scotia. Available online at: www.communityconservation.net/resources/governance.

vitality, it can also undermine public health, environmental sustainability, and the mental and social well-being of individuals and communities. To address these challenges, tourism must be developed and managed with a focus on sustainability, community engagement, and integrated health planning. Policymakers and stakeholders must work collaboratively to ensure that tourism supports, rather than undermines, the long-term health and well-being of all those involved.

Harnessing Social Justice, Gender, and Sustainable Development

Beyond simply protecting the environment, sustainable development requires strategies that consider social justice and cultural integrity. Women and gender-diverse people often face disproportionate impacts (care burdens, wage gaps, limited access to land/credit) and are underrepresented in decision-making about climate policy. While women continue to be underrepresented in decision-making processes, they are frequently those most impacted by environmental degradation, especially in marginalised and indigenous communities. Better outcomes can be achieved when women lead adaptation programs. For example, research indicates that inclusive and community-centred strategies increase the likelihood of success for women-led climate projects. At the same time, traditional lifestyles that have accumulated centuries' worth of sustainable knowledge are also in danger due to climate change. Development initiatives that ignore these realities may exacerbate inequality and undermine cultural heritage. Recognising that gender equality is both a goal and a catalyst for greater advancement is necessary to harness sustainable development (Carranza et al., 2018). More effective solutions to global issues, such as poverty and climate change, are made possible by providing these groups with equitable access to resources, decision-making authority, and education. However, in the long term, equitable outcomes should be ensured when gender perspectives are integrated into development policies.

Natural resource management is typically more transparent and sustainable when women are involved in environmental governance and conservation (World Bank, 2012). In the same vein, removing gender-based obstacles to social services, infrastructure, and clean energy improves the standard of living for entire communities. Ultimately, inclusive frameworks that enable all genders to fully and fairly participate in shaping the future are essential for sustainable development (UN, 2015). To achieve gender equality in sustainable development, it is also necessary to question deeply ingrained institutional and cultural practices that perpetuate inequality. To ensure equal rights to inheritance, land, and property, as well as to stop discrimination and violence against women, legal frameworks and policy tools must be reinforced. For example, according to the World Bank (2023), women are granted equal rights to property and assets in only 40% of nations worldwide. Women are more likely to invest in community well-being and environmental conservation when they have stable land ownership and financial independence, leading to more durable development outcomes.

Moreover, avoiding one-size-fits-all solutions and ensuring that the requirements of every group are met are two benefits of creating development initiatives using participatory approaches that accommodate a variety of gender perspectives. To further close the representation gap in policymaking areas, funding for gender-sensitive education and leadership development is essential. Initiatives to build capacity must be implemented to enable women and marginalised genders to take the lead in fields such as technology innovation, governance, and climate science. According to UNDP (2022), countries with greater representation of women in political engagement tend to implement more comprehensive social welfare and environmental policies. Therefore, enhancing the visibility and voice of women in leadership roles improves the usefulness and responsiveness of development programs. Normalising gender-diverse leadership encourages future generations to take up political and environmental causes while also challenging traditional gender norms. As a result, investing in gender equity is not only morally necessary but also crucial to creating equitable and sustainable societies.

Furthermore, women business owners tend to reinvest a larger percentage of their profits back into their communities and families than those owned by men and thus have a greater social impact (Thomas, 2024). Women are often at the forefront of managing water, food, and energy resources, particularly in rural areas, but their voices are frequently excluded from environmental decision-making. Incorporating gender perspectives into environmental policies improves environmental outcomes. In Nepal, for example, community forest groups that include women have been shown to manage forests more sustainably, and women's participation in climate adaptation projects has led to more resilient, sustainable solutions in climate-vulnerable areas (Thomas, 2025). One powerful instrument for bringing about social and personal transformation is education. Women with higher levels of education typically break the cycle of poverty by investing more in their children's education and having smaller, healthier families[5]. Women who have leadership positions in business, politics, or grassroots movements also frequently support laws that advance inclusive growth, social welfare, and environmental conservation.

Climate change is one of the major challenges to sustainable development, especially in vulnerable regions of the Global South. The impacts of rising temperatures, extreme weather events, sea-level rise, and environmental degradation are closely linked to issues such as food insecurity, water scarcity, biodiversity loss, and community displacement (IPCC, 2023). These environmental challenges threaten to undo development gains and deepen inequalities, with those marginalised having the least resources to adapt. For example, erratic rainfall and prolonged droughts are driving declining crop yields, undermining local economies and threatening the livelihoods of subsistence farmers in sub-Saharan Africa (DP, 2021). However, with the right strategies and policies in place, tourism can also be a powerful tool for promoting sustainable development and combating climate change.

One of the keyways tourisms can contribute to sustainable development is by promoting eco-friendly practices and initiatives. This can include measures such as reducing energy consumption, promoting waste reduction and recycling and

---

[5] Carranza, E., Dhakal, C., & Love, I. Female entrepreneurs: How and why are they different? 2018. World Bank, Washington, DC. License: Creative Commons Attribution CC BY 3.0 IGO

supporting local conservation efforts. By implementing these practices, tourism operators can minimise their environmental impact and help preserve the natural resources essential to their industry (Scott, 2021). Responsible travel practices can include encouraging tourists to minimise their carbon footprint by choosing eco-friendly transportation options, supporting local businesses and communities and respecting the cultural and natural heritage of the destinations they visit. Jong et al. (2022) argue that promoting responsible travel can help ensure that the benefits of tourism are shared equitably and sustainably.

In addition to promoting eco-friendly practices and responsible travel, tourism can also play a crucial role in raising awareness about climate change and promoting sustainable development more broadly (ICOMOS, 1999). By showcasing the impacts of climate change on popular tourist destinations, tourism operators can help educate tourists about the importance of taking action to combat it. This can include promoting sustainable tourism practices, supporting local conservation efforts, and advocating for policies that protect the environment and promote sustainability. Tourism thus has the potential to be a powerful force for promoting sustainable development and combating climate change (Jong et al., 2022).

Co-management, Sustainability, Funding, and Resource Allocation

Ndoro and Pwiti (2001) observe that "in all southern African countries except South Africa, the government or the state agency owns designated ancient and national monuments. In South Africa, national monuments can be owned by individuals or institutions. Thus, the legislation gives guidelines on how to look after nationally valued property" (p. 24). Co-management is the process by which two or more social actors agree to a fair division of management duties, rights, and responsibilities for a particular territory, area, or collection of natural resources (Borrini-Feyerabend et al., 2007). Co-management refers to the preservation, setting clear goals, and establishing policies and accountability to align conservation with education, tourism, and local development (e.g., a site that hosts school programs, interpretive trails, and research partnerships). Improving decision-making should be done in line with data, permits, and existing governance structures (Ballet et al., 2009). It emphasises the importance of maintaining cultural diversity, traditional knowledge systems, languages, and collective memory as essential to societal well-being and resilience. For culture to be sustainable, it supports communities' ability to retain their distinctiveness and cohesion in the face of globalisation, modernisation, and social change. It fosters a sense of belonging, continuity, and purpose, which are crucial for holistic human development (ICOMOS, 1999). Co-management between managers and local communities and/or Indigenous groups should be strengthened to enhance local livelihoods, improve legitimacy, and improve compliance.

Co-management aligns conservation with local livelihoods, enhances legitimacy, and improves compliance[6]. Moreover, it acknowledges that culture is dynamic, encouraging the trans-

---

[6] Berdej, S., D. Armitage & A. Charles. Governance and Community Conservation. 2015. Community Conservation Research Network. Halifax, Nova Scotia. Available online at: www.communityconservation.net/resources/governance.

mission and adaptation of traditions that remain relevant to current and future generations. Promoting cultural sustainability involves inclusive education, supportive policy frameworks, community engagement, and institutional protection of heritage and creative expressions. Developing diverse and reliable financial streams can help in covering conservation, interpretation, and community benefits[7]. The integration of ecological restoration with heritage interpretation can help maintain both biodiversity and cultural narratives. Prioritise high-impact initiatives to stabilise an unstable wall over cosmetic improvements. Equitable budgets for both preservation and inclusive visitor education should balance conservation, access, and education[8]. For example, the town can develop guided tours of its cultural heritage sites, featuring traditional music and dance performances and handicraft demonstrations.

Infrastructure Development, Education and Training and Site Integrity

Community-based cultural initiatives are another way to harness cultural sustainability for sustainable development[9]. This involves empowering local communities to take ownership of

---

[7] SAHRA. The Management and Conservation of Heritage Objects housed in State Departments or supported bodies. 2021. Available online from: https://www.theheritageportal.co.za/article/ manage m ent-and-conservation-heritage-objects-housed-state-departments-or-supported-bodies. Accessed on 23/02/2026.

[8] Ballet, J., Kouamékan J., Koffi, M., and Komena, K.B. Co-management of natural resources in developing Countries: the importance of Context. 2009. Économie Internationale 120 (2009), p. 53-76.

[9] Tsintskiladze, M. Role of Community Empowerment in the sustainable cultural heritage Management: A review. 2024. Proceedings of the International Conference on Business, Management and Economics. 1 (1), 22-31.

their cultural heritage and develop initiatives that promote cultural preservation and exchange. Cultural education and training are a way to harness cultural sustainability for sustainable development. This involves providing education and training programs that promote cultural awareness and preservation. The use of cultural festivals and events is another way to harness cultural sustainability for sustainable development. This involves promoting environmentally friendly, socially responsible cultural festivals and events. According to Quinn (2017), sustainable cultural festivals and events can contribute to local economic development and community engagement.

Conclusion

Culture and heritage conservation can contribute to the preservation of cultural heritage and community development. The road forward calls for a comprehensive approach that considers the diverse character of conservation and encourages collaboration among local communities, governments, and international organizations. The relationship between tourism and livelihood diversification is multifaceted and fraught with challenges. While tourism can provide significant economic opportunities, it can also create dependence, environmental degradation, and social inequality. By promoting responsible practices, enhancing local capacity, and encouraging collaboration, communities can harness the benefits of tourism while diversifying their livelihoods. Ultimately, sustainable tourism development requires concerted effort from all stakeholders to ensure benefits are shared equitably, thereby fostering resilience and long-term economic stability. By addressing these challenges, Southern Africa can work toward a future in which its natural heritage is protected while meeting the needs of its people.

References

Abrahams, E., & Tichaawa, T. M. (2025). Telling our story, holding our ground: Heritage interpretation as a tool for resilience and inclusive tourism in a South African National Park. *Geojournal of Tourism and Geosites, 62*(4), 2478–2485.

Abrahams, E., & Tichaawa, T.M. (2025). Telling our story, holding our ground: Heritage interpretation as a tool for resilience and inclusive tourism in a South African National Park. Geojournal of Tourism and Geosites, 62(4), 2478–2485. https://doi.org/10.30892/gtg.62442-1608

Adams, J. M. (2018). The value of wellness. *Public Health Reports, 133*(2), 127–129.

Adler, D. M., Finkelstein, C., & Huang, H.P. (2003). Preferences and rational choice: New perspectives and legal implications: Introduction, *151 U. PA. L. REV. 707*. https://scholar.law.colorado.edu/articles/526.

Ainsworth, S. H. (Ed.) (2020). *Rational choice theory in political decision making*. Oxford Research Encyclopedia of Politics. Oxford University Press.

Amarilla B., & Conti A. (2012). *Built heritage and sustainable tourism: Conceptual, economic and social variables.* In C. Ghenai (Ed.), *Sustainable development. Policy and urban development: Tourism, life science, management and environment* (pp. 147–174). Intech.

Anderson, B. (1983). Imagined Communities: Reflections on the Origin and Spread of Nationalism. London: Verso.

Anderson, B. (1983). Imagined communities: Reflections on the origin and spread of nationalism. Verso.

Anderson, P. (1976). *Considerations on western Marxism.* New Left Books.

Apostolopoulos, Y., Sonmez, S., & Timothy, D. J. (2001). *Women in tourism: Challenges and opportunities.* Routledge.

April 2012Journal of Brand Management 19(6):484-499. DOI:10.1057/bm.2011.51

Arrow, K. J. (1951). *Social choice and individual values.* Yale University Press.

Ashley, C. & Ntshona, Z. (2003). *Transforming roles but not reality? Private sector and community involvement in tourism and forestry development on the Wild Coast.* Foreign, Commonwealth & Development Office. Gov.uk.https://www.gov.uk/research-for-development-outputs/transforming-roles-but-not-reality-private-sector-and-community-involvement-in-tourism-and-forestry-development-on-the-wild-coast-south-africa

Ashley, S.L., Terry, A., & Lapace, J. (2018). Introduction: Critical Heritage Studies in Canada / Études critiques du patrimoine au Canada. *Journal of Canadian Studies/Revue d'études canadiennes 52*(1), 1–10. https://muse.jhu.edu/article/703424.

Aurindo, M. J., & Machado, C. (2016). MUVITUR (virtual museum of tourism): A new approach to tourism history. *Journal of Tourism History, 8*(3), 300–309.

Ballet, J., Kouamékan J., Koffi, M., & Komena, K. B. (2009). Co-management of natural resources in developing countries: The importance of Context. *Économie Internationale, 120,* 53–76.

Ballet, J., Kouamékan J., Koffi, M., and Komena, K.B. (2009). Co-management of natural resources in developing Countries: the importance of Context. Économie internationale 120 (2009), p. 53-76.

Barrère, C. (2016). Cultural heritage: From official to informal. *City, Culture & Society, 15*(2), 181–203.

Barsalou, J. & Baxter, V. (2007). The urge to remember: The role of memorials in social reconstruction and transitional justice. *United States Institute of Peace Stabilisation and Reconstruction Series No. 5* January 2007. Retrieved [12 December 2025] from [http://www.usip.org/sites/default/files/srs5.pdf]

Basik, S. (2024). Exploring urban toponymic verticality: An initial note. *Urban Governance, 4*, 193–197.

Baum, T. (2006). *Human resource management for tourism, hospitality, and leisure*. Thomson.

Becken, S. & Job, H. (2014). Protected areas in a changing world: The need for a regional perspective in Southern Africa. *Tourism Geographies, 16*(2), 278–299.

Bennett, J., McIntyre, & Choi, Y. (20 I 9). The role of local food in sustainable tourism development. *Journal of Sustainable Tourism,* 27(4), 517–533.

Berdej, S., D. Armitage & A. Charles. (2015). Governance and Community Conservation. Community Conservation Research Network. Halifax, Nova Scotia. Available online at: ww.communityconservation.net/ resources/ governance.

Bianchi, C. (2006). Making online monuments more accessible through interface design. In L. MacDonald (Ed.), Digital heritage, applying digital imaging to cultural heritage (pp. 445–466), Butterworth-Heinemann.

Bianchi, R. V. (2004). *Tourism, the world system, and 'the other'*. In D. T. Herbert (Ed.), Geographies of tourism and global change (pp. 58–73). Pearson Education.

Bikhchandani, S., Hirshleifer, D. & Welch, I. (1998). Learning from the behaviour of others: Conformity, fads and informational cascades. *Journal of Economic Perspectives, 12*, 151–170.

Bimms, T. (2002). Tourism, gender and empowerment: A case study of a women's tourism cooperative in Zanzibar. *Progress in Development Studies*, 2(1), 39–53.

Blackstock, K. (2005). A critical look at community-based tourism. *Community Development Journal*, 40(1), 39–49.

Borges, A. L., Hammami, F., & Wangel, J. (2020). Article reviewing neighbourhood sustainability assessment tools through critical heritage studies. *Sustainability 2020, 12*, 1605.

Born, J., Linder, H. P. & Desmet, P. (2007). The Greater Cape Floristic Region (GCFR). *Journal of Biogeography, 34*(1), 147–162.

Borrini-Feyerabend, G., Farvar, T.M., Nguinguiri, C.J., & Ndangang, A.V. (2007). Co-management of Natural Resources: Organising, Negotiating and Learning-by-Doing. Kasparek Verlag, Mönchhofstr. 16, Heidelberg, Germany.

Borrini-Feyerabend, G., Farvar, T.M., Nguinguiri, C.J., & Ndangang, A.V. (2007). Co-management of natural resources: Organising, negotiating and learning-by-doing. Kasparek Verlag.

Bramwell, B., & Lane, B. (2011). *Tourism planning: Subverting sustainability*. Routledge.

Breen, C. (2007). Advocacy, international development, and world heritage sites in sub-Saharan Africa. *World Arch, 39*, 355–370.

Briedenhann, J. (2017). Sustainable tourism and local economic development. *Journal of Sustainable Tourism, 25*(1), 1–15.

Brown-Luthango, M., Reyes, E. & Gubevu, M. (2017). Informal settlement upgrading and safety: experiences from Cape Town, South Africa. *Journal of Housing and the Built Environment, 32*, 471–493.

Caffo, R. (2014). Digital cultural heritage projects: Opportunities and future challenges. *Procedia Computer Science, 38*, 12–17.

Calaminus, G., & Barr, R. (2008). Economic evaluation and health-related quality of life. *Paediatric Blood & Cancer, 50*(S5), 1112–1115.

Cameron, F., & Kenderdine, S. (2017). *Theorising digital cultural heritage: A critical discourse.* MIT Press.

Cannas, R. (2012). An overview of tourism seasonality: Key concepts and policy. *Alma Tourism*, 3(5): 40–58.

Carranza, E., Dhakal, C., & Love, I. (2018). Female entrepreneurs: How and why are they different? World Bank, Washington, DC. License: Creative Commons Attribution CC BY 3.0 IGO.

Carranza, E., Dhakal, C., & Love, I. (2018). Female entrepreneurs: How and why are they different? World Bank.

Cherchi, E. (2009, December). *Modelling Individual Preferences: State of the Art, Recent Advances, and Future Directions* [Conference presentation]. 12th International Conference on Travel Behaviour Research, Jaipur, India.

Chikodzi, D., Hamo, G., Dube, K. & Chapungu, L. (2022). Climate change risk assessment of heritage tourism sites within South African national parks. *International Journal of Geoheritage and Parks, 10*(3), 417–434.

Chimhundu, H. (2016). Language policy in Zimbabwe: The historical and current trends. *Language Matters, 47*(2), 192–208.

Chirikure, S. (2013). Heritage conservation in Africa: The good, the bad, and the challenges. *South African Journal of Science, 109*(1-2), 1–3.

Chiwawa, N. & Wissink, H. (2023). Sustainable tourism for local and regional development in South Africa: Unlocking economic potential through responsible tourism strategies. *African Journal of Hospitality, Tourism and Leisure,* 12(3), 1163–1175.

Chng, K. S. & Narayanan, S. (2017). Culture and social identity in preserving cultural heritage: An experimental study. *International Journal of Social Economics, 44*(8), 1078- 1091.

Chuang F, Manley E, Petersen A. (2020). The role of worldviews in the governance of sustainable mobility. Proc Natl Acad Sci U S A. 2020 Feb 25;117(8):4034-4042. doi: 10.1073/pnas.1916936117. Epub 2020 Feb 7. PMID: 32034101; PMCID: PMC7049160.

Chuang, F., Manley, E., & Petersen, A. (2020). The role of worldviews in the governance of sustainable mobility. *Proc Natl Acad Sci., 117*(8), 4034–4042.

Cocks, M., Vetter, S. & Wiersum, K.F. (2017). From universal to local: perspectives on cultural landscape heritage in South Africa, International Journal of Heritage Studies, DOI: 10.1080/13527258.2017.1362573

Cocks, M., Vetter, S. & Wiersum, K.F. (2017). From universal to local: Perspectives on cultural landscape heritage in South Africa. *International Journal of Heritage Studies, 24*(1), 35–52

Conti, A. (2011). The impact of tourism on World Heritage towns in Latin America. *Proceedings from the World Heritage and tourism: Managing for the global and the local Conference.* Presses de l'Université Laval, Québec, 385–398.

Córdoba Azcárate, M. (2025). Tourism, space, and place: bridging past, present and future research. *Tourism Geographies, 27*(3–4), 735–755.

Crowley, K., Jackson, R., O'Connell, S., Karunarthna, D., Anantasari, E., Retnowati, A., & Niemand, D. (2022) Cultural heritage and risk assessments: Gaps, challenges, and future research directions for the inclusion of heritage within climate change adaptation and disaster management. Climate Resil Sustain., 1, e45. https://doi.org/10.1002/cli2.45

Crowley, K., Jackson, R., O'Connell, S., Karunarthna, D., Anantasari, E., Retnowati, A., & Niemand, D. (2022). Cultural heritage and risk assessments: Gaps, challenges, and future research directions for the inclusion of heritage within climate change adaptation and disaster management. *Climate Resil Sustain., 1*, e45.

Cudny, W. & Appelblad, H. (2019). Monuments and their functions in urban public space. Norsk Geografisk Tidsskrift - Norwegian Journal of Geography, 73(5), 273–289,

Daly, C. (2014). *A cultural heritage management methodology for assessing the vulnerabilities of archaeological sites to predicted climate change, focusing on Ireland's two world heritage sites.* [Doctoral dissertation, Technological University Dublin]. https://arrow .tudublin.ie/builtdoc/13/.

Dangi, T. B. & Jamal, T. (2016). An integrated approach to "sustainable community-based tourism". *Sustainability, 8*(5), 1475.

Davis, B. J. (2003). *The theory of the individual in economics.* Routledge.

DEAT (2002). National Responsible Tourism Development Guidelines for South Africa. Department of Environmental Affairs and Tourism. Available online from: https:// www. tourism.gov.za/CurrentProjects/ResponsibleTourism/Responsible%20Tourism/Responsible%20Tourism%20Guidelines.pdf. Accessed on 22/02/2026.

DEAT (2002). National Responsible Tourism Development Guidelines for South Africa. Department of Environmental Affairs and Tourism. https:// www. tourism.gov.za/CurrentProjects/ResponsibleTourism/Responsible%20Tourism/Responsible%20Tourism%20Guidelines.pdf.

Denis, P. (2015). Memory and commemoration as a subject of enquiry for African Christianity scholars. Studia Historiae Ecclesiasticae, 41 (3), https://doi.org/10.17159/2412-4265/2015/450

Denis, P. (2015). Memory and commemoration as a subject of enquiry for African Christianity scholars. *Studia Historiae Ecclesiasticae, 41*(3), 4–22.

Dias, Á., Viana, J., & Pereira, L. (2026). Barriers and policies affecting the implementation of sustainable tourism: the Portuguese experience. Journal of Policy Research in Tourism, Leisure and Events, 18(1), 184–202. https://doi.org/10.1080/19407963.2024.2314514

Dias, Á., Viana, J., & Pereira, L. (2026). Barriers and policies affecting the implementation of sustainable tourism: the Portuguese experience. Journal of Policy Research in Tourism, Leisure and Events, 18(1), 184–202.

Dladla, A., Ndlovu, J. & Phoofolo, T. (2023). Incorporating cultural heritage into the local tourism development strategy in Kwa Ndebele: A systematic review. *African Journal of Hospitality, Tourism and Leisure, 12*(5SE):1740–1753.

Dodman, D. & Millin, D. (2013). Challenges for community-based adaptation: Discovering the potential for transformation. *Journal of International Development*, *25*(5), 640–659.

Dondolo, L. (2005). Intangible heritage: the production of indigenous knowledge in various aspects of social life. Indilinga African Journal of Indigenous Knowledge Systems, 4 (1). https://hdl.handle.net/10520/EJC61483

Dondolo, L. (2005). Intangible heritage: the production of indigenous knowledge in various aspects of social life. *Indilinga African Journal of Indigenous Knowledge Systems, 4*(1).

Doro, W. (2017). World heritage and development in Sub-Saharan Africa, *American Anthropologist, 119(*1), 129-131.

Dube, K., Nhamo, G. & Chikodzi, D. (2021). Rising sea level and its implications on coastal tourism development in Cape Town, South Africa. *Journal of Outdoor Recreation and Tourism, 33*, 00346.

Dutt, A. K., & Wilber, C. K. (2010). *Individual Preferences, Efficiency, and Cost-Benefit Analysis.* In A. K. Dutt & C. K. Wilber, *Economics and ethics*. London.

Duval, B. S. (2012). Rock art tourism in the uKhahlamba/Drakensberg World Heritage Site. *Obstacles to the Development of Sustainable Tourism*, 21(1), 134–153.

Ehlers, T. B., & Main, K. (1998). Women and the new tourism. *Annals of Tourism Research, 25*(3), 698–714.

Eichhorn, V. & Buhalis, D. (2011). Accessibility: A key objective for the tourism industry. In D. Buhalis & S. Darcy (Eds.), *Accessible tourism: Concepts and issues* (pp. 46-61). Channel View Publications.

Eichler, J. (2021). Intangible cultural heritage, inequalities and participation: who decides on heritage? The International Journal of Human Rights, 25(5), 793–814. https://doi.org/10.1080/13642987.2020.1822821

Eichler, J. (2021). Intangible cultural heritage, inequalities and participation: Who decides on heritage? *The International Journal of Human Rights, 25*(5), 793–814.

Enloe, C. (1989). *Bananas, beaches, and bases: Making feminist sense of international politics.* University of California Press.

EPA (Environmental Protection Agency) (2010). *Guidelines for preparing economic analyses.* National Centre for Environmental Economics.

Eslava, L. and Pahuja, S. (2020). The state and International Law: A Reading from the Global South. Hunanity and International Journal of Human rights, Humanitarianism and Development. 11 (1), 118-138.

Evaldsson, A & Wessels, A. (2003). To commemorate or not to commemorate: Three important commemorative events in twentieth century South Africa. *Journal for Contemporary History, 28*(1).

Evaldsson, A and Wessels, A. (2003). To commemorate or not to commemorate: three important commemorative events in twentieth century South Africa. Journal for Contemporary History. 28, (1). https://hdl.handle.net/10520/EJC28270

Evans, M. (2007). The Wretched of the Empire: Politics, Ideology and Counterinsurgency in Rhodesia, 1965–80. Small Wars & Insurgencies, 18(2), 175–195. https://doi.org/10.1080/09574040701400601

Evans, M. (2007). The wretched of the empire: Politics, ideology and counterinsurgency in Rhodesia, 1965–80. *Small Wars & Insurgencies, 18*(2), 175–195.

Fajinmi, O. O., Olarewaju O. O., & Van Staden J. (2023). Propagation of medicinal plants for sustainable livelihoods, economic development, and biodiversity conservation in South Africa. *Plants (Basel), 12*(5), 1174.

Faria, R., Azevedo, R., Kraemer, M.U., Souza, R., Cunha, M.S., Hill, S.C., Theze, J., Bonsall, M.B., Bowden, T.A., Rissanen, I. & Rocco, J.M. (2016). Zika virus in the Americas: Early epidemiological and genetic findings. *Science, 352*(6283), 345-349.

Feakinsa, C., Barrett, E. & Bower, M. (2024). Trauma-heritage: towards a trauma-informed understanding of heritage. International Journal of Heritage Studies. 2024, VOL. 30, NO. 8, 857–871. https://doi.org/10.1080/13527258.2024.2342286.

Feakinsa, C., Barrett, E. & Bower, M. (2024). Trauma-heritage: Towards a trauma-informed understanding of heritage. *International Journal of Heritage Studies, 30*(8), 857–871.

Finlay, A. (2015). *Community media in South Africa: The struggle for survival and sustainability.* MISA.

Garidzirai, R. & Pasara, M. T. (2020). An analysis of the contribution of tourism on economic growth in South African provinces: A panel analysis. *GeoJournal of Tourism and Geosites, 29*(2), 554–564. https://doi.org/10.30892/gtg.29214-489

Garidzirai, R. & Pasara, M.T. (2020). An analysis of the contribution of tourism on economic growth in South African provinces: A panel analysis. GeoJournal of Tourism and Geosites, 29(2), 554–564. https://doi.org/10.30892/gtg.29214-489

Gkarane, S. & Vassiliadis, C. (2024). *Breaking the seasonality barrier in tourism. a literature review of policies and strategies.* In A. Kavoura, T. Borges-Tiago, F. Tiago (Eds.), Strategic Innovative Marketing and Tourism. ICSIMAT 2023. Springer Proceedings in Business and Economics (pp. 211–218). Springer, Cham.

Godovykh, M., Baker, C. & Fyall, A. (2022). VR in tourism: A new call for virtual tourism experience amid and after the COVID-19 pandemic. *Tourism and Hospitality, 3*(1), 265–275.

Goldblatt, P. & Manning, J. C. (2002). Plant diversity of the Cape region of southern Africa. *Annals of the Missouri Botanical Garden, 89*(2), 281–302.

Goldblatt, P. (1997). Floristic diversity in the Cape flora of South Africa. *Biodiversity & Conservation, 6*, 359–377.

Gonda, T. (2024). The importance of infrastructure in the development of accessible tourism. *Journal of Infrastructure, Policy and Development, 8*(2), 2735.

González-Reverté, F., Corrons, A., & Gomis-López, M.J. (2025). Exploring the role of memorable tourism experiences and place attachment in the revisit intention of tourists staying in short-term rentals. *Journal of Hospitality and Tourism Insights, 8*(11), 79–99.

González-Reverté, F., Corrons, A., and Gomis-López, M.J. (2025). Exploring the role of memorable tourism experiences and place attachment in the revisit intention of tourists staying in short-term rentals. Journal of Hospitality and Tourism Insights. 8 (11), 79-99. https://doi.org/10.1108/JHTI-05-2024-0451

Goodwin, H. & Santilli, R. (2009). Community-based tourism: A success? *ICRT Occasional Paper, 11*(1), 1–24.

Gordhan, P. (2018). T*ourism marketing in Southern Africa: Challenges and opportunities*. University of Pretoria Press.

Goss, J. (1993). The 'sex' tourism industry: A commentary on the commodification of the female body in the global tourism industry. *International Journal of Urban and Regional Research, 17*(3), 477–497.

Gossling, S. (2002). Global environmental consequences of tourism. *Global Environmental Change, 12*(4), 283–302.

Gossling, S., Scott, D. & Hall, C. M., (2020). Pandemics, tourism and global change: A rapid assessment of COVID-19. *Journal of Sustainable Tourism, 29*(1), 1–20.

Greenwood, C., & Quinn, M. (2017). Digital amnesia and the future tourist. *Journal of Tourism Futures, 3(*1), 73–76.

Guenthe, E. (2015). Women's empowerment through tourism: A case study of community-based tourism in Kenya. *Journal of Sustainable Tourism, 23*(11),1614–1631.

Gundlach, H. & Neville, A.N. (2012). Authenticity: Further theoretical and practical development

Gundlach, H. & Neville, A.N. (2012). Authenticity: Further theoretical and practical development. *Journal of Brand Management 19*(6), 484-499.

Gweshengwe, B., & Hassan, N. H. (2020). Defining the characteristics of poverty and their implications for poverty analysis. Cogent Social Sciences, 6(1). https://doi.org/10.1080/23311886.2020.1768669

Gweshengwe, B., & Hassan, N. H. (2020). Defining the characteristics of poverty and their implications for poverty analysis. *Cogent Social Sciences, 6*(1).

Hamo, G., Dube, K. & Saurombe, T. (2021). Impact of tropical Cyclone Idai on tourism attractions and related infrastructure in Chimanimani, Zimbabwe. In G. Nhamo & D. Chikodzi (Eds.), *Cyclones in Southern Africa (Vol. 3), Implications for the sustainable development goals* (pp. 245–264). Springer Nature.

Hanafiah, M. H., Azman, I., Jamaluddin, M. R., & Aminuddin, N. (2016). Responsible tourism practices and quality of life: Perspective of Langkawi Island communities. *Procedia-Social and Behavioural Sciences, 222*(1), 406–413.

Harrison, D. (2020). *Tourism, politics, and social issues in Southern Africa.* South African Tourism Academy.

Harrison, R. (2015). Beyond "natural" and "cultural" heritage: Toward an ontological politics of heritage in the age of anthropocene. *Herit. Soc., 8*, 24–42.

Hasan, M., & Siddique, Z. R. (2016). Impacts of tourism development on the local community: A study on Shalban Vihara. *Bangladesh Journal of Tourism, 1*(1), 74–82.

Hawkins, R., & Mowatt, R. (2019). The social impact of tourism: Enhancing social wellness through community engagement. *Journal of Tourism and Cultural Change, 17*(1), 1–16.

Heehs, P. (1994). Myth, History, and Theory. History and Theory, 33(1), 1–19. https://doi.org/10.2307/2505649

Heehs, P. (1994). Myth, history, and theory. *History and Theory, 33*(1), 1–19.

Henama, S. U. (2017). Marikana: Opportunities for heritage tourism. *African Journal of Hospitality, Tourism and Leisure, 6*(4).

Henama, S.U. (2017). Marikana: Opportunities for Heritage Tourism. African Journal of Hospitality, Tourism and Leisure, Volume 6 (4) - (2017).

Hilgart, A. (2024). Home languages in early childhood development in South Africa, viewed n.d., from https://starfish-greathearts.org/blog/blog-template-25.

Hlongwane, K. A. & Ndlovu, M. S. (2019). *Public history and culture in South Africa: Memorialisation and liberation heritage sites in Johannesburg and the Township Space.* Springer Nature.

Hoelscher, S. & Alderman, H. D. (2004). Memory and place: Geographies of a critical relationship. *Cultural Geography*, 5(3), 347–355.

Hugentobler, L. (2025). Memories Set in Stone—How Visitors Make Sense of Memorials On-Site and Online Experiences of Public Memory at Two Dr. King Memorials in DC. Universität Zü rich, Zü rich, Switzerland: Springer.

Hugentobler, L. (2025). *Memories set in stone—how visitors make sense of memorials on-site and online experiences of public memory at two Dr. King memorials in DC*. Springer.

Hutton, J., Adams, W. M. & Murombedzi, J. C., (2005). Back to the barriers? Changing narratives in biodiversity conservation. *Forum for Development Studies, 32*(2), 341–370.

ICOMOS (2019). *The future of our Pasts: Engaging cultural heritage in climate action. https://civvih.icomos.org/wp-content/uploads/Future-of-Our-Pasts-Report-min.pdf*

ICOMOS (International Council on Monuments and Sites). (1999). *International Cultural Tourism Charter. Managing tourism at places of heritage significance.* [http://www.icomos.org/en/charters-and-texts.

IPCC (2014). Climate Change 2014: Impacts, vulnerability, and adaptation. Part A: Global and sectoral aspects. *Contribution of*

Working Group II to the Fifth Assessment Report of the Intergovernmental Panel on Climate Change. Cambridge University Press.

Ireland, T., Brown, S., Bagnall, K., Lydon, J., Sherratt, T., & Veale, S. (2025). Engaging the everyday: The concept and practice of 'everyday heritage'. *International Journal of Heritage Studies, 31*(2), 192–215.

Ireland, T., Harrison, A., & Brockwell, S. (2020). 'Materialities, mobilities and multiple modernities: Exploring new approaches to Australia's 'heritage of the air'. *Historic Environment, 32*(3), 14–31.

Ishida, N. (2021). Thorstein Veblen on economic man: Toward a new method of describing human nature, society, and history. *Evolutionary and Institutional Economics Review, 18*, 527–547.

Jackson, W.A. (2013). The decolonising of economic theory. International Journal of Social Economics, 40 (9), 809-825.

Janssen-Lauret, F. (2024). Naturalistic Dualistic and Putnam's paradox. Australasian Philosophical review, 8(1), 48-59.

Jigyasu, R., Murthy, M., Boccardi, G., Marrion, C.E., Douglas, D., King, J., O'Brien, G., Dolcemascolo, G., Kim, Y., Albrito, P., & Osihn, M. (2013). *Heritage and resilience: issues and opportunities for reducing disaster risks*. UNESCO.

Jokilehto, J. (2017). *A history of architectural conservation*. Routledge.

Jong, M., Soh, A. & Puah, C. (2022). Tourism sustainability: Climate change emissions in South Africa. *International Journal of Energy Economics and Policy, 12*(6), 412–417.

Kalla M, & Metaxas, T. (2024). Cultural and Heritage Tourism, Urban Resilience, and Sustainable Development. Comparative Analysis of the Strategies of Athens and Rome. Journal of Sustainable Research, 2024;6(4): e240073. https://doi.org/10.20900/jsr20240073

Kalla, M., & Metaxas, T. (2024). Cultural and heritage tourism, urban resilience, and sustainable development. Comparative analysis of the strategies of Athens and Rome. *Journal of Sustainable Research, 6*(4), e240073.

Kamel Ahmed, E. (2015). What to conserve? Heritage, memory, and management of meanings. *International Journal of Architectural Research, 9*(1), 67–76.

Kaschula, R. H. & Mostert, B. (2011). Technology and mother-tongue education in South Africa: A case study. *Perspectives in Education, 29*(4), 1–10.

Katapidi, I. (2026). Reframing Living Rural Heritage: Local Ontologies of Nature–Culture Symbiosis and the Challenge of Sustainable Management in Greece. Sustainability, 18(1), 422. https://doi.org/10.3390/su18010422

Katapidi, I. (2026). Reframing living rural heritage: Local ontologies of nature–culture symbiosis and the challenge of sustainable management in Greece. *Sustainability, 18*(1), 422.

Kavita, E., & Saarinen, J. (2016). Tourism and rural community development in Namibia: Policy issues review. Fennia, 194(1), 79-88. https://doi.org/10.11143/46331

Kavita, E., & Saarinen, J. (2016). Tourism and rural community development in Namibia: Policy issues review. *Fennia, 194*(1), 79-88.

Keita, L. (2012). Revealed preference theory, rationality, and neoclassical economics: science or ideology. *Africa Development, 37*(4), 73–116.

Khadaroo, J. & Seetanah, B. (2008). The role of transport infrastructure in international tourism development: A gravity model approach. *Tourism Management, 29*(5), 831–840.

Kidd, J. (2019). With new eyes I see: Embodiment, empathy and silence in digital heritage interpretation. *International Journal of Heritage Studies, 25*(1), 54.

Kim, K., Uysal, M. & Sirgy, M. J. (2013). How does tourism in a community impact the quality of life of community residents? *Tourism Management, 36*, 527–540.

Kinnaird, V., & Hall, D. (1994). *Tourism: A gender analysis*. Wiley.

Klamer, A. (2016). Cultural heritage management and community engagement. *Journal of Cultural Heritage Management, 1*(1), 1-15.

Klostermann, J., van de Sandt, K., Harley, M., Hilden, M., Leiter, T., van Minnen, J., Pieterse, N. and van Bree, L. (20 I 8). Towards a framework to assess, compare and develop monitoring and evaluation of climate change adaptation in Europe. *Mitigation and Adaptation Strategies for Global Change, 23*, 187–209.

Kontoleon, A., Macrory, R., & Swanson, T. (2002). Individual preference-based values and environmental decision making: Should valuation have its day in court? *Research in Law and Economics, 20*, 179–216.

Kornhauser, A. L. (2003). The domain of preference. *University of Pennsylvania Law Review, 151*(3), 717–746.

Kraaij, T. & van Wilgen, B.W. (2014). Drivers, ecology, and management of fire in fynbos. *Fynbos: Ecology, evolution, and conservation of a megadiverse region, 15*(1), 47-72.

Kryder-Reid, E. (2018). Introduction: Tools for a critical heritage. *International Journal of Heritage Studies, 24(7)*, 691–693.

Lähdesmäki, T., & Vlase, I. (2023). Mapping the research on gender, LGBTQI minorities and heritage across social sciences and humanities. International Journal of Heritage Studies, 29(8), 743–758. https://doi.org/10.1080/13527258.2023.2220298

Lähdesmäki, T., & Vlase, I. (2023). Mapping the research on gender, LGBTQI minorities and heritage across social sciences and humanities. *International Journal of Heritage Studies, 29*(8), 743–758.

Lee, J., & Scott, D. (2016). The effects of outdoor tourism on health and well-being: A review of the literature. *Tourism Management, 57,* 120–132.

Levin, J. D., & Milgrom, P. R. (2004). *Introduction to choice theory.* https://web.stanford.edu/~jdlevin/Econ%20202/Choice%20Theory.pdf

Light, D. (2015). Heritage and tourism. In E. Waterton & S. Watson (Eds.), *The Palgrave handbook of contemporary heritage research* (pp. 144–153). Palgrave Macmillan.

Linda, N. & Nzama, A. T. (2020). Tourism crime, safety and security issues: The case of a local South African municipality. *African Journal of Hospitality, Tourism and Leisure, 9*(3), 372–381.

Loewenstein, E. G., & Prelec, D. (1993). Preferences for sequences of outcomes. *Psychology Review, 100*(1), 91–108.

Loftus, W. J. (2013). *Strategic adaptive management and the efficiency of invasive alien plant management in South African national parks.* [Master's dissertation, Nelson Mandela Metropolitan University].

Madandola, M., & Boussaa, D. (2023). Cultural heritage tourism as a catalyst for sustainable development; the case of old Oyo town in Nigeria. International Journal of Heritage Studies, 29(1–2), 21–38. https://doi.org/10.1080/13527258.2023.2169332

Madandola, M., & Boussaa, D. (2023). Cultural heritage tourism as a catalyst for sustainable development; the case of old Oyo town in Nigeria. *International Journal of Heritage Studies, 29*(1–2), 21–38.

Maller, C., Townsend, M., Pryor, A., Brown, P., & St Leger, L. (2008). Healthy parks, healthy people: The health benefits of contact with nature in a park context. *Visitor Studies, 11*(2), 245–262.

Mamvura, Z. (2023). By what authority? The contested politics of urban toponymic inscription in Zimbabwe. *Urban Geography, 44*(1), 198–220.

Mangwiro M, Chikuta O & Kabote F (2025). Agritourism in Southern Africa: a policy analysis. Front. Sustain. Tour. 4:1501008. https://doi: 10.3389/frsut.2025.1501008

Mangwiro, M., Chikuta, O. & Kabote, F. (2025). Agritourism in Southern Africa: A policy analysis. *Front. Sustain. Tour., 4,* 1501008.

Manwa H. A. (2007). Is Zimbabwe ready to venture into the cultural tourism market? *Development Southern Africa, 24*(3), 465–474.

Manyara, G., & Jones, E. (2007). Community-based tourism enterprises: A case study of Kenya's community-based tourism development. *Journal of Sustainable Tourism, 15*(6), 629–644.

Marschall, S. (2010*). Landscape of Memory: Commemorative monuments, memorials, and public statuary in post-apartheid South Africa*. Brill, Hotei Publishing.

Marschall, S. (2017). Negotiating heritage and development on Robben Island. *African Heritage Review, 14*(2), 87–102.

Maseko, P. & Vale, P. (2016). Languages and the construction of cultural identity: The case of South Africa. *Journal of Multilingual and Multicultural Development, 37*(1), 42–52.

Masilela, N., Hoogendoorn, G. & Visser, G. (2023). Cultural Tourism in South Africa: A Case Study of the Experiences of Employees. African Journal of Hospitality, Tourism and Leisure, 12(1):326338. DOI: https://doi.org/10.46222/ajhtl.19770720.370

Masilela, N., Hoogendoorn, G. & Visser, G. (2023). Cultural tourism in South Africa: A case study of the experiences of employees. *African Journal of Hospitality, Tourism and Leisure, 12*(1):326338.

Masilela, N., Hoogendoorn, G., & Visser, G. (2023). Cultural Tourism in South Africa: A Case Study of the Experiences of Employees. African Journal of Hospitality, Tourism and Leisure, 12(1), 326-338. https://doi.org/10.46222/ajhtl.19770720.370

Masilela, N., Hoogendoorn, G., & Visser, G. (2023). Cultural tourism in South Africa: A case study of the experiences of employees. *African Journal of Hospitality, Tourism and Leisure, 12*(1), 326-338.

Mathew, P. V. (2021). Sustainable tourism development: Discerning the impact of responsible tourism on community well-being. *Journal of Hospitality and Tourism Insights, 5*(5), 987–1001.

Mathew, P. V., & Sreejesh, S. (2017). Impact of responsible tourism on destination sustainability and the quality of life of the community in tourism destinations. *Journal of Hospitality and Tourism Management, 31*, 83–89.

Matti, L. & Woodley, E. (2010). *Biocultural diversity conservation: A global sourcebook. Earthscan.*

Mautle, G. (2004). Language planning and policy in Botswana. *Current Issues in Language Planning, 5*(4), 385–401.

Mbaiwa, J. (2005). The impact of tourism development on rural livelihoods in Botswana. *Journal of Contemporary African Studies, 23*(2), 161–184.

Mbaiwa, J. E. & Kolawole, O. O. (2013). *Tourism and biodiversity conservation: The case of community-based natural resource management in Southern Africa. CABI Reviews, 8*(10), 1–10.

McConnell, R. (2022). Heritage tourism: From problems to possibilities, *The Asia Pacific Journal of Anthropology, 23*(4-5), 410–412.

Mejabi, E. I. (2018). *The impact of events on sustainable tourism development in Durban: An evidence-based enquiry* [Doctoral dissertation, University of KwaZulu-Natal].

Mekonnen, H., Bires, Z. & Berhanu, K. (2022). Practices and challenges of cultural heritage conservation in historical and religious heritage sites: evidence from North Shoa Zone, Amhara Region, Ethiopia. Herit Sci 10, 172 (2022). https://doi.org/10.1186/s40494-022-00802-6

Mekonnen, H., Bires, Z. & Berhanu, K. (2022). Practices and challenges of cultural heritage conservation in historical and religious heritage sites: Evidence from North Shoa Zone, Amhara Region, Ethiopia. *Herit Sci, 10*, 172.

Menozzi, F. (2024). The postcolonial museum and nonsynchronous heritage. Interventions, 1-23. https://doi.org/10.1080/1369801X.2024.2402470

Meque, A., Gamedze, S., Moitihobogi, T., Booneeady, P., Samuel, S. & Mpalang, L. (2021). Numerical weather prediction and climate modelling: Challenges and opportunities for improving climate services delivery in Southern Africa. *Climate Services*, 23, 100243.

Meskell, L. (2011). *The nature of heritage: The new South Africa*. John Wiley & Sons.

Meskell, L. (2018). A future in ruins: UNESCO, world heritage and the dream of peace. Oxford University Press.

Meskell, L. M., & Scheermeyer, C. (2008). Heritage as therapy: Set pieces from the new South Africa. *Journal of Material Culture*, 13, 153–173.

Meyer, H. (2019). *Sustainable tourism development in Namibia: Strategies for growth and conservation*. Namibian Tourism Board.

Mgadle, A. (2022). *An examination of climate change impacts on coastal tourism in Durban, South Africa.* [Master's thesis, Vaal University of Technology]. ProQuest.

Mhlanga, B. (2013) Ethnicity or tribalism? The discursive construction of Zimbabwean national identity, African Identities, 11:1, 47–60, DOI: 10.1080/14725843.2013.775840

Mhlanga, B. (2013) Ethnicity or tribalism? The discursive construction of Zimbabwean national identity. *African Identities, 11*(1), 47–60.

Mitchell, J. (2018). Cultural heritage conservation and community development. *Journal of Sustainable Tourism, 26*(1), 1–15.

Mitchell, K. (2003). Monuments, memorials, and the politics of memory. *Urban Geography, 24*(5), 442–459.

Mollel, D. (2024). Promoting the Progression of Expeditions and Implementing Policies to Enhance Sustainable Tourism Development in Tanzania. Journal of Financial Risk Management, 13, 305-324. doi: 10.4236/jfrm.2024.132014.

Mollel, D. (2024). Promoting the progression of expeditions and implementing policies to enhance sustainable tourism development in Tanzania. *Journal of Financial Risk Management, 13*, 305–324.

Morrow, J. D. (1994). *Game theory for political scientists*. Princeton.

Mowforth, M., & Munt, l. (2016). *Tourism and sustainability: Development, globalisation and new tourism in the Third World* (4th ed.). Routledge.

Msunda, C. O. (2023). New dispensation, new kids on the block. 'Ama 2000' and the 2023 Harmonised Elections in Zimbabwe. *The Strategic Review for Southern Africa, 45*(2).

Msunda, C.O. (2023). New Dispensation, New Kids on the Block. 'Ama 2000' and the 2023 Harmonised Elections in Zimbabwe. (2023). The Strategic Review for Southern Africa, 45(2). https://doi.org/10.35293/srsa.v45i2.4893

Mtapuri, O., Daitai, J., Camilleri, M.A., & Dluzewska, A (Eds.) (2024). Sustainable tourism development: Insights from South Africa and the continent. In: *Tourism planning and destination marketing, Second Edition* (pp. 95–116), Emerald Publishing Limited.

Mtapuri, O., Daitai, J., Camilleri, M.A., & Dluzewska, A. (2024). Sustainable tourism development: Insights from South Africa and the continent, Tourism Planning and Destination Marketing, Second Edition, 95–116, Emerald Publishing Limited, Leeds, United Kingdom, https://doi.org/10.1108/978-1-80455-888- 120241006

Mtshali, M., Mtapuri, O., & Shamase, S. P. (2017). Experiences of black-owned small, medium, and micro enterprises in the accommodation tourism-sub sector in selected Durban townships, KwaZulu-Natal. *African Journal of Hospitality, Tourism and Leisure, 6*(3), 30–141.

Munaretto, S., Vellinga, P. & Tobi, H. (2012). Flood protection in Venice under conditions of sea-level rise: An analysis of institutional and technical measures. *Coastal Management, 40*(4), 355–380.

Mushandu, T.A. & Zhang, R. (2024). Design and social influence of the Great Zimbabwe ruins. *Open Journal of Social Sciences,* 12(8), 465–493.

Mutanga a, N. C., Masunga, G. S., Kolawole, D. O., Gondo, R., & Mbaiwa, E. J. (2025). *Scientific African, 29,* e02876.

Mutanga a, N.C., Masunga, G.S., Kolawole, D.O., Gondo, R., and Mbaiwa, E.J. (2025). Scientific African, 29, 9September 2025), e02876. https://doi.org/10.1016/j.sciaf.2025.e02876

Ndoro, W. & Pwiti. G. (2001). Heritage management in southern Africa: Local, national and international discourse. *Public Archaeology,* 2(1), 21–34.

Nelson, F. (2010). *Community rights, conservation & contested land: The politics of natural resource governance in Africa.* Earthscan.

Nicolaides, A. (2014). Authenticity and the tourist's search for Being. *African Journal of Hospitality, Tourism and Leisure, 3*(1).

Nwauche, E. S. (2014). The UNESCO Convention for the protection and promotion of the diversity of cultural expressions: Implications for African trade and cultural policy. In T. Moyo (Ed.), *Trade and industrial development in Africa: Rethinking strategy and policy,* (pp.245–274). JSTOR.

Nyakunu, E. & Rogerson, M. C. (2014). Tourism policy analysis: The case of post-independence Namibia. *African Journal of Hospitality, Tourism and Leisure, 3*(1).

Nyathi, M., & Ncube, M. (2020). The 2017 military coup in Zimbabwe: Implications for human rights and the rule of law. *African Human Rights Law Journal, 20*(2), 825–851.

Nyika, N. (2009). Mother tongue as a medium of instruction in Zimbabwean primary schools: A rights-based analysis. *NAWA Journal of Language and Communication, 3*(1), 138–148.

Odhiambo, N. M. (2021). Tourism development and poverty alleviation in sub-Saharan African countries: an empirical investigation. Development Studies Research, 8(1), 396–406. https://doi.org/10.1080/21665095.2021.2007782

Odhiambo, N. M. (2021). Tourism development and poverty alleviation in sub-Saharan African countries: an empirical investigation. *Development Studies Research,* 8(1), 396–406.

Oelkers, E. H. and Cole, D.R. (2008). Carbon dioxide sequestration is a solution to a global problem. *Elements,* 4(5), 305–310.

Ogu, I.M., (2013). Rational choice theory: assumptions, strengths, and greatest weaknesses in application outside the Western milieu context. Arabian Journal of Business and Management Review (Nigerian Chapter), *1*(3), 90–100.

Oloidi, A.J. (2020). Theory of symbolic interactionism in heritage tourism: Assumptions, criticisms

Oloidi, A.J. (2020). Theory of symbolic interactionism in heritage tourism: assumptions, criticisms

Oloso, S. E. (2025). Evaluating the Role of Government Policies in Enhancing Sustainable Practices in the Hospitality Industry. International Journal of Research and Innovation in Social Science

(IJRIS), 9 (5) 4176-4191.
https://dx.doi.org/10.47772/IJRISS.2025.905000318

Oloso, S. E. (2025). Evaluating the role of government policies in enhancing sustainable practices in the hospitality industry. *International Journal of Research and Innovation in Social Science (IJRIS), 9*(5), 4176–4191.

Oppermann, M. (1999). Sex tourism and prostitution. *Journal of Sustainable Tourism, 7*(1), 47–63.

Orr, S. A., Richards, J. & Fatoric, S. (2021). Climate change and cultural heritage: A systematic literature review (2016-2020). *The Historic Environment: Policy & Practice, 12*(3-4), 434–477.

Padin, C. (2012). A sustainable tourism planning model: Components and relationships. *European Business Review, 24*(6), 510–518.

Palalane, J., Larson, M., Hanson, H., & Juizo, D. (2016). Coastal erosion in Mozambique: Governing processes and remedial measures. *Journal of Coastal Research, 32*(3), 700–718.

Pansiri, J. (2023). Methodological choices in tourism: A review of the application of symbolic interactionism in tourism and hospitality studies. *African Journal of Hospitality, Tourism and Leisure, 12*(1), 351–369.

Phori, M. M., Hermann, U. P., & Grobbelaar, L. (2024). Residents' perceptions of sustainable heritage tourism development in a rural municipality. Development Southern Africa, 41(3), 551–569. https://doi.org/10.1080/0376835X.2024.2350391

Phori, M. M., Hermann, U. P., & Grobbelaar, L. (2024). Residents' perceptions of sustainable heritage tourism development in a rural municipality. *Development Southern Africa, 41*(3), 551–569.

Pomering, A. (2013). A review of: 'The Tourist Gaze 3.0'. In J. Urry & J. Larsen, Sage Publications Ltd, 2011. 282 pp., £75, ISBN 978-1-84920-376-0 (hc). *Tourism Geographies, 15*(4), 691–693.

Pomering, A. (2013). A review of: 'The Tourist Gaze 3.0': John Urry & Jonas Larsen London, Sage Publications Ltd, 2011. 282 pp., £75, ISBN 978-1-84920-376-0 (hc). Tourism Geographies, 15(4), 691–693. https://doi.org/10.1080/14616688.2012.699095

Pyke, S., Hartwell, H., Blake, A., & Hemingway, A. (2016). Exploring well-being as a tourism product resource. *Tourism Management, 55,* 94–105.

Quan, X., Song, X. & Nguyen, T. P. (2025). From cognition to conservation: Applying grid–group cultural theory to manage natural resources. *Sustainability, 17,* 4613.

Quan, X., Song, X. & Nguyen, T.P. (2025). From Cognition to Conservation: Applying Grid–Group Cultural Theory to Manage Natural Resources. Sustainability 2025, 17, 4613. https://doi.org/10.3390/su17104613

Rabin, M. (1998). Psychology and economics. *Journal of Economic Literature, 36,* 11–46.

Reading, A. (2015). *Making feminist heritage work: Gender and heritage.* In E. Waterton & S. Watson (Eds.), The *Palgrave handbook of contemporary heritage research* (pp. 397-410). Palgrave Macmillan.

Reid, R. (2024). World Heritage Sites in South Africa and why to visit them. Available online from: https://www.roxannereid.co.za/blog/world-heritage-sites-in-south-africa-and-why-to-visit-them. Accessed on: 16/02/2026.

Reid, R. (2024). World Heritage Sites in South Africa and why to visit them. https://www.roxannereid.co.za/blog/world-heritage-sites-in-south-africa-and-why-to-visit-them.

Republic of South Africa (2021). *Tourism: South Africa's economic engine.* Pretoria: Department of Tourism.

Richardson, M., Butler, W.C., Alcock, I., Tindley, A., Sheffield, D., & White, L. C. P. (2025). Introducing heritage connectedness:

Connections to people, nature, and place across time are associated with wellbeing and environmentalism. *The Historic Environment: Policy & Practice, 16*(1), 38–58.

Rogers, L. (2023). *The safeguarding and protection of intangible cultural heritage in international law and policy* [Doctoral dissertation, Deakin University].

Rogerson, C. (2006). Women in tourism: Empowerment through entrepreneurship. *Journal of Tourism and Cultural Change, 4*(1), 1–15.

Rogerson, C. M. (2017). Tourism and local development in Southern Africa: Challenges and opportunities. *GeoJournal of Tourism and Geosites, 20*(2), 192–203.

Rogerson, R. & Shimer, R. (2011). *Search in macroeconomic models of the labour market. In Handbook of Labour Economics, 4*, 619–700.

RSA (2026). Tourism on latest growth figures from Statistics South Africa. Available online: https://www.gov.za/news/media-statements/tourism-latest-growth-figures-statistics-south-africa-03-feb-2025. Accessed on 09/02/2026.

RSA (2026). Tourism on latest growth figures from Statistics South Africa. https://www.gov.za/news/media-statements/tourism-latest-growth-figures-statistics-south-africa-03-feb-2025

Saayman, M. & Saayman, A. (2014). Economic impact of tourism in major parks in South Africa. *Koedoe, 56*(2), 1–8.

Saayman, M., Rossouw, R., & Krugell, W. (2012). The impact of tourism on poverty in South Africa. Development Southern Africa, 29(3), 462–487. https://doi.org/10.1080/0376835X.2012.706041

Saayman, M., Rossouw, R., & Krugell, W. (2012). The impact of tourism on poverty in South Africa. *Development Southern Africa, 29*(3), 462–487.

SAHRA (2021). The Management and conservation of heritage objects housed in state departments or supported bodies.

https://www.theheritageportal.co.za/article/ manage m ent-and-conservation-heritage-objects-housed-state-departments-or-supported-bodies

Salazar, N. B. & Graburn, N. H. H. (Eds.) (2014). *Tourism imaginaries: Anthropological approaches.* Berghahn.

Salazar, N. B. & Zhang, Y. (2013). Seasonal lifestyle tourism: The case of Chinese elites. *Annals of Tourism Research, 43*(4), 81–99.

Salazar, N. B. (2005). Tourism and glocalisation: "Local" tour guiding. *Annals of Tourism Research, 32*(3), 628–646.

Salazar, N. B. (2006). Touristifying Tanzania: Global discourse, local guides. *Annals of Tourism Research, 33*(3), 833–852.

Schelling, T.C. (1978). *Micromotives and macrobehavior*. W.W. Norton.

Scheyvens, R. (1999). Ecotourism and the empowerment of local communities. *Tourism Management, 20*(2), 245-249.

Scheyvens, R. (2000). Promoting women's empowerment through involvement in ecotourism: Experiences from the Third World. *Journal of Sustainable Tourism, 8*(3), 232–249.

Scheyvens, R. (2011). *Tourism and poverty.* Routledge

Scott, D. (2021). Sustainable tourism and the grand challenge of climate change. *Sustainability, 13*(4).

Seduikyte, L., Grazuleviciute-Vileniske, I., Mlinkauskienė, A., & Januškienė, E. (2025). Fostering Resilient Communities Through the Interaction of Heritage, Policy, and Participation: Insights from a Lithuanian Case Study. *Sustainability, 17(*9), 3883.

Seduikyte, L., Grazuleviciute-Vileniske, I., Mlinkauskienė, A., and Januškienė, E. (2025). Fostering Resilient Communities Through the Interaction of Heritage, Policy, and Participation: Insights from a Lithuanian Case Study. Sustainability 2025, 17(9), 3883. https://doi.org/10.3390/su17093883

Segadika, P. (2006). Managing intangible heritage at Tsodilo Hills, Botswana: A consultant's perspective. *Conservation and Management of Archaeological Sites, 7*(3), 173–184.

Semov, S. I. (2009). The strength of the Veblenian critique of neoclassical economics. *Gettysburg Economic Review, 3,* Art. 8, 98–109.

Seraphin, H., Sheeran, P. & Pilato, M. (2018). Over-tourism and the fall of Venice as a destination. *Journal of Destination Marketing & Management, 9*, 374–376.

Sethaba, R. M. H. & Scholes, M. (2021). Management guidelines for the conservation of heritage resources in Wakkerstroom, Mpumalanga, *Koedoe, 63*(1), a1647.

Sha, P. J. (2009). Tourism, power, and power relations: The role of the state. *Tourism Geographies, 11*(4), 468–486.

Sharma, G. D., Taheri, B., Chopra, R., & Parihar, J. S. (2025). Relationship between climate change and tourism: An integrative review, *The Service Industries Journal, 45*(3-4), 426–453.

Sharma, G.D., Taheri, B., Chopra, R., & Parihar, J. S. (2025). Relationship between climate change and tourism: An integrative review. *The Service Industries Journal, 45*(3-4), 426–453.

Siambombe, H. & Hupile, M. (2024). Zimbabwe's economic challenges beyond sanctions. *African Journal of Inclusive Societies*, 4(1), 109.

Sibanda, R. & Tshehla, L. P. (2025). From mother tongue to English: A language policy shift at a multilingual township school in Gauteng, *South African Journal of Childhood Education, 15*(1), a1598.

Sinclair, J. T. (1997). *Gender: Work and tourism*. Routledge.

Skoura, A. (2023). Mapping everyday heritage practices: Tivoli Barber Shop on North Street. In A. Martire, B. Hausleitner, & J. Clossick (Eds.), *everyday streets: Inclusive approaches to understanding and designing streets* (pp. 313–318). UCL Press.

Smith, M. A. D. A. (2017). Tourism and wellbeing. *Annals of Tourism Research, 66*,1–13.

Snyman, S. L. (2017). The role of tourism employment in poverty reduction and community perceptions of conservation and tourism in Southern Africa. In R. Scheyvens (Ed.), *Tourism and poverty reduction* (pp. 145–166). Routledge.

South African Government (2023). *Languages of South Africa*. https: www.gov.za/about-salsouth-africas-people.

South African History Online. (2013, August 16). Marikana Massacre - 16 August 2012. https://sahistory.org.za/article/marikana-massacre-16-august-2012

Specian, P. (2025). Consensus, Prediction and Economic Education. 3rd Economics and Finance Conference, Rome, Italy, April 14-17 and the 4th Economic and Finance Conference, London, UK, August 25-28. Procedia Economics and Finance, 30(2025) 836-841.

Spenceley, A. (2008). *Responsible tourism: Critical issues for conservation and development.* Earthscan.

Staiff, R., Watson, S., & Bushell, R. (2013). Introduction: Place, encounter, engagement: context and themes. In R. Staiff, R. Bushell, & S. Watson (Eds.) *Heritage and tourism: Place, encounter, engagement* (pp. 1–23). Routledge.

Sterling, C., Bauduin, T., & Caicedo, S. M. (2024). Critical heritage ecologies. *AHM Conference 2024: 'Heritage, Memory and Material Culture: Research-Teaching-Society Nexus', 3*, 96–99.

Stojcic, N., Pavlic, I., Puh, B., & Svilokos, T. (2026). Reinventing carrying capacity for living heritage sites. *Tourism Planning & Development*, 1–31.

Stronza, A. (2001). The economic impact of ecotourism on local communities: A critical analysis. *Tourism Economics, 7*(1), 29–42.

Swain, M. B. (1993). Women producers of ethnic crafts. *Annals of Tourism Research, 20*(1), 32–47.

Swanson, K. (2014). Souvenirs, tourists, and tourism. In A. A. Lew, C. M. Hall, & A. M. Williams (Eds.), *The Wiley Blackwell companion to tourism* (pp. 179–188). John Wiley & Sons.

Tapper, R. (2001). Tourism and socio-economic development: UK tour operators' business approaches in the context of the new international agenda. *International Journal of Tourism Research, 3*(5), 351–366.

Tapper, R. (2010). *Tourism and biodiversity: Achieving common goals towards sustainability*. World Tourism Organisation Publications.

Telfer, D. J. & Sharpley, R. (2015). *Tourism and development in the developing world.* Routledge.

Thomas, A. (2024). The role of women's entrepreneurship in achieving Sustainable Development Goals (SDGs): A Comprehensive Review. *Journal of Biotechnology & Bioinformatics Research, 6*(2), 1–11.

Tiberghien, G., Bremner, H., & Milne, S. (2020). Authenticity and disorientation in the tourism experience. *Journal of Outdoor Recreation and Tourism, 30,* 100283

Timothy, D. J. & Yaupane, G. P. (Eds.) (2009*). Cultural heritage and tourism in the developing world*. Routledge.

Toorzani, A. A & Rassafi, A. A. (2022). The effect of cultural values on pro-environmental attitude in the context of travel mode choice: A hierarchical approach. Transportation Research Part F. *Traffic Psychology and Behaviour, 88,* 291–308.

Tourism in Africa: harnessing tourism for growth and improved livelihoods (English). Africa Development forum. World Bank Group.

Tuan, T.H. & Navrud, S. (2008). Capturing the benefits of preserving cultural heritage. *Journal of Cultural Heritage, 9(3),* 326–337.

UNEP (United Nations Environment Programme) (2019). *sustainable consumption and production: A handbook for policymakers.* https://wedocs.unep.org/handle/20.500.11822/9660

UNESCO (United Nations Educational, Scientific and Cultural Organisation) (2016). *If you don't understand, how can you learn?* Policy Paper 24. https://unesdoc.unesco.org/ark:/48223/pf0000243713

UNESCO, (2021). *International Decade of Indigenous Languages (2022-2032).* https://www.unesco.org/en/decades/indigenous-languages.

UNESCO. (2021). *Robben Island: Report of the World Heritage Centre on its activities and the implementation of the World Heritage Committee's decisions.* https://unesdoc.unesco.org/ark:/48223/pf0000379139

UNWTO (2020). *Tourism and Jobs: a better future for all.* https://www.untourism.int/world-tourism-day-2019

UNWTO (2019). *Tourism for sustainable development coal.* United Nations World Tourism Organisation. https://www.untourism.int/world-tourism-day-2019

UNWTO (2025). Guiding Principles for Sustainable Investment in Tourism. United Nations and World Tourism Organisation. https://unctad.org/system/files/official-document/diae2024d6_en.pdf.

UNWTO (United Nations World Tourism Organisation) (2019). *Global report on women in tourism.* 2nd Ed. https://doi.org/10.18111/9789284420384

van Zyl, C. J. (2005). *The role of tourism in the conservation of cultural heritage, with particular relevance for South Africa* [Doctoral dissertation, University of Stellenbosch].

Verovšek, P.J. (2016). Collective memory, politics, and the influence of politics. *Social Semiotics*, 22(2), 143–153.

Visser, G. (2017). *Urban tourism in the developing world: The South African experience.* Routledge.

Vollgraaff, H. (2015). A vision for museums in South Africa: A review of policy proposals, *South African Museums Association Bulletin, 37*(1), 41–45.

Waligo, V., Clarke, J., & Hawkins, R. (2015). Embedding stakeholders in sustainable tourism strategies. *Annals of Tourism Research, 55,* 90–93.

Walpole, M. J., & Goodwin, H. J. (2000). Local economic impacts of dragon tourism in Tanzania. *Journal of Sustainable Tourism, 8*(4), 292–306.

Waterton, E. (2013). Heritage tourism and its representations. In R. Staiff, R. Bushell, and S. Watson (Eds.) *Heritage and tourism: Place, encounter, engagement.* Routledge.

Watson, S. & González-Rodríguez, R. M. (2015). Heritage economies: The past meets the future in the mall. In E. Waterton & S. Watson (Eds), *The Palgrave handbook of contemporary heritage research* (pp. 458–473). Palgrave Macmillan.

Weaver, D. B., & Lawton, L. J. (2002). Overnight ecotourist market segmentation in the Gold Coast hinterland of Australia. *Journal of Travel Research, 40*(3), 270–280.

Weedon, C. & Jordan, G. (2012). Collective memory: theory and politics. *Social Semiotics, 22*(2), 143–153.

Winberry, J. J. (1983). 'Lest we forget': The Confederate monument and the southern townscape. *Southeastern Geographer, 23,* 107–121.

Winstanley, L. (2022). Acts of culture: Representations of memory in postcolonial literature. *PhiN-Beiheft, 29,* 39–45.

Winter, T. (2013). Clarifying the critical in critical heritage studies. *International Journal of Heritage Studies, 19*(6), 532–545.

Winter, T. (2013). Clarifying the critical in critical heritage studies. *International Journal of Heritage Studies, 19*(6), 532–545.

Wong, P. P. (Ed.) (1993). *Tourism vs environment: The case for coastal areas*. GeoJournal Library (Vol. 26). Springer Science & Business Media.

World Bank (1999) *Sustainable tourism and cultural heritage: A review of development assistance and its potential to promote sustainability.* https://documents1.worldbank.org/curated/en/551751468176048723/pdf/369931culture0fulltext.pdf

World Bank (2012). *World development report 2012: Gender equality and development.* World Bank.

Woyo, E. & Musavengane, R. (2023). Has community-based tourism been a useful tool for poverty eradication in Southern African rural destinations? *African Journal of Hospitality, Tourism and Leisure, 12*(2), 251–534.

Woyo, E. & Woyo, E. (2018). Towards the Development of Cultural Tourism as an Alternative for Tourism Growth in Northern Zimbabwe. Journal of Cultural Heritage Management and Sustainable Development, 9 (1), 74-92.

Woyo, E. & Woyo, E. (2018). Towards the development of cultural tourism as an alternative for tourism growth in Northern Zimbabwe. *Journal of Cultural Heritage Management and Sustainable Development, 9*(1), 74–92.

WTTC (World Travel & Tourism Council) (2020). *Economic Impact Reports.* https://researchhub.wttc.org/product/south-africa-economic-impact-report

Wu K, Su L, Zhang S, Yang S, Xing A, & Zhou J. (2025). Cultural distortion risk and tourist loyalty at Silk Road heritage: The mediating roles of perceived value and satisfaction. PLoS One. 2025

Nov 5;20(11): e0335476. doi: 10.1371/journal.pone.0335476. PMID: 41191642; PMCID: PMC12588480.

Wu, C., & Young, C. (2023). Critical toponymies beyond the power-resistance nexus: Multiple toponymies and everyday life in the (re-)naming of South China Sea Islands. *Social & Cultural Geography, 24*(10), 1732–1751.

Wu, K., Su, L., Zhang, S., Yang, S., Xing, A., & Zhou, J. (2025). Cultural distortion risk and tourist loyalty at Silk Road heritage: The mediating roles of perceived value and satisfaction. *PLoS One, 20*(11), e0335476.

Xiong, Y. & Tang, X. (2023). *Tourism during health disasters: Exploring the role of health system quality, transport infrastructure, and environmental expenditures in the revival of the global tourism industry. PLoS One, 18*(9), e0290252.

Xu, Y. (2021). Heritage tourism: from problems to possibilities. *Journal of Tourism and Cultural Change*, 20(1-2), 309–310.

Yükseka, G., and Sökmenb, S. (2018). Digital cultural heritage: Some critical reflections. *Journal of Tourism, Leisure and Hospitality, 3*(2), 138-142.

Zhang, Q., & Mohamad, D. B. (2025). Mapping identity dynamics in heritage tourism: A bibliometric and theoretical review. *Cogent Social Sciences, 11*(1).

Zhong, L., Deng, B., Morrison, A., Coca-Stefaniak, J., & Yang, L. (2021). Medical, health and wellness tourism research: A review of the literature (1970- 2020) and research agenda. *International Journal of Environmental Research* on *Public Health, 18*(20), 10875.

Zhong, L., Qi, X., Sun, S., Liu, J., & Law, R. (2025). Symbolic interactionism: Exploring the experience of traditional costume in a destination. *Current Issues in Tourism, 28*(7), 1100–1115.

Zhu, Y. (2021). *Heritage tourism: From problems to possibilities.* Cambridge University Press.

Zunckel, K. (2007, 9-12 September). The Maloti Drakensberg trans frontier conservation and development programme: A cooperative initiative between Lesotho and South Africa. *Peace, Parks, and Partnership Conference, Waterton Lakes National Park, Alberta, Canada.*